BEST-SELLING AUTHOR
DON COLBERT SAYS:

Finally—a wonderful resource on the issues of sexuality from a Christian perspective. Dr. Scott Farhart is a compassionate, accomplished and caring physician who shares his experience and knowledge on a subject so sensitive to some Christians that it is often never discussed openly.

Intimate and Unashamed is an excellent teaching tool for singles, newlyweds and married couples alike, as it will offer answers to those questions that many are reluctant or too embarrassed to ask. As a physician myself, I strongly recommend this book, which I found to be highly informative and filled with spiritual and physical insight on sexuality.

—DON COLBERT, M.D.

Intimate & Unashamed

SCOTT FARHART, M.D.

SILOAM®
A STRANG COMPANY

INTIMATE AND UNASHAMED by Scott Farhart, M.D.
Published by Siloam
A Strang Company
600 Rinehart Road
Lake Mary, Florida 32746
www.siloam.com

Unless otherwise noted, all Scripture quotations are from the Holy Bible, New International Version. Copyright © 1973, 1978, 1984, International Bible Society. Used by permission.

Scripture quotations marked KJV are from the King James Version of the Bible.

Scripture quotations marked NKJV are from the New King James Version of the Bible. Copyright © 1979, 1980, 1982 by Thomas Nelson, Inc., publishers. Used by permission.

Scripture quotations marked THE MESSAGE are from *The Message*, copyright © 1993, 1994, 1995. Used by permission of NavPress Publishing Group.

Cover design by Judith McKittrick

This book is not intended to provide medical advice or to take the place of medical advice and treatment from your personal physician. Readers are advised to consult their own doctors or other qualified health professionals regarding the treatment of their medical problems. Neither the publisher nor the author takes any responsibility for any possible consequences from any treatment, action or application of medicine, supplement, herb or preparation to any person reading or following the information in this book. If readers are taking prescription medications, they should consult with their physicians and not take themselves off of medicines to start supplementation without the proper supervision of a physician.

Library of Congress Cataloging-in-Publication Data

Farhart, Scott, 1959-
 Intimate and unashamed / Scott Farhart.
    p. cm.
 Includes bibliographical references (p.).
 ISBN 0-88419-944-4 (trade paper)
 1. Sex—Religious aspects—Christianity. I. Title.
BT708.F37 2003
241'.66—dc21
            2003002377

03 04 05 06 07 — 9 8 7 6 5 4 3 2
Printed in the United States of America.

To my wife, Sandy—the one person with whom I can truly be intimate and unashamed

Acknowledgments

I would like to thank Pastor John and Diana Hagee for encouraging me to speak out about sexual issues in the church and giving me a forum to do so. Their marriage has been a true inspiration to me.

I also want to express my appreciation to the following:

- To Terry Thompson at John Hagee Ministries for his unwavering support of this project and his "connections" that got my foot in the door

- To Don and Mary Colbert for laying a path for me to follow

- To Stephen Strang, Carol Noe and the team at Strang Communications who gave me far more attention than I ever expected for a first-time author

- To Rev. John Gross and Rev. John Rangel, who have helped me in ways only they know. I am forever indebted to their ministries.

- To Tony Navarro for helping Sandy and me in our quest for intimacy

- To my "Twelve," who have had to put up with less attention from me than they deserved while I wrote this book. Their sacrifices are appreciated.

- To my partners at Northeast Ob/Gyn Associates, who have created a work environment that allows me to pursue my dreams, yet stay close to home

- And finally, to my wife, Sandy, and my children, Jordan and Jared. I love you all very much and I could not have written this without your patience and understanding. Thanks for supporting me every step of the way.

Contents

Foreword

It is my pleasure to highly recommend to you Dr. Scott Farhart's courageous and enlightening book, *Intimate and Unashamed.*

Dr. Farhart, one of the premier Christian physicians of San Antonio, approaches traditionally forbidden topics boldly. As the keynote speaker at highly successful seminars, Dr. Farhart answers the questions Christian men and women of America are asking. His answers are not pious platitudes but are truthful, insightful, biblical and often heart stopping.

Intimate and Unashamed will be the last book on this topic you will need to purchase for yourself, your son or daughter entering puberty or anyone you know who is about to get married. This book covers the waterfront of intimacy with breathtaking boldness.

Because this book is biblically based, it is timeless! The truth of *Intimate and Unashamed* can be passed from generation to generation as a guiding light in an area of absolute darkness to most Christians. *Intimate and Unashamed* should be required reading in every Christian household.

If you only read one book this year, make it *Intimate and Unashamed.* Enjoy!

—Dr. John C. Hagee

Chapter **One**

A BIBLICAL PERSPECTIVE ON OUR SEXUALITY

> God blessed them and said to them, "Be
> fruitful and increase in number." ...God saw all
> that he had made, and it was very good.
> —*Genesis 1:28, 31*

As a Christian gynecologist, I have had the privilege of treating thousands of women in my community over the past two decades. Many of them have had the courage to ask questions about one of the most private aspects of their lives—their sexuality. The issues have ranged from the values of virginity to sexually transmitted diseases; from wedding night romance to the challenges of geriatric sexual relations; from birth control to plastic surgery.

Over time, these women also have asked questions regarding issues of concern for their husband such as how to be a better lover, how to know appropriate boundaries for Christian sexual activity and how to find answers for erectile dysfunction.

IT'S OK TO HAVE QUESTIONS

The majority of couples struggle with these sensitive and important issues of marriage in a spiritual vacuum. They wonder how their faith in Christ and their human sexuality can peacefully coexist. Sensing that there must be more to their sexual lives than they are experiencing but wondering if God really approves of these secret desires, they ask themselves: *Is sex the forbidden fruit after all, except in the most plain and sterile variety?*

Many of my patients struggle to be *holy* and *righteous*, while their flesh floods them with feelings and desires they don't think *Christians* should have. Men and women often argue with their spouses about this area of their lives; it seems they may never be truly satisfied. As individuals, they feel that this battle over sex may be the one area of their lives that threatens their personal relationship with God more than any other.

If you identify with these couples, you know what I am talking about.

Your thought life intrudes into your quiet time with God. It seems you are bombarded with "messages" about sex from the secular world that cause you to doubt your integrity regarding your sexual life.

Courageously seeking for answers

To whom can you turn with your fears and frustrations? If you approach your pastor, will he or she think you are less spiritual and holy than they once believed? Would your friends understand your struggles and guard your secrets, or will they "share" their concerns about you with others?

Will your spouse think you are *demonized*? Could you ever pray to a holy God about the struggles you are having, being the man or woman you think you are supposed to be—and have faith to receive an answer? Giving in to these fears, you have kept quiet, thinking this is your "thorn in the flesh," your cross to bear. So you turn to this book, hoping for an anonymous consultation with a Christian gynecologist. I congratulate you for having the courage to seek answers that will satisfy your most sensitive questions of life, and I do not plan to disappoint you.

Over the years, as I sought answers for my patients who have had the courage to ask these questions in my office under the cover of confidentiality, I began looking for Christian resources I could give them in addition to the acceptable answers my medical training provided.

In my search, I attended a meeting where Dr. James Dobson introduced a Christian gynecologist, Dr. Joe McIlhaney, who had dedicated his life to teaching abstinence-based sexual education for our youth from a medical perspective. As I sat there in a room filled with gynecologists, Dr. McIlhaney displayed graphic slides showing the horrors of sexually transmitted diseases and told shocking statistics of the epidemic of these diseases, of which I was unaware even as a practicing physician.[1]

Armed with his slides and outlines and a passion to protect our young people, I presented this material to our local Christian high school biology class. As word spread of the effectiveness of this presentation, the public demand for me to provide biblically based, scientific information on sex and sexuality increased dramatically.

Diana Hagee, wife of television evangelist John Hagee, asked me to speak to a group of five hundred women whom she was mentoring. I solicited questions in advance and discovered an honest hunger for knowledge on very practical sexual issues with which these lades were grappling, either as single adults or in their marital lives. The help these women received resulted in my being asked to share these biblically based, scientific answers for our sexuality as Christians at a men's conference, which followed shortly thereafter. Their honest response was similar to that of the ladies.

Recognizing the needs of her church, Diana Hagee asked me to contribute to her book, *The King's Daughter*.[2] Two television interviews followed on the Hagees' national interview show, *John Hagee Today*, which brought a tremendous response from viewers. I realized that for most of the church, questions about sex and sexuality were pressing issues, which have been sparsely addressed from the pulpit. I understood that most Christians do not have a source, other than the secular media, as a model on which to base their sexual relations.

GOD IS INTERESTED IN YOUR SEX LIFE

Of the many hundreds of questions I have been asked, the fundamental theme remains: *Is God really interested in my sex life? What does He think about sex?* The answer I give is the response I received from my pastor in my youth when I asked the same question: *It's God's idea!*

God created the sexes and sexual intercourse. He instilled the sexual drive into our bodies, knowing it would work its way into our thoughts and minds. He is not ashamed of our sexuality, nor does He regret creating it. From the beginning of Scripture, in the second chapter of Genesis, we can read how God weaves His plan for our sexuality, which continues throughout the pages of Scripture. And from one passage to the next, the theme is one of pleasure, joy and fulfillment within the boundaries He has created.

No one would suggest that just because God commanded that Adam and Eve not eat of the tree of the knowledge of good and evil, making its *forbidden fruit* off-limits to them, that the rest of the garden ceased to be Paradise to them. The beautiful flowers and majestic creatures the Lord had created still filled Adam and Eve with wonder as they discovered a new aspect of the creation each day and began to take dominion over all the Lord had given them.

IS GOD REALLY INTERESTED IN MY SEX LIFE?

Paradise was filled with joy and delight for this first couple. If this were not true, I do not believe being banished from this garden would have caused them such sorrow. (See Genesis 3.) Yet, many Christians mistakenly perceive that the few hedges of protection that God placed around our sexuality indicate that God is *against* sex; they feel that sex represents our *forbidden fruit.*

SEX IS NOT A FORBIDDEN FRUIT

While few areas of our lives have been as distorted since the Fall as our sexuality, it is still God's desire for us to experience all that He had in mind for our sexuality when He created us. He hasn't changed His mind, nor does He secretly wish we had never been introduced to sex. Our sexuality is still God's gift to us, not just for reproduction, as many in the church seem to believe, but for intimacy and pleasure in the comfort of marriage. And yes, He knows how much fun it is. He made it feel that way!

The faulty perception of thinking that God is against sex is like thinking He is against music because of some musical expressions that are unacceptable, such as music with violent, satanic lyrics. God demonstrated His desire for music when He ordained that King David and others write the Book of Psalms, reminding us that music was meant for a higher purpose— the praise and worship of our Lord. And the world is full of wonderful, heart-inspiring hymns and songs, both traditional and contemporary, that give us but a glimpse of the heavenly worship we will someday enjoy around the throne of God. But for so long, the church has looked at the way the fallen world has expressed itself sexually and closed its doors to all discussions of sex, seemingly fearing that the influences of the secular world would corrupt the holiness of the church.

The sometimes irresponsible approach of the church to human sexuality has left many sincere Christians sitting in their church pews each Sunday wondering if God is for or against sex. Is God condemning them as they struggle with questions for which they desperately need answers, and for feelings that threaten their very walk with Him? The answer is, *absolutely not!*

I can tell you on the authority of the Word of God that He is definitely interested in your sexual life—and not just so He can say, "Don't do that!" He longs for you to experience all He has created you for from the beginning. While we may not achieve what we would have had in the Garden of Eden, we can surely take hold of a lot more than we currently enjoy, and we can do it without the guilt and condemnation that has so often hounded the sincere Christian.

Consider God's motivation for creating a companion for Adam and His ultimate design for their relationship. During God's creation process, He said:

> "It is not good for the man to be alone. I will make a helper suitable for him"…Then the LORD God made a woman from the rib he had taken out of the man, and he brought her to the man. The man said, "This is now bone of my bones and flesh of my flesh."…For this reason a man will leave his father and mother and be united to his wife, and they will be *one flesh*. The man and his wife were both naked, and they felt no shame.
>
> —*Genesis 2:18, 22–25, emphasis added*

It was God who created a beautiful woman and brought her to Adam as

His precious gift to him. When Adam looked upon her, he saw the differences and knew what it was to be a man. He saw *woman* and, for the first time, perceived himself to be *man*, with all the unique qualities created in him.

What happened in the garden?

Eve was human yet different from Adam, and those differences revealed the plan of God for each of them. When Adam saw how Eve was made, he also learned how his body *fit* together with hers. The erect penis had a place, designed by God, that it fit into, and it all made sense to Adam. The two became *one flesh*, which is how the rest of us got here! But God's plan also involved a beautiful gift of intimacy, as Adam discovered as he held Eve close to his flesh and felt the two of them meld into one unit. This was satisfaction that Adam could find with no other creature on earth. Sex is more than a physical union just as we are more than flesh and bones, as we will discuss later. But it is a wonderful gift of God to be enjoyed.

> **ADAM SAW *WOMAN* AND, FOR THE FIRST TIME, PERCEIVED HIMSELF TO BE *MAN*.**

God's first command to them was to "be fruitful and increase in number" (Gen. 1:28). In other words, God told them to have intercourse; it was their first assignment as a couple. It is difficult for us to imagine the Father of all Creation peering down into the garden to watch Adam and Eve making love. For some, it would seem like making God a "peeping Tom." And yet we can be sure that God was present at this love scene.

When God presented Eve to him, Adam's physical body responded with an erection, and either God explained to him what to do with it or Adam discovered it for himself. As the two perfectly formed beings explored the different parts of the other's body, they discovered sensitive areas created by God for their pleasure, and they freely enjoyed themselves whenever they wanted, without fear that God would *catch* them or feeling that what they were doing was *wrong* or *filthy*. Sin had not yet entered the garden; there were no limits placed on them except for the tree of the knowledge of good and evil.

Yet, even with this clear biblical picture of God's design in creation, we struggle fiercely with the idea that a holy God could want anything to do with our sex lives. We somehow pretend that He and all the angels flee to the backside of heaven whenever we make love. There is no reassuring consciousness of a loving Father standing by to give us wisdom and knowledge about how He created this body we live in, or teaching us how to please the partner with whom He has joined us—in holy unity.

For many, the very idea of God in our bedrooms is a shocking thought; yet it is a reality. If we think otherwise, we do not understand the powerful indwelling of Christ in the believer. Do we leave the Holy Spirit waiting in the bathroom while we have intercourse? Do we ask the Son of God, who promised He would never leave us or forsake us, to stay downstairs and watch TV while we make love? Do we somehow think God would be offended by what He saw, the uniting of two people into one, just as His Word says He created us to become?

Though mankind's disobedience to God's command in the garden not to eat of the tree of the knowledge of good and evil caused them to fall from relationship with God, it did not change God's original intention for us, that we have the very best in intimacy and sexual pleasure in our marriages. There is other scriptural basis to support the fact that God intends for sex to be more than simply for the purpose of reproduction. He intends for His children to view themselves as sexual beings, filled with desires for their spouse and possessing the need for those desires to be fulfilled. He created the marriage bed for that very purpose.

A look at the Song of Solomon

Probably one of the least read or least quoted books of the Bible is the Song of Solomon. Many Christians seem embarrassed that it is even in their Bibles, and many clergy avoid all reference to it. To read it from the pulpit opens up an area of life they would rather not discuss in church. And yet it is exactly what we need to hear—the truth. The images of love and its verbal expressions in the Song of Solomon affirm that we are created as sensual beings with God-given sexual needs that are powerful. We are designed to be desired by the other person with all the senses—sight, smell, taste, hearing and touch. And in all these ways, we are created to give and receive pleasure.

What first attracted most of us to our spouses was what we saw. Something (or everything) about the way they were formed drew us to them like a powerful magnet. Most couples can tell you something about their spouse that first caught their attention: broad shoulders, piercing blue eyes or firm buttocks; a slender neck, flowing black hair or an hourglass figure. For me it was the beauty of my wife's face and the shape of her legs. They still remain my favorite things to look upon after twenty years of marriage.

Some women clutch the sweater or shirt of a distant "beloved" in order to smell their scent and ease the loneliness that physical separation has brought to their home. People often have a "signature" perfume or cologne, which, when smelled in the air, tells the partner their loved one is near. The whisper of your partner's voice can send chills through your body, and their touch can cause all of your muscles to tighten in anticipation.

Are all of these sensations the evil works of the flesh? No, definitely not; they are the genius of God exploding through a thousand nerve endings with such repercussions that even medical science cannot begin to grasp.

The most complicated of all the created beings on earth is programmed by God to experience ecstasy with another being of God's creation through the five senses, and sex is no exception.

Each of the senses is used by the lovers in the Song of Solomon as a biblical reminder of the gift that our body is to each other. For example, the bride describes her husband, the object of her intense desire, in very powerful terms. I am going to quote it here since many of you are too afraid to read it in your own Bibles:

> My lover is radiant and ruddy, outstanding among ten thousand. His head is purest gold; his hair is wavy and black as a raven. His eyes are like doves...His lips are like lilies dripping with myrrh. His arms are rods of gold set with chrysolite. His body is like polished ivory decorated with sapphires. His legs are pillars of marble...His mouth is sweetness itself; he is altogether lovely.
>
> —*Song of Solomon 5:10–16*

In modern terms, her beloved is a *hunk*! She does not describe to her friends his intelligence, his social standing or his wealth. There is no talk of his wit or wisdom, his gentleness or kindness or any other virtue. In fact, his spiritual nature is never even mentioned. She longs for his *body*, the object of her desire. Only he can satisfy the burning passion that has been awakened in her. There is no shame or secrecy about this. She tells her friends openly about her beloved and extols his beauty to all who will listen to her.

When was the last time you thought about the different parts of your husband's body and felt so powerfully drawn to him that you could not eat or sleep until he was again in your arms? For so many, the passion of the early years has faded, and their conversation has turned to topics like what a good father he is; what a faithful provider he is; how well he is doing at the office. It is little wonder that spouses "grow apart" in their marriages, which results in devastating consequences.

Later in the Song of Solomon, the man's description of his wife is even more detailed and more graphic!

> Your graceful legs are like jewels...Your navel is a rounded goblet that never lacks blended wine. Your waist is a mound of wheat encircled by lilies. Your breasts are like two fawns, twins of a gazelle. Your neck is like an ivory tower...How beautiful you are and how pleasing, O love, with your delights!
>
> —*Song of Solomon 7:1–4, 6*

He even goes on to describe his intentions toward her:

> Your stature is like that of the palm, and your breasts like clusters of

fruit. I said "I will climb the palm tree; I will take hold of its fruit."

—*Song of Solomon 7:7–8*

Why did God put these sensuous descriptions in the Bible? When the early church leaders were deciding which writings were the inspired Word of God, how did they ever choose this book? Surely God could have gotten this one thrown out somewhere along the way before it showed up in my Bible! It is simply because He wanted His people to know that the desires and drives they feel are a legitimate part of what it means to be men and women. They are not meant to be a cause of shame or a reason to hide from God. These desires are to be satisfied in all their intensity and richness within the protective hedge of marriage ordained by God.

I'm well aware that there are other valid, more spiritual analogies that can be taken from the Song of Solomon. But they do not make void the simple, literal descriptions of sexual desire and intimacy that we read about in the Song of Solomon.

BECOMING ONE FLESH IS MORE THAN A PHYSICAL UNION

Within every adolescent there are sexual feelings and desires. This is not a reflection of our fallen state. It is an affirmation that for each generation, God continues to plant within us these powerful desires that drive us to seek the companionship and intimacy in marriage that can be found in no other creature, hobby, profession or sport on the face of the earth. It is a natural, even divine, call to find that perfect helpmate that will bring us into completeness in marriage as a human being. This relationship is also a powerful reflection to the rest of the world of the dual nature of God.

God possesses both the male and female within Himself. This is a difficult concept for our finite minds to grasp, considering the invisible realm where God dwells. But in creation we see all of the attributes of God on display. He has an intense desire to experience intimacy with us—to know us and allow us to know Him at the deepest level of human consciousness— our spirits. When God made man and woman as intimate creatures, the invisible God was giving us a natural portrait of the divine, spiritual intimacy He desires to share with each of us, Spirit to spirit.

The Scriptures give us this understanding:

> For this reason a man will leave his father and mother and be united
> to his wife, and the two will become one flesh. This is a profound
> mystery—but I am talking about Christ and the church.

—*Ephesians 5:31–32*

The apostle Paul is teaching us that just as a man and woman become *one flesh* in sexual union, so can Christ (our Bridegroom) and the church (His bride) become one in spiritual union. When you seek an intimate relationship with God, it is a union of His spirit with yours. It is God's hope that we will see the power of such a union between two people and grasp the possibility of a powerful spiritual union with Him. If our spouse can bring us comfort, peace and solace, how much more can a perfect Creator give to us what we lack?

What is perhaps the area of our greatest struggle is meant to be a source of great intimacy, pleasure and joy. I believe that is why the devil wants to keep the church ignorant about God's purpose for sexuality. If the divorce rate in the church stopped being the same as it is for the rest of society…if we could enjoy heaven on earth in our marital relationships…if the pressures of life melted away in the loving and nurturing haven of our spouse's embrace, a Christian marriage should be bliss. The devil knows the world could be drawn to a God who provides such happiness in the midst of a world otherwise filled with chaos. The marital bed, as God ordained it, is a powerful agent for healing, restoration, fulfillment and joy that most of us rarely enjoy to the fullest. This lack of fulfillment is not the design or the will of God.

Searching for role models

Many of us became Christians after we had already engaged in sexual activity. Enjoying the freedom of the *new creation* in Christ that we experienced in so many areas of our lives, it is easy to assume that the *old man,* our sinful nature, died sexually as well. To some extent that is true. Our old way of looking at sex simply to fulfill a sexual need or drive has been replaced.

We no longer seek to use another person simply to gratify our sexual desires or fill an emptiness we feel inside. Our new man cares about the opposite sex as brothers and sisters of the faith, not objects of exploitation. We desire to know God as our source of comfort, our refuge and our strength. We don't need anyone else to *complete* us because we are complete in Him. But where does that leave us as sexual beings? How do we honor God and have sexual relationships at the same time?

If we search for role models in the Old Testament, we soon discover men whose sexual life was their spiritual, and often their physical, undoing. For example, the great warrior Samson led Israel for twenty years, but his lusts brought him to a woman named Delilah. Although he was a Nazirite, set apart to God since his birth, he allowed her to rob him of his strength, and Scripture says that the Lord left him (Judg. 16:20).

According to the Scriptures, King Solomon was the most powerful, the wealthiest and the wisest man of his day (2 Chron. 9:22). Yet Solomon could not control himself sexually and slept with over a thousand different women, most of whom were forbidden partners by God due to their pagan religious backgrounds. As he grew older, these pagan women turned Solomon's heart away from the Lord. Although God had twice appeared to him in person and he had been allowed to build the Lord's temple, experiencing the awesome presence of the glory of God, Solomon began worshiping the gods of the women with whom he had slept. As a result, the Lord took the kingdom from him (1 Kings 11).

Even a seemingly innocent woman was the downfall of one of the most powerful men in the Old Testament. King David, a man after God's own heart (1 Sam. 13:14), was unable to restrain his passions for Bathsheba, another man's wife. After summoning her to the palace where he committed adultery with her, David conceived a plan to murder her husband, an honorable commander in his army.

As a result, David was forbidden to build the Lord's temple, which was one of his greatest desires in life. And the son conceived from their union died shortly after birth, causing them deep grief. (See 2 Samuel 12.) Amnon, another of David's sons, followed his father's poor example and committed sexual sin. He wanted his sister Tamar so badly that he raped her, leading to his death at the hands of his brother Absalom. This tragic event forced Absalom to hide in exile for three years and planted the seeds of hatred that culminated in civil war, with Absalom trying to overthrow his own father's kingdom.

What happens when we take God out of our sex lives?

Whole chapters in the Old Testament are devoted to the regulation of sexual activity. (See Leviticus 18; 20.) In the pagan cultures that surrounded the people of Israel, sexual activity between father and daughter, mother and son, brother and sister, or men and animals was not uncommon. It is in these chapters where God also defines homosexuality. He places boundaries for His people and commands them not to engage in these types of sexual activity. For example, He declares:

> Keep all my decrees and laws and follow them, so that the land where I am bringing you to live may not vomit you out. You must not live according to the customs of the nations I am going to drive out before you. Because they did all these things, I abhorred them. But I said to you, "You will possess their land; I will give it to you as an inheritance, a land flowing with milk and honey." I am the LORD your God, who has set you apart from the nations.
>
> —*Leviticus 20:22–24*

These few rules were designed to distinguish the Israelites from the pagan cultures around them. But they were also a hedge of protection around the sanctity of the family, where sinful sexual practices had destroyed the foundation of those pagan societies. God did not want the nation of Israel to fall victim to the same fate.

But some Christians read chapters 18 and 20 of Leviticus, where the punishment of sexual sin is death by stoning, and conclude that God is fierce and vengeful, ready at any moment to strike them down if they sin sexually. They forget that God is also a God of grace and forgiveness. The boundaries still exist to protect us, but the stones stay on the ground; forgiveness is ours for the asking because of Calvary.

New Testament heroes reveal little information of their marital lives to us. Of course, Jesus and Paul were both celibate. And Paul teaches us to present our bodies as living sacrifices, holy unto God (Rom. 12:1–2). He reminds us that our body is the temple of the Holy Spirit and that we must strive to honor God with it (1 Cor. 6:18–20).

So how does one honor God with his body, be an acceptable temple for the Holy Spirit, live holy before God, and yet experience the joys and delights of sexual union? Many of us have thought that when the Bible says to present our bodies as living sacrifices, it really means sacrificing a fulfilling and exciting sex life.

Under this guilt canopy, we find ourselves envying those television and movie "role models" who seem to enjoy sex with guiltless abandon. Some of us escape into the fantasy world of romance novels, soap operas or worse, pornographic videos, to become spectators of a dark and lonely life from which we have been set free. This dilemma seems especially difficult for those of us who carry memories of a pre-conversion sexual life that was fulfilling.

While the secular world has, admittedly, pushed the envelope of sexual exploration to extremes, we as a church have been robbed of our inheritance in Christ. The lack of proper scriptural interpretation and explanation of God's true design for marriage hinders a mutually satisfying intimacy with our spouse. We have had too few champions from the pulpit to encourage us to reclaim what has been stolen from us. Much preaching that touches the topic of sexuality has emphasized the sins of sex with little, if any, reference to the joy of sex that God ordained. It is only recently that Christian couples, preparing to begin their married lives together, could find any written resource materials in their local Christian bookstore.

A NEW LOOK AT BIBLICAL
AND MEDICAL TRUTHS

Thankfully, times are changing, and a new generation of spiritual leaders is dedicated to reclaiming the sexually broken and discarded and to teaching young adults a godly pattern for beginning their marriages. We are living with an epidemic of divorce, adultery, fornication, sexually transmitted diseases and pornography. Yet, God has revealed wonderful promises from His Word to all who would hear and be set free by its truth. And, perhaps surprisingly, the Bible reveals beautiful examples of the pleasures that proper sexual expression should bring to our lives.

We have already discovered the Song of Solomon. While it is the largest and most detailed biblical example of the beauty of sexual life God intended us to share, it is by no means the only example. The Book of Proverbs warns against adultery while extolling the pleasures of intimacy in your own house:

> Drink water from your own cistern, running water from your own well…Let them be yours alone, never to be shared with strangers. May your fountain be blessed, and may you rejoice in the wife of your youth. A loving doe, a graceful deer—may her breasts satisfy you always, may you ever be captivated by her love.
>
> —*Proverbs 5:15, 17–19*

This passage contains simple instruction about enjoying sexuality in a healthy way. In the New Testament, Jesus quotes from the Book of Genesis regarding God's intention for marriage:

> But at the beginning of creation God made them male and female. "For this reason a man will leave his father and mother and be united to his wife, and the two will become one flesh." So they are no longer two, but one. Therefore what God has joined together, let man not separate.
>
> —*Mark 10:6–9*

Jesus reminds us that from the very beginning it was God's intention that man and woman come together sexually and become one flesh, a condition that only occurs in intercourse. This drive to unite is so strong that a man will leave the comforts of home and all that is familiar to begin a new life with his wife. This bond is so important to God that He commands that no man separate it.

I am, of course, aware of the teachings of Paul recommending celibacy, preferring a devotion to the work of the Lord instead of to marriage. However, most of us do not have the gift of celibacy this lifestyle requires, a fact that the apostle Paul readily admits. (See 1 Corinthians 7.) Since you are reading this book, I can safely assume that you are not called to a life of celibacy! With that understanding, let us begin to examine biblical and medical truths to discover who we are as males and females and allow these truths to guide us in fulfilling our destinies as human beings who were created for physical intimacy.

An honest evaluation

Throughout this book I will examine various issues dealing with sex and sexuality from a medical, biblical and practical viewpoint. While I am not a pastor or Bible scholar, I am an elder in a church with seventeen thousand members. I will refer to scriptural principles as the foundation upon which to base my answers. I will also be sharing the stories of men and women whose questions have inspired this book. Their names and certain facts have been changed to protect them from detection, but the questions they have asked are real. And I will answer them in frank and honest terms.

Some of the issues we will cover in this book may not specifically apply to your personal situation, but I encourage you to read each chapter. The knowledge gained from it will be needed for the chapter that follows, and you may need to be a source of truth to someone else you meet along the way.

We will look at our bodies as God created them, how they function and the areas where they suffer affliction. We will explore the issue of abstinence until marriage, based on medical and biblical teachings, and examine the very real consequences of violating this safeguard in a world filled with STDs (sexually transmitted diseases) and AIDS. For married couples, we will discover what it means to love your spouse and discuss how to meet each other's deepest sexual and relational needs. For those who have been wounded by past relationships, we will introduce healing. And we will examine sexual relations for the older couple, as a guide for those who need it presently as well as a compass for the future of the young.

The underlying truth to all of these issues that we have tried to express is that God wants you to have great and satisfying sex; it is His idea. Of course, that can only become a reality when we do things His way. By following some very specific and true boundaries, we can have a life and marriage not only satisfying to us, but also pleasing to the One who made us.

Chapter **Two**

HOW GOD
MADE A WOMAN

> Then the LORD God made a woman from the rib
> he had taken out of the man, and he brought
> her to the man. The man said, "This is now
> bone of my bones, and flesh of my flesh; she
> shall be called 'woman,' for she was taken out
> of man."
>
> *—Genesis 2:22–23*

G od did one of His greatest acts of creation when He created woman. A
unique creature was formed who was like man but different in so
many complementary ways. In many respects, women are far more complex than men (a fact that most married men have already discovered for
themselves). To fully appreciate what the Lord created, it is helpful to look
at women from an anatomic, hormonal and emotional viewpoint. In this
way, we will better understand a woman's sexual makeup.

THE WONDER OF BEING FEMALE

Embryologically, it is as if the Creation story is backward to procreation as we
understand it. In Creation, the male was formed first, then the female.
However, medically, we understand that a developing fetus will automatically
take a *female* form if not influenced early on by the male hormone testosterone regardless of whether the fetus has male or female chromosomes.

In a rare condition, called *testicular feminization,* a fetus that is *chromo-
somally* male "turns into" a female-looking human being because its cells
lack the ability to recognize testosterone. It is this male hormone testosterone that closes the vagina, makes the labia turn into a scrotum and elon-
gates the clitoris to form a penis. Without the influence of this hormone, a
normal-appearing female will be formed, complete with breast development and a vagina, even though that person has the chromosomes of a
male. It is often when no uterus or ovaries are found that the diagnosis of
the condition testicular feminization is made. Without the proper influence

of testosterone, the fetus will automatically become female. So being female is the easy and natural process. Far more complex changes must take place to create the male anatomy.

I have said all this to dispel the notion that women are lesser persons who lack the right *equipment*—the so-called "penis envy" syndrome. Women who are treated equally and fairly will celebrate the uniqueness of their bodies and the reproductive power that lies within them. They do not feel they are lesser human beings because they lack a penis. Those women who have learned to truly celebrate their femaleness have an appreciation of their unique makeup. Anyway, it has been my experience that the only people who suffer from penis envy are other men!

Her ovaries

The ovaries are the dominant organs of women. Nearly all of the sex hormones come from the ovaries, and they hold the key to much of what it means to be female. These oval structures are about the size of almonds and are located on each side of the uterus. They produce the female sex hormones of estrogen and progesterone, and they store all of the eggs needed for later reproduction.

Each month, dozens of eggs compete with each other to select the one egg that will be released for fertilization in a process called ovulation. In a complex interaction between the brain and the ovaries, one dominant egg reaches maturity and is released into the pelvic cavity where the fallopian tube takes it into itself. It is there that waiting sperm fertilize it. The resulting embryo journeys into the uterus to begin its new life.

The working premise of most birth control pills is to stop the ovulation process by replacing the hormones made in the ovaries with ones taken orally, thus putting the ovaries into a state of *rest*. The ovaries make estrogen every day from puberty until menopause. It is this hormone that keeps the voice high, develops breasts, changes the shape of the pelvic bones to accommodate pregnancy and grows a uterine lining for later use in reproduction.

Estrogen has been found to interact with almost every organ of the body in a powerful way. It causes calcium to bind to bone (the loss of estrogen is the primary cause of osteoporosis in women). It increases the good cholesterol (HDL) and lowers the bad cholesterol (LDL), delaying the onset of heart attack and stroke in women compared to men. And its influence on the brain is legendary!

When the egg is released in the middle of the menstrual cycle, a second hormone called progesterone is made. Its principle job is to prepare the uterine lining to receive an embryo. Without this preparation, the embryo would float by and fall out of the cervix, never implanting and never causing "pregnancy." If an embryo does not implant and signal its existence to the ovary, the progesterone levels will fall and the uterine lining will tear away, beginning the familiar process of menstruation.

Her uterus

The uterus, as mentioned above, is the place where the embryo develops into the fetus and then is delivered by a series of contractions as a live baby. It is commonly called the *womb*. The end of the uterus that protrudes into the vagina is called the *cervix*. While the uterus and the cervix have different functions and different cellular makeup, they essentially blend together into one organ. The uterus is the "house" for the fetus, and the cervix is the "door" for the house.

The uterus is a series of muscles lined by cells that will hold and nourish an embryo, making a place for the placenta to attach and begin the exchange of all the oxygen and nutrients the developing fetus will need. Its primarily muscular nature is responsible for menstrual cramps that squeeze out the old lining and for labor contractions that bring delivery of the baby.

These contractions cause the cervix to open and release the developed baby. Damage to the cervix from surgical procedures—for example, to correct conditions detected by abnormal Pap smears or from past abortions—can weaken its ability to hold a pregnancy to term and can cause loss of the fetus. Apart from its function in pregnancy, the cervix serves as a source of lubrication for intercourse. It also releases its own unique secretions during the fertile phase of each cycle that nourish the sperm and aid their passage into the uterus.

Her fallopian tubes

Attached to the upper sides of the uterus are the fallopian tubes that bring egg and sperm together and transport the created embryo to the uterus. Scarring of the tubes from previous infection is a common cause of infertility. Complete loss of the tubes' ability to unite egg and sperm has led to the development of *in vitro fertilization* (IVF), commonly referred to as "test-tube" babies.

Through IVF, embryos are created in the lab with the parents' sperm and eggs. The embryos are then placed into the uterus directly. When there is only partial blockage of the tube, couples can conceive on their own, but the embryo may develop in the tube instead of the uterus. This serious condition is called a tubal or ectopic pregnancy and is a leading cause of death due to pregnancy. As the placenta buries itself in the thin wall of the tube, it can rupture the tube, causing massive blood loss. The fallopian tubes are among the most delicate of the female organs, yet so vitally important to the procreation process.

Her vagina

The vagina is a three- to four-inch muscular tube leading from the cervix to the outer labial opening. It is lined by cells that secrete lubrication to aid in intercourse, and it is capable of expanding during sexual excitement to hold the erect penis. The vagina is able to accommodate any size penis; in fact, a fully developed baby can journey through it during birth.

The vagina is surrounded by the bladder above and the rectum below. Childbirth injuries to the vaginal walls, as well as aging of the muscles, can cause the uterus, bladder and/or rectum to "fall" into it, as we will discuss in a later chapter. While the vagina is the main location of intercourse and is capable of feeling its own unique sensations, it is not the primary place where the pleasure of intercourse is experienced for a woman. That is left to the clitoris.

Her clitoris

The clitoris is the most sensitive receiver of sexual pleasure in a woman's body. I have been amazed in my practice to learn how many women do not even know the clitoris exists or that it is supposed to be involved in giving them sexual satisfaction. Its counterpart in men is the head of the penis. Imagine expecting men to be sexually fulfilled but ignoring the head of the penis. That is unthinkable, yet many women have had their clitoris ignored by their spouse as a sexual organ.

The clitoris is filled with sensitive nerves that transmit pleasurable sensations. It is also capable of an erection, and when erect, it protrudes from under a hood of skin formed by the joining of the tops of the labia (or lips). During intercourse, the inward thrusting of the penis pulls on the labia, and the hood of the clitoris rubs against it, causing sensation to be transmitted to the clitoris. With enough sensation, a woman will achieve orgasm.

I will never forget the reaction of one sixty-four-year-old woman who had just discovered there was an organ called the clitoris and that it was an important source of her sexual pleasure. She was indignant that she had never been told it existed and that her husband of forty-five years had been ignorant of its function. Looking back on her marriage, she felt she had been cheated out of her inheritance. There was anger in her voice mixed with great sorrow over what might have been.

Her hormones

As mentioned earlier, the ovaries are the source of most of the hormones that make a woman female. Besides the familiar estrogen and progesterone that dominate the menstrual cycle, a small amount of testosterone is also made which, when produced in its normal amount, increases energy, helps form muscle mass and fuels the sexual drive (or libido). Imbalances in these hormones can cause tremendous problems for women and their spouses.

In a common condition called *polycystic ovarian syndrome* (PCOS), the ovaries secrete too much testosterone beginning shortly after puberty. This leads to increased acne and thickening of facial, chest and abdominal hair. There is also an increase in insulin production, which encourages deposits into the fat cells, leading to rapid increases in weight during the teens and early twenties. At the same time, the hormonal imbalance stops ovulation, resulting in irregular or even absent menstrual periods and later infertility.

PCOS can be treated with birth control pills to put the ovaries at "rest" and stop the imbalance that is occurring. This treatment will regulate the menstrual cycle and stop further unwanted hair growth. A newer brand of birth control pills specifically designed for PCOS is called Yasmin. It has a mild diuretic that daily flushes out the water retention and bloating commonly experienced by patients during their menstrual cycles.

Fertility medications may be necessary to overcome problems of poor ovulation. Medications such as clomiphene citrate (or Clomid) have been popular remedies. Recently, fertility has been enhanced with medications commonly used to treat diabetes. By bringing down the insulin levels surrounding the ovaries, restoration of normal fertility is possible without the risk of multiple births that are common with fertility drugs. The expense is also greatly reduced, as are the side effects.

Her cycle

A mysterious condition affecting women during their monthly menstrual cycle is called *premenstrual syndrome,* or PMS. It can range from mild to severe, but nearly every woman experiences some degree of symptoms at one time or another, peaking between the ages of thirty and forty-five. A small percentage of women have a severe form of PMS called *premenstrual dysphoric disorder,* or PMDD. It seems there is a spectrum of disease with symptoms ranging from physical changes on one hand to mental changes on the other. Many women suffer more physical discomforts than mental, while a minority have severe emotional changes.

There are one hundred fifty separate symptoms that have been identified as belonging to the spectrum of PMS. While no woman has all of these, most will experience several symptoms in the few days prior to her period. Physical changes include headache, breast tenderness, fluid retention, abdominal bloating, fatigue and insomnia. Mental changes include forgetfulness, confusion, depression, irritability, anger, tearfulness and anxiety. These symptoms usually occur in the second half of the menstrual cycle, between ovulation and menstruation, increasing in severity until menstrual flow begins.

It is believed that the hormone progesterone, which is only made by the ovaries in the second half of the cycle, is one of the keys to PMS. It is only as these levels decline that the symptoms begin to manifest. Just prior to menstruation there is a rapid decline in progesterone, corresponding to an increase in PMS symptoms.

By using birth control pills, women receive a steady dose of progesterone for twenty-one days of the cycle, leaving only two days of progesterone decline to trigger menstruation. The pills that are the most successful at treating PMS are those that have the same dose every day and are not "triphasic," changing doses (and colors) each week of the pill pack.

Those women who prefer a more natural approach can supplement with progesterone cream made from wild yam. This is available at most health food and vitamin retailers. Other herbal preparations that can be effective for some women include evening primrose oil, chasteberry (vitex), dong quai, black cohosh and soy. The precise formulations of these and other herbal supplements can be found in Dr. Don Colbert's *The Bible Cure for PMS and Mood Swings.*[1]

Two minerals that are active in regulating our cellular functions at almost every level include calcium and magnesium. Women who supplemented 1,200 milligrams per day of calcium and 200 milligrams per day of magnesium had significant reductions in PMS. The addition of 400 units of vitamin E was also helpful.[2]

Preventative measures include regular exercise, decreasing dietary salt and reducing sugar, caffeine and alcohol. For that small percentage of women who find that neither hormonal therapy nor natural methods bring relief of emotional symptoms, the diagnosis of PMDD may be more accurate. A deficiency in the chemical serotonin has been linked to this disorder. A new class of antidepressants called SSRIs increase serotonin levels in the brain. Two FDA-approved medications, Sarafem and Zoloft, treat the physical as well as the mental changes. They can bring great relief and comfort to a home that has been victimized by this disorder.

THE STRENGTH OF A WOMAN

Knowledge of the emotional and spiritual makeup of women is just as important as understanding the anatomic and hormonal qualities they possess. God created women to be different from men, yet complementary to them.

Men and women have different strengths and weaknesses, as we will discuss. Women's weaknesses are to be covered by men's strengths, and female strengths can fill in the gaps of male weakness. God beautifully designed us so that, in union together, all of the strengths would operate at their fullest capacity and each one's weaknesses would be covered. It is only when each partner is using his or her strengths to their fullest, without being overwhelmed by their weaknesses, that a couple reaches their divine destiny.

Scripture refers to the strength that comes when two people choose to unite their lives together:

> Two are better than one, because they have a good return for their work: if one falls down, his friend can help him up. But pity the man who falls and has no one to help him up! Also, if two lie down together, they will keep warm. But how can one keep warm alone? Though one may be overpowered, two can defend themselves.
>
> —*Ecclesiastes 4:9–12*

The New Testament teaches the power two people have in prayer together:

> If two of you on earth agree about anything you ask for, it will be done for you by my Father in heaven.
>
> —*Matthew 18:19*

These are wonderful, divine promises for husband and wife, as well as for believers in the body of Christ. However, in marriage, often the two people involved will approach the same situation differently because they were created to be different from each other.

In his book *Pursuing Sexual Wholeness*, Andrew Comiskey helps us understand the impact of these created differences.[3] Both men and women are created with divine strengths that differ from each other. However, these strengths can also become weaknesses if misused by either gender.

Women are formed in the feminine image of God, who gave them His wonderful ability to be *receivers* with a divine capacity to simply *be*—in human relationships, in their relationship with the Lord and with themselves. Women are not consumed with the drive that men experience for *becoming* something; they can just be themselves. They have a great ability to listen and hear from God and man *before* acting. They are able to yield and follow more readily then men, much as Jesus did with His Father, without feeling inferior.

Women don't generally define themselves by what they *do,* but by who they *are.* They are the nurturers, the comforters and the restorers. When the husband or children come home bruised and bleeding from the hostile world they live in, it is the woman who holds them and makes everything all right. It is she who listens to their war stories and calmly builds them back up, making them ready to face the challenges of another day. These are divine strengths given to the female psyche.

But these same strengths can be weaknesses as well. Because women are more intuitive than men, women make judgments more on feelings than facts. As a result, they can be more easily deceived by people who would lead them astray from the truth. They must guard against people who would entice them, with kind words or deeds, to believe a lie. Women often feel unsure in new situations and can be reluctant to enter uncharted territory. They naturally shy away from conflict and war. This characteristic can be a weakness or strength, depending upon the situation.

Together, men and women share the divine capacities for life that we see demonstrated between the Father and the Son: each with different characteristics, but sharing equal position. We are all a composite of God's masculine and feminine characteristics. But men are usually more dominant in the masculine traits than the feminine, with the opposite being true for women. The problems in relationships arise when men want women to think and act as a man would, and women expect their husbands to respond as a woman does. This faulty perception is perhaps no more strongly illustrated than in the terrible battle over sexual intercourse, with no capacity more profoundly affected than the area of the sexual drive, which we will discuss later.

Chapter Three

HOW GOD MADE A MAN

> "Haven't you read," he replied, "that at the beginning the Creator 'made them male and female'?"
>
> —*Matthew 19:4*

K nowledge of the male reproductive system is crucial to understanding the very essence of masculinity. In a way completely different from women, men symbolize their sexuality in one organ—the penis. Many cultures, both past and present, have glorified and even worshiped this organ. In biblical times, Baal worship included the Asherah poles, symbolizing an erect penis. Many pagan figurines and statues feature this grossly oversized organ as well. Its size and erectness have been equated with dominance and power for centuries. It is no wonder that even modern man derives most of his masculine self-esteem from his perception of this organ and its ability to perform on command.

THE WONDER OF BEING MALE

Man is set apart from all of the other creatures as being in the very image of God. When God created the heavens and the earth, the creatures of the land, the sea and the sky, He called all of it *good*. And the Scriptures declare: "Then God said, 'Let us make man in our image, in our likeness'" (Gen. 1:26). To appreciate fully what God has made, we will look at the anatomical aspects of the body that are uniquely male.

His penis

The penis is made up of three parts: the *head* (or glans), the *body* (or shaft) and the *root* (or crus). The head of the penis is covered at birth by a foreskin that is removed in circumcision. From a purely medical standpoint, circumcision is an optional practice, probably originally intended to prevent infection and penile cancer. Uncircumcised males have a more sensitive glans because it is protected in its flaccid state by the foreskin.

The opening of the urethra is at the tip of the glans, allowing both urine and semen to pass from the body. The base of the glans is called the *corona* (or crown), for its shape, and it forms a seal with the woman's vagina walls, increasing friction and sensation, which leads to ejaculation. The majority of the sexual sensations of the penis are located in the glans.

The shaft of the penis is made up of three structures: two upper cylinders called the *corpora cavernosa,* and a lower cylinder called the *corpus spongiosum.* At the center of each corpus cavernosum is an artery that pumps blood into the shaft, flattening the veins so that blood cannot escape. This produces an erection. Blood also flows through the corpus spongiosum, aiding erection of both the shaft and the head of the penis.

One question men ask me is why their penis curves, especially with erection. The answer is that this curvature is caused by a condition called Peyronie's disease, in which the lining of the shaft of the penis develops fibrous tissue that pulls it in one direction. There is no known cause, and often the surgical attempts to correct it lead only to recurrence. If there is no hindrance to urination or ejaculation, it is better left alone.

The base of the penis is formed by the splitting of the corpora cavernosa to attach to the pubic bone on each side of the penis. This connection accounts for the change in angle when the penis is erect. This portion of the penis is buried beneath the pubic region and is not visible. Those men with longer external length have a shorter base length. When the penis is erect, it may continue to point downward. Men with shorter external length have more buried in the attachments and achieve a higher angle with erection. However, over time, these internal connections stretch, and older men lose the angle of erection.

Many men are concerned with the length of their penis. The Internet is filled with websites devoted to devices and techniques to stretch the penis; even plastic surgeons have begun offering such procedures. Most of the surgical techniques involve bringing the part of the body of the penis that is hidden under the pubic region to a more forward position, usually by cutting or stretching the ligaments attached to the pubic bone. This gives the appearance of a longer penis in its flaccid state, although its erect state is only minimally changed.

With this procedure, the angle of erection is sacrificed by the cutting of the ligaments. Since it makes no impact on intercourse, the only reason to do this procedure is to improve the appearance of the penis in its flaccid state. This has more to do with how the penis looks in comparison to other men, such as in locker rooms, dormitories or military barracks, than it does with pleasing a spouse.

As we mentioned, the size of the penis has long been equated with male power and superiority in many cultures and for many centuries. While rarely verbalizing it, a man is often concerned with how he compares with other men, especially if his wife had other sexual relationships before him. It is unfortunate, as well, if in their early years men were exposed to pornography, because that industry tends to choose men with a penis size on the larger end of the spectrum. Most average viewers would find themselves on the smaller side if these "role models" were used as the standard for comparison.

It is also common for men to believe that larger size equals increased female satisfaction. This belief has been reinforced by our culture through various media. The fact is, however, that in my many years of medical practice, I have almost never heard a woman complain about her husband being too small to satisfy her. But I hear complaints from several women each month who resist intercourse because they perceive that their partner is too large for them. Many women complain of pain as a result, and I have met couples unable to consummate their marriage because of this.

Virtually none of my female patients would ever want their spouses to have surgery to create a larger appearance to the penis. In many ways, that procedure is very different from breast augmentation, which is often done for the viewing pleasure of the husband. Attempts at penile enlargement are almost never done to please the spouse; rather, it is a way to bolster male ego.

His testes and sperm

There are other organs to consider in this survey of male anatomy. The testicles, while not the main focus of male pride, are nonetheless carefully guarded due to the risk of injury and severe pain. Each testicle is similar to the female ovary; reproductive cells and male hormones are both made in this organ. The sperm are manufactured in the testes and, unlike women, who have all the eggs they will ever have at birth, men continue to produce new sperm every minute of every day from puberty to old age. The maturation process of sperm takes about seventy days.

The sperm leave the testicle and enter a coiled duct called the epididymis. This structure sits next to the testicle and can be a startling finding on self-examination if its presence is not expected. It is here that the sperm acquire their final feature, the ability to swim. These sperm swim out of the epididymis and enter the vas deferens, a tube about a foot long leading to the penis. A *vasectomy* is the cutting of this tube to interrupt the passage of sperm.

Unlike the female, male hormone production has little monthly variation. There is no "cycle" and no real "menopause" for men. Testosterone levels gradually decline with age, but there is no distinct or sudden decline that is noticeable to men, and there are no male episodes similar to female PMS. It may be for this reason that men find the hormonal fluctuations of women, sometimes an hourly event, so difficult to understand.

The testicles are housed in a sac called the scrotum that is lined with muscle fibers. These can tighten, bringing the testicles closer to the body for warmth, or loosen to pull them away from the body when the environment is too warm. The scrotum will also contract with perceived danger, probably as a defense mechanism to prevent injury. The testicle is very sensitive to heat, medications, drug abuse, radiation and injury.

The sperm are mixed with fluids that nourish them and constitute the main product of ejaculation, or the semen. It is made by the seminal vesicles on each side and the centrally located prostate gland, all of which are located beneath the bladder. The urethra passes through the prostate gland. With impending ejaculation, the semen is deposited into the back of the urethra for passage through the penis. Even in men who have had a vasectomy, the semen is still ejaculated normally. It simply lacks the addition of sperm, an amount that is not noticeable to men and will not affect the quality or quantity of the ejaculate.

UNLIKE THE FEMALE, MALE HORMONE PRODUCTION HAS LITTLE MONTHLY VARIATION.

His prostate gland

The prostate gland is perhaps the most mysterious male reproductive organ because it cannot be seen and is also difficult to feel. This walnut-sized gland is located in front of the rectum and surrounds the base of the bladder. Its main function is to release fluid into the urethra through a series of muscular contractions during ejaculation. This fluid gives energy to the sperm and balances the pH of the vagina, making it less acidic and more hospitable to sperm.

BPH and treatment

As men age, the prostate gland begins to grow and can lead to an enlarged prostate condition called BPH (benign prostatic hypertrophy). It rarely occurs in men under the age of forty, but more than 50 percent of men in their sixties and nearly 90 percent of men in their seventies and eighties experience some symptoms of BPH.[1]

The main symptoms of BPH are urinary in nature. As the prostate swells, the urethra becomes constricted, limiting the flow of urine and occasionally obstructing flow completely. As the bladder contracts harder to force the urine out, its walls thicken and become irritable. This can lead to a sensation of urgency, feeling the need to urinate even when only small amounts of urine are present. At some point, the bladder can weaken and lose its ability to empty itself.

Men who suffer with BPH make frequent trips to the bathroom and have a weakened urinary stream, taking far longer to void than when they were younger. Many will awaken throughout the night with a need to void, which robs them of needed rest.

The causes of BPH are unknown but appear to be linked to testosterone, specifically a by-product called dihydrotestosterone (DHT). This hormone accumulates in the hair follicles as well as the prostate gland, leading to male baldness.

Prolonged, untreated BPH can lead to irreversible damage to the bladder and kidneys. It is important to seek medical help when this condition is present. While eight out of ten cases will be benign, prostate cancer may also present with similar symptoms.

Treatments for BPH include drug therapy, nonsurgical and surgical therapies. Several medications are FDA-approved for the treatment of BPH. Some target DHT and cause shrinkage of the gland. Others relax the muscles of the prostate to improve urine flow.

Nonsurgical treatments include microwave therapy that heats and destroys excess prostate tissue. This is performed as an outpatient procedure without the need for general anesthesia. It does not cure BPH, but it reduces the urgency, frequency and straining associated with BPH. Needle ablation delivers radio-frequency energy to the prostate to burn away unwanted glandular tissue to improve urine flow. Neither the microwave or needle ablation procedures have been found to cause incontinence or impotence.

The impact of prostate surgery

The best long-term solution for BPH currently available is the removal of the enlarged portion of the prostate gland through surgery. This can be done by three methods. Ninety percent of all the surgical procedures for BPH are done through the urethra by a technique called transurethral resection of the prostate (TURP). An instrument is inserted through the opening of the penis that includes a scope for visualization and a wire loop that cuts pieces of the prostate gland. The remnants are flushed through the urethra at the end of the case.

For those men with extremely large prostate glands or bladder damage, an open procedure is done with an incision made between the scrotum and anus. Side effects can include retrograde ejaculation, where male orgasm carries the semen backward into the bladder instead of forward through the penis.

A newer approach includes use of a laser to shrink prostate tissue. It causes less blood loss and faster recovery but is limited by prostate size. Its long-term effectiveness is not yet known. As with any treatment decision, careful consultation with a skilled urologist is crucial.

Many men are concerned about the impact of prostate surgery on their sexual function. This may cause them to delay seeking treatment. The truth is that the longer the disease has been active, the longer it will take to recover from treatment. While urinary recovery is more rapid, complete recovery of sexual function may take a year.

While surgery rarely impacts the ability to have an erection, it will not improve potency that was missing before surgery. The problem of retrograde ejaculation, already mentioned, which causes the semen to go backward into the bladder, will cause men who suffer this complication to be sterile. However, since BPH is mainly a condition relating to older men, this is often not a significant loss. A "dry climax" does not impact the sensation of orgasm, and most men find intercourse as pleasurable as before.

Treatment for BPH is not a permanent cure, but it can give relief for up to fifteen years. Only 10 percent of men who have surgical therapy require a second operation in their lifetime.[2]

Cancer of the prostate

An unrelated but far more serious condition than BPH is *prostate cancer*. As mentioned earlier, symptoms of prostate cancer can be very similar to BPH. This cancer is the second leading cause of cancer deaths among men, behind lung cancer. It accounts for 11 percent of all male cancer deaths in the United States. Prostate cancer is also extremely common. While only one in thirty-two men will die of prostate cancer, one in six will contract it in their lifetime, making it the most common cancer in men, excluding skin cancers.[3]

Most prostate cancers grow very slowly and may exist for decades before symptoms appear. A digital rectal exam (DRE) is the first screening test done by a physician. A gloved finger is inserted through the rectum to palpate the prostate gland for any enlargement, bumps or abnormal areas. The National Cancer Institute recommends this exam be done annually for every man age fifty and older. For African American men, who have a higher incidence of prostate cancer, and men who have a close male relative with the disease (father or brother), the exams should begin between age forty and forty-five.

It is the discomfort and embarrassment caused by this exam that has kept many men away from their physicians. Sadly, by the time symptoms cause the person to seek medical attention, it may be too late for a cure.

The second screening tool for prostate cancer is the prostate-specific antigen, or PSA. This test measures the amount of PSA in the bloodstream and can be elevated in both benign and malignant conditions. It is just a screening tool. An elevated PSA does not mean a person has cancer. In men over age fifty, 15 percent will have an elevated PSA, but only 3 percent will have cancer.[4] In other words, 80 percent of the men with a high PSA will have a noncancerous condition such as prostatitis (an inflamed prostate) or BPH. The higher the PSA, the greater is the likelihood that the patient has cancer. To confirm this, an ultrasound-guided biopsy of the prostate is required.

Treatments for prostate cancer vary with patient age and stage of disease. Radiation can be used externally or can be implanted directly into the prostate gland. Hormone therapy to reduce testosterone, or castration itself, can be used to prolong life in advanced cases. Radical prostate surgery to remove the entire gland is commonly offered. All of these treatments carry significant risks to the patient. Some will experience urinary incontinence, impotence or even rectal difficulties. A careful and thorough review of all options is required.

Obviously, treatment of prostate cancer carries tremendous implications for male sexual function because of the damage to nerves and arteries that such treatment can cause. We will discuss treatments for impotence in a later chapter.

I strongly encourage all wives to use whatever means are necessary to ensure that their husbands receive a thorough physical examination each year. I believe you should follow the apostle Paul's instruction to women: "The husband's body does not belong to him alone but also to his wife" (1 Cor. 7:4). Take good care of your property!

THE STRENGTH OF A MAN

Many men often do not understand why women don't react and respond to a given situation in the way that a man would, and they become frustrated when women see things differently from the way they perceive them. The simple answer to their different responses is that men are different from women, created that way by God Himself.

Men are formed in the masculine image of God the Creator, who gave them the ability to initiate, to effect change, to push through to victory against all resistance, to act on one's deeply held convictions, to protect and defend, and to pursue a goal until it is achieved. These are divine strengths given to the male psyche. Even the masculine sex organ, the penis, symbolizes this creative ability to go forward into unknown territory and take charge.

The key to a man's strength lies in having a relationship with God. God called King David "a man after my own heart" (Acts 13:22). What kind of man was he, and what characteristics did he possess that we as men are endowed with by God for His use?

As a teenager, David was a humble and gentle servant, tending sheep while his brothers vied to be anointed king by the prophet Samuel. Young David's strength did not lie in the way he looked, but in his character. God taught His prophet not to be impressed with the way a man looked. He said to him: "Do not consider his appearance or his height...The LORD does not look at the things man looks at. Man looks at the outward appearance, but the LORD looks at the heart" (1 Sam. 16:7).

David was an anointed worshiper who was able to comfort and soothe King Saul with his music. He was not afraid or embarrassed about worship after he became king. He commanded the people to sing, lift their hands and dance before the Lord as he did.

He was also a mighty warrior for God, understanding that his strength did not come from himself but from God. He called upon the Lord: "Keep me safe, O God, for in you I take refuge...You are my Lord: apart from you I have no good thing" (Ps. 16:1–2).

But like other men, David had his weaknesses, most profoundly in the area of lust. David looked upon the naked Bathsheba and desired her for his wife. Even though she was the wife of his loyal soldier Uriah, he sent for her and slept with her. When she conceived his child, David had her husband killed in battle and took her to be his own wife. His lust cost him the life of his son and the greatest desire of his heart—to build the temple of God.

God has given men a wonderful potential to become mighty warriors for their families, their churches and their communities, standing for the righteousness of God. But without a strong relationship with God, they can become abusive, domineering, obsessive and lust-driven. The key to their strength, as we stated, is in becoming a man after God's own heart.

Chapter **Four**

UNDERSTANDING OUR
SEX DRIVE

Isaac brought her into the tent of his mother
Sarah, and he married Rebekah. So she
became his wife; and he loved her; and Isaac
was comforted after his mother's death.
—Genesis 24:67

In spite of God's good plan for sexual fulfillment in marriage, in seminar after seminar I am asked the same question from men: "Why doesn't my wife ever initiate sex?" The flip side of that question comes from the women: "Why is my sexual drive so low compared to my husband's?" These questions expose a complex issue involving many factors; the answers are vital to any couple struggling in their sexual relationship.

And it seems to be an issue that has only recently surfaced with the "sexual" revolution of the 1960s. Generations past did not struggle so intensely with the idea of unequal sexual drive. It was seen as *normal* for the man to possess a greater drive for intercourse than the woman. But with the emphasis placed on sex in our culture and the infusion of the women's rights movement, there is a new perception that men and women should have an equal sexual drive. When that does not manifest itself in "real" life, both the husband and wife want to know, *Why not?*

WHAT THE MEDIA
PORTRAY IS FICTION

As we discussed earlier, men are created with a stronger tendency to initiate, while women are often better able to receive. It is within these God-given roles that men would naturally be the initiators of intercourse and women the receivers of their love. And there would be less problem with misunderstanding these roles if the world hadn't interfered by injecting its ungodly "standards."

Hollywood's influence

On televisions and movie screens, in books and magazines, in music videos and video games, the role is portrayed of a woman who is sexually desirable taking charge over the man: ripping off his shirt, unbuttoning his pants and taking control. This scenario has become every man's fantasy because it is Hollywood's fantasy. However, this perception of a woman's role is a complete reversal of the way God made us. This model of sexual activity should never be perceived as the norm.

Much of the discrepancy expressed by men and women concerning sexual drive is a matter of perception: It involves what you *think* you should be doing or what your spouse *wants* you to do. And some of the sense of "lower" sexual drive in women is actually a reflection of how they perceive a "good" Christian woman should behave. In their proper rejection of Hollywood's version of the oversexed, promiscuous harlot, women may unwittingly reject the natural desires God placed within them. This lack of understanding of what is normal and acceptable in a godly sexual relationship plagues many women.

Biblical freedom

While men are routinely taught that their sex drive is a strong aspect of what it is to be a man, women rarely receive such positive reinforcement, especially from the Christian community. Women can confuse the godly understanding of being submitted to their husbands with being "submissive," passively waiting for him to initiate sexual activity. They wrongly interpret a desire to have intercourse with their spouse as outside their rights, a product of their "flesh" that the Bible commands us to crucify.

The Bible teaches us the proper perspective to have regarding marital sex and sets us free from the world's distorted perceptions. For example, the apostle Paul commands the husband to fulfill his marital duty to his wife and the wife to her husband:

> The husband should fulfill his marital duty to his wife, and likewise the wife to her husband. The wife's body does not belong to her alone but also to her husband. In the same way, the husband's body does not belong to him alone but also to his wife. Do not deprive each other...
>
> *—1 Corinthians 7:3–5*

This mutual sharing of each other's body as taught by the Scriptures gives freedom to the Christian couple to understand that both the man and the woman have a right to have sex without fearing they are somehow displeasing God. The apostle Paul warns them not to deprive one another, except for a period of time they would devote to prayer, lest Satan tempt them to be unfaithful (1 Cor. 7:5).

Just discovering this truth can increase a woman's sexual desire for her husband because she now realizes she has a right to it. And a husband's understanding of the God-given differences between the initiator he is and the receiver she is may give him more reasonable (godly) expectations of his wife.

The role of hormones

There is another important difference between men and women that affects the natural sex drive—the hormone *testosterone*. In men, testosterone is the primary sex hormone, whereas in women it is a very small part of their hormonal makeup. Testosterone fuels the sexual drive, so the differences in levels of testosterone between male and female also contribute to what many couples see as an imbalance in sexual drive. The bottom line reality is that men and women are created by God with drastically different sexual drives; if we accept this fact, we can come to a much healthier idea of what "normal" really is.

ISSUES THAT DECREASE A WOMAN'S SEX DRIVE

Some women who attend my seminars express frustration because their sexual drive is lower than it used to be. They compare their current desire with their past selves and sense a problem. This too can be a reality for several reasons.

Hormonal changes

Depending on the woman's age, many have noticed that as they approach or proceed through menopause, their sexual desire declines. This decline occurs because the ovaries begin to decrease production of all the sex hormones, particularly estrogen. When this happens, the lining that covers the vagina and clitoris thins, making it more fragile and easier to traumatize. The amount of natural lubrication lessens, increasing the friction in intercourse and the likelihood of tearing the lining. This makes the act of intercourse painful, and anything painful is avoided.

Why would your body express a desire for something that it knows will hurt you? So, as a protective mechanism, a woman's desire will decline if she perceives that the act will be painful. Each time intercourse is uncomfortable, it only reinforces this response, and the cycle of ever-lowering sexual drive continues.

Use of birth control pills

Even younger women can find themselves with lower testosterone levels than they used to have due to the effects of birth control pills. As we discussed earlier, the birth control pill suppresses the ovaries' natural production of hormones and replaces it with its own formula. This is often accompanied by a decrease in previous testosterone levels. It is one of the reasons the pill is used to treat female acne, a testosterone-driven condition. But many women complain to me about loss of sexual drive after beginning to take the birth control pill. Often changing to a brand with a different formula will alleviate this loss, and her sexual drive will return to more acceptable levels.

Other medications

The most common medications that affect the sex drive include those used to treat high blood pressure, depression and other psychiatric conditions. These can inhibit not only sexual desire but also the ability to achieve an orgasm. Consultation with your physician can determine if a change in prescription might benefit your sexual drive without compromising your health.

Decreased energy

Many women today have accepted more roles and responsibilities than God ever created them to handle. The average woman works forty hours a week, cooks dinner, helps with her children's homework, cleans the house, pays the bills, bathes and puts the kids to bed, and is supposed to have something left at the end of the long day to take care of her husband's sexual needs—and hers. It's not going to happen! With everyone taking away pieces of her throughout the day, it is easy to find there is nothing left to give. Or she may feel that the last little piece she has belongs to her, and she will be reluctant to let it go.

A wise husband will share the duties at home and relieve some of the burden from his wife's shoulders. This may be contrary to the role model of fathers they observed while growing up. But if the wife works full time outside of the home, there must be some sharing of the domestic responsibilities. It is ultimately in the husband's best interest to share household duties if he wants his wife to have any energy left for sex.

While we are addressing the issue of energy, it is important that you understand that a physically active woman (or man) has much more stamina than a sedentary one. She will be in a much better position to handle the rigors of being a wife and mother if her body is strong.

I hear so many people complain that they are too tired to exercise. What they fail to realize is that exercise itself builds strength and stamina and will leave you less tired at the end of the day. If you could begin to exercise, in faith, even when you feel tired, within a few short weeks you would be surprised at how much more energy you have. And the sexual benefits of increased exercise have been well documented.

Quality of relationship

Another factor that affects sexual drive in women, which men too often ignore, is quality of relationship. Women need commitments of time, intimacy and caring from their husbands. They need to know that their views have been heard and that they have shared their lives with the person they will be uniting themselves with in intercourse. This doesn't happen in a conversation over the rim of a newspaper or while channel-surfing cable television. For a woman to desire to be "known" sexually by her husband, she must first have her desire to be known in all other aspects of herself satisfied.

Lack of communication, lack of attention and marital discord poison the well of sexual desire for women. They want to be treated to the same intensity of relationship by their man as when they were being courted. Pressures of job, money, children and even church work and social activities can take us away from our first love for our spouses. For a woman, this is a key factor in feeling less willing to give of herself sexually to someone who has not first given of himself to her the consideration of time and attention.

Pain

Was intercourse a pleasurable or painful experience for her? If her partner rushed into penile penetration before she had adequate foreplay that allowed her to be well lubricated, the process of intercourse could be painful for her. Arousal in women causes the vagina to lengthen by 30 percent and pulls the internal organs away from penile contact.[1] Entering the vagina before arousal is fully developed can lead to bumping of the internal organs. The equivalent pain in men would be a result of the testicles being bumped repeatedly!

As we stated earlier, anything that is consistently painful will be avoided. Gynecologic conditions such as endometriosis, uterine fibroids or pelvic scar tissue can also be painful and diminish pleasure for the woman, and should be discussed with a knowledgeable physician.

Pain need not be *physical* in order to diminish pleasure and cause a decrease in sexual drive. Emotional pain is as vigorously avoided as physical pain. It is estimated that 25 percent of women have been either physically or sexually abused during their lives.[2] As a result, their emotional pain may cause them to unconsciously separate themselves from the sexual experience as a defense against further pain.

Even in a relationship that is now free from danger and harm, the body may respond to sexual advances with avoidance behavior. Counseling is often needed for these women to be able to recapture what has been stolen from them so they can enjoy the intimate pleasures God had in store for them from the beginning.

Even without a history of abuse, a wife may experience emotional hurt.

If the experience of intercourse does not leave her feeling better about herself or her relationship with her husband, the desire to experience that activity again will diminish. And her perception of the event will color the reality of it. If she feels she did not perform well or is no longer satisfying to her husband, her sexual drive will diminish. And she could wrongly interpret his erectile dysfunction as a reflection on her ability to arouse desire, when it may have nothing to do with her. It could be a medical condition for which her husband needs to seek professional help.

Misconceptions

If the sexual experience is always one-sided, the woman will grow frustrated or resentful. Many women do not know they have a right to orgasm or don't know what it takes to achieve one. Misconceptions, often fueled by Hollywood or romance novels, lead women to believe that orgasm should be achieved automatically during vaginal intercourse alone. She wonders, *Everyone else seems to experience simultaneous and mutually satisfying orgasm in this way. What's wrong with me?*

But scientific studies document that only 30 percent of women will achieve orgasm solely on the basis of vaginal intercourse.[3] Most women need more than that, but for many couples, both the woman and her spouse are ignorant of what it takes to achieve her satisfaction. Consequently, women often leave the experience of intercourse feeling that it was rather one-sided. And while it is nice to please one's husband, that alone will wear thin over time, and the desire to participate in such activity will be very low. We will explore this area in more detail in a later chapter.

In the next chapter, we will look at the final hindrance to female sexual drive—body image. We will discuss the part that increased weight gain, poor muscle tone and other anatomic changes wrought by aging and pregnancy play in diminishing sexual desire. But first, let me share the story of a couple that represents what we have been discussing so you can see how this plays out in real life.

Real Life

Twenty-five-year-old Karen, an attractive professional woman, came to my office for her yearly examination. She and her husband, Richard, have been married for three years. Karen works as a legal secretary, and Richard is an insurance adjuster. They have an eight-month-old son, Jake, whom they both adore. Their marriage seems to be wonderful, even to those who know them well.

During the examination, Karen and I exchanged small talk, and I asked her if she was still breast-feeding. She replied that when she went back to work four months ago it became difficult to continue pumping milk at work, so she only nursed him in the morning and then at night before he went to bed. She had recently begun a mini-pill for birth control that contains no estrogen so as not to interfere with milk production, and she had not had a period since delivery.

As I began to write her a refill prescription for birth control, I asked her if there was anything else she needed or would like to bring up at this visit. Hesitantly, she stated that her sexual drive was not what it was before Jake was born, and as the months went by, Richard became increasingly frustrated by her reluctance to have sex. In fact, he was so concerned that he had come to the appointment with her and was in the waiting room, hoping that I as her doctor would provide the key to unlock their shackled sexual life.

Since Richard had come with her, I asked Karen if it would be all right for him to come back to the consultation room with her while we discussed this problem. With Richard sitting beside her, I began the conversation by telling him that Karen had noticed a change in her sexual drive since delivering Jake and had asked for my help. In a concerned and loving way, Richard agreed that the situation was becoming a problem for them and that many arguments had occurred because of her refusal to be intimate sexually with him. He felt he had been very patient and had given her plenty of time, but after eight months, he expected things to be the way they used to be. While Richard loved Jake very much, at times he found himself regretting that they had ever had a child, as he felt a wedge growing between the once happy union he enjoyed with his wife.

Richard was taking more and more assignments out of town, in part to make more money to replace what had been forfeited during Karen's maternity leave, and in part to avoid her rejections at night. It was easier for him to sleep alone in a hotel room than to lie next to his wife and know he was unwelcome. He wondered if she even loved him anymore. And he knew that with the temptations that presented themselves on the road, he was vulnerable to an affair should the situation at home fail to improve.

As I listened to Richard, I noticed that several statements seemed to catch Karen off-guard, as if she were hearing them for the very first time. I realized that the arguments they had had over this issue had not involved true sharing and receiving of information, but involved, instead, a barrage of hurt and pain. Karen, of course, had her own story to tell.

She and Richard had looked forward to Jake's birth with great anticipation. When he was born, they were excited and overjoyed to be parents. He was perfect in every way, and they took him home from the hospital, ready to begin their new family. Richard had agreed with Karen's desire to stay home with Jake as long as possible. Between maternity leave and money they had set aside, Karen was able to stay home with him for four months. Her employers were very understanding and did not replace her position, but left everything as it was until she could return to work. This meant that she was instantly overwhelmed by the workload that had accumulated during her four-month absence.

Karen struggled at first with breast-feeding, but she began to enjoy the bonding she was receiving from Jake and the fulfillment that came from watching him grow from her breast milk alone. It was a sense of accomplishment she had never felt before. At Karen's six-week postpartum visit, I had examined her episiotomy site and found it well healed, telling her that she was able to become sexually active again and that she should consider birth control other than what breast-feeding alone offered. Karen was familiar with oral contraception and chose a mini-pill that was compatible with breast-feeding.

Richard was ready and waiting when she returned from that visit, and Karen admitted that she also felt desire for him after such a long waiting period. After getting Jake asleep, they began to make love in their usual style, and she was surprised by the lack of lubrication she was experiencing. She and Richard had never needed artificial lubrication before, so they were unprepared for this situation. Friction from vaginal dryness or tenderness from the episiotomy scar caused Karen to experience pain with that first act of intercourse. Fortunately, Richard was so excited to be making love that the experience lasted only a couple minutes and was mercifully finished.

Karen assumed that things would progressively improve, but they did not. In fact, she noticed that several things seemed to be happening at the same time to sabotage even her best efforts to be a willing sexual partner. While she loved breast-feeding, by the end of the day she longed for her body to be left alone. Now, it seemed as if Richard was one more person to "feed." Some days even the thought of him lying on her made her retreat to her corner of the bed, hiding behind a book or magazine.

Jake often woke for feedings at the same time they were preparing to go to sleep. Sometimes when she would agree to have sex, she couldn't help but have one ear trained to the baby monitor. Every whimper or cry would distract her, and this seemed to make Richard rush to climax for fear that he would be discarded in mid-coitus for the baby.

When I questioned Karen, she could not remember achieving orgasm since Jake was born. It had always taken her some time to reach climax, but their new lovemaking style seemed geared toward a more rapid conclusion. In Richard's defense, he feared that his window of opportunity was so brief it might close on him at any moment, and he developed a habit of rushing climax so he would not be frustrated.

Several other issues were addressed during that session. Because intercourse was now uncomfortable for Karen, she had a natural tendency to avoid it. The lack of estrogen from breast-feeding and the mini-pill caused decreased vaginal lubrication and increased friction, especially over her episiotomy scar. Every time of intercourse that was physically unpleasant only reinforced a pattern that led Karen, even unconsciously, to avoid the experience.

Even when intercourse wasn't uncomfortable, it seemed to offer very little in a positive dimension for Karen. It was so brief and one-sided that she was receiving no pleasure from it at all. And while she acknowledged her responsibility for creating the limitations of the new routine, it nevertheless made intercourse for her just another task she was expected to do for someone else.

When she returned to work it became even worse. Not only was she overwhelmed by all the work that had been left waiting for her return, but when she came home there was still housekeeping and cooking to do, not to mention giving herself to Jake to make up for the time he had spent in day care.

By the end of the day, Karen felt that all the pieces of herself had been taken away. And if she had managed to cling desperately to one final piece, here came Richard asking for it, in the form of intercourse. I explained to them that while she felt she could not control the pieces her job took, or the house took, or Jake took, that last piece belonged to her and she could control that one. Withholding from Richard was not as much about denying him as it was about preserving some small sense of self, something left at the end of the day that she could hold on to.

What should have been a beautiful exchange of pieces between them was furthered sabotaged by their new lovemaking "style." Had Karen experienced sexual fulfillment and satisfaction from the experience, she would have been far better off than to lie in bed alone. But instead, intercourse had turned into an uncomfortable and one-sided chore. Not only that, but I suspected that as Richard began spending more time at work, she resented having to do everything at home and still work full time. And his absences sent signals to her that she misinterpreted as being due to her lack of physical attractiveness since giving birth.

My prescription that day involved several sets of instructions:

- First, Karen had to realize that she was not Superwoman. She could not do it all. Jake was taking pieces from her that she had previously given to Richard. She was still working, keeping house and cooking as she has always done. Something needed to change. Depending on their financial ability, I suggested that Karen hire someone to come in once or twice a week to clean her house and do her laundry.

- Richard could take turns cooking, or he could bring food home with him. While Karen was getting dinner ready, he could bathe Jake and enjoy some bonding time with his son instead of burying his head in papers he brought home from the office. I suggested that Richard put Jake to bed whenever possible while Karen prepared for her own bed-time routine. Maybe a relaxing bath or a glass of wine would help melt away the stresses of her workday.

- I also told Karen to turn the baby monitor down and place her focus on Richard during their time of intercourse. He in turn was to be given, as much as was possible, the time to be the lover he had been in the past. Artificial lubrication was to become part of foreplay, and he was to enter vaginally only when she was ready. Whatever she needed to do to achieve orgasm was his goal; his focus was to be on Karen. I wanted her to discover that intercourse was not a piece that was taken away, but in a very real way, it was an exchange that would leave her feeling full again, not empty.

We were realistic in stating that these criteria would not always be achieved, but the goals and ideals were set forth clearly to work toward. Richard had a new appreciation for the demands that were placed on Karen from all sides, and Karen made a commitment to discover again a passion for her husband that she had sacrificed for her nurturing of Jake.

Several months later I had the opportunity to see Karen in the office again, and when I asked her how she and her husband were doing, she spontaneously flashed a broad, satisfied smile. Somewhere, I was sure Richard was smiling, too.

Chapter **Five**

HOW BODY IMAGE
AFFECTS A WOMAN

> The young woman was lovely and beautiful...
> The king loved Esther more than all the other
> women, and she obtained grace and favor in
> his sight more than all the virgins.
> —*Esther 2:7, 17*, NKJV

The well-known cliché "Beauty is in the eye of the beholder" is only partially accurate; it depends on whose values have influenced the "eye." Wall Street has saturated every department store and women's magazine, as well as print and television commercials, with its version of the "ideal woman." A composite description of their beautiful woman would read like this:

> She is six feet tall, wafer thin, has oversized breasts, with perfect hair, teeth and skin to match. She seems to possess all of these features with little effort, and she has become the force behind the fashion and cosmetics industries.

THE ILLUSION OF PERFECTION

In truth, this image of the "perfect" woman is an illusion; if she exists, she is the product of dangerous dieting, smoking, cocaine use, plastic surgery, airbrushing and digital refinements not available to the average woman living on this planet. However, many women unfairly compare themselves with this hypothetical "ideal" and become gripped with the defeating thought that they do not "measure up." Their painful perception often translates into a conviction that they are not sexually desirable, which can lead to women's varied attempts to avoid sexual intimacy.

WALL STREET'S IMAGE OF A "PERFECT" WOMAN IS AN ILLUSION.

Laboring under this illusion of physical perfection, a woman may fear her husband will reject her because of a few extra pounds she has gained, breasts that have fallen from breast-feeding, stretch marks that cover her stomach or hair turning gray with age. If a woman is not comfortable with the way she looks, she will shrink from the light of scrutiny. A few ill-timed comments by her husband about how poorly she looks or how great someone else appears will cement these fears into devastating reality in her psyche.

A double standard

While life may have left a man with a beer gut, a bald head and more facial lines than a road map, he rarely questions whether he looks physically pleasing to his wife. The world's standards have not placed pressures of appearance upon him, and he is relatively immune to male-oriented advertising that would suggest the contrary. He can have a 102-degree fever and fail to bathe for a week—and still desire sex! Society has a double standard in this regard.

THE FEAR OF INTIMACY

But for women, part of sex is intimacy, a deep connection of the soul that is both physical and emotional. It is the peeling back of the layers of protection we so often place around our souls to protect us. For men, the emotional aspect of intimacy may be far more difficult to achieve than the physical. But for women, the physical part of intimacy involves risking that what is discovered about her appearance may lead to rejection in her most vulnerable state. Even if her husband never says a word, she has already accepted the judgment of the advertising world's standards and placed a sentence upon herself. She needs reassurance from her husband to the contrary.

> IF A WOMAN DOES NOT FEEL ATTRACTIVE AND DESIRABLE, SHE WILL NOT SEEK OUT VULNERABLE SITUATIONS WHERE REJECTION IS A POSSIBILITY.

Society's "sentence" of judgment tells her she is unattractive and unworthy of sexual attention. She concludes that if her husband wants sex with her, it can't be because he finds her desirable and attractive; he is only satisfying his own needs, and she is the easy answer. If a woman does not feel attractive and desirable, she will not seek out vulnerable situations where rejection is a possibility. A woman who feels she has nothing to offer will not want to participate in sexual intercourse.

COPING WITH CHANGES
AFTER SURGERY

I also see this reluctance to engage in sex in women who have had surgery that changes their physical appearance for the "worse." An example of this would be trauma of the post-mastectomy patient. Some time after the breast cancer treatments have concluded and the fear of dying has subsided, her husband will want to resume the sex life they once enjoyed. But many women who have had mastectomies, especially if reconstructive surgery has not been done, no longer view themselves as sexually desirable. Losing her breast, in a woman's mind, equates to losing her sexual appeal, and she feels less attractive to her husband, whether or not that is true for her husband.[1]

The truth is that almost every husband I talk to is so grateful for his spouse's restored health, so appreciative of his "second chance" to enjoy her, that he feels even more attracted to her than before the cancer appeared. He no longer takes his wife for granted; having faced the awful prospect of losing her, he now views her as more precious than before.

The way men express this reality is through sexual activity. Unfortunately, many times the woman is telling herself she is not attractive any longer and that he only wants to have sex to meet his needs or as an expression of pity for her. For these women, the battle of the physical disease may have been conquered, but the battle of the mind is just beginning. A husband needs to be sensitive to these often unspoken fears and reassure his wife of his love for her.

HOW A MAN HURTS HIS
WIFE'S SELF-IMAGE

In many situations, however, it is not just Hollywood or the fashion industry that contributes to the low self-esteem many women possess because of poor body image. The man who desires sex poisons the well of his wife's sexual attentions with his demeaning comments and behaviors. A husband's wayward glances at other women, those who pass by and those who capture his attention in film or print, reinforce the conviction in his wife's mind that she no longer has what it takes to arouse him.

A husband's preoccupation with his job can also translate easily in her mind as rejection of her because of how she looks. Devotion to a particular hobby or sport is often misinterpreted as his desire to avoid spending time with her. Although the husband may not be aware of the impact these behaviors are having on his wife, the result is the same—a deflated female sexual drive and a frustrated husband, who then spends more time away, setting in motion a vicious cycle.

WHAT WOMEN CAN DO
TO HELP THEMSELVES

There is a simple reality also that while few women will ever look like a swimsuit model all of their lives, most can look better than they do, even after years of marriage. I see a large percentage of women in my office who diet and exercise to look their best on their wedding day. However, when they are settled into the marital routine, exercise and good nutritional habits fall away, and significant weight gain follows.

Sometimes when I see a woman after a few years of marriage, she no longer resembles the person she used to be, and her self-esteem has plummeted. She complains that her husband no longer shows her the attention or affection she once enjoyed while courting, but she does not realize the simple reason is that the man she married feels betrayed.

In his book *His Needs, Her Needs*, Willard Harley lists "attractive spouse" among the top five needs of men.[2] Many men see the attractiveness of their wives as a reflection on themselves. The husband feels more capable and successful if he can attract a beautiful woman to marry him. And many men feel betrayed when their once beautiful, physically fit and energetic wife becomes tired, overweight and unkempt. As Harley points out, men are not all looking for the perfect "ten"; they just want the woman they originally fell in love with.

While no woman can cheat the hands of time, most could lose weight, tone their bodies, dress more attractively and use cosmetics and hair products to their advantage, helping them to age gracefully. When they make this effort, not only will their chances for receiving the attention they desire from their husbands improve, but also their own self-esteem will rise. While this reality affects many aspects of life besides sexual drive, it is a fact that women who feel more attractive will be more sexual. And women who satisfy their husbands feel more successful as spouses and more secure about their marriages.

I am always amazed at the physical transformation a woman will undergo when she is divorcing, which she would not do when she was married. It is not uncommon for me to see a patient in the office who has lost twenty or thirty pounds since her last annual exam, only to discover that she is getting a divorce. The separation has caused her to take a hard look at life in the single lane again, and she begins to get back into shape to attract another spouse. If only she had taken these steps while she was still married.

"Trophy" maintenance

Among professionals, one often sees an older man walking with an attractive and much younger woman by his side. She is most often wife number two, the "trophy" wife. She is his "prize" for being successful. Having thoughtlessly discarded the mother of his children, who stood faithfully by him through the lean years before he became successful, he now feels entitled to a woman worthy of his success.

While my wife and I are often amused by these pairings, I occasionally remind her that although she is my first wife, she is also my "trophy." I have no intentions of trading her in for a newer model, but I don't want my trophy to get tarnished or dented either! This frees her to spend some of our income on "trophy maintenance."

It is a shortsighted husband who would complain about his wife spending money on her appearance. While every household has its budget, the physical appearance of the wife should be a line item. Men regularly spend money to maintain cars, lawns and houses, but they complain about their wives' new hair color or dress. This faulty prioritizing is both sexual and relational suicide.

I know this next statement may seem sexist and outdated, but it is simply the truth: Women do not place male attractiveness as high on their list for husbands as they do his being a good provider and making a stable home for their children. But men place a very high value on their wives' appearance, even if, in their ignorance, they sabotage those efforts by complaining about the money their wives spend to improve it. The honest man will tell you that it is important to him. Those who say it is not may be lying!

Beating the competition

In a country with a 50 percent divorce rate, which, tragically, includes the Christian community, it is in the best interest of a woman (and her children) to make every effort to keep the marriage together.[3] An attractive wife who keeps her husband sexually satisfied does much to chase away the competition. And believe me, the competition is out there.

Another positive result for a wife who keeps herself attractive is that she feels better about herself. Women enjoy sex more when they feel attractive, and the intimacy that sexual activity brings makes them feel more secure and more highly favored. It recharges them and influences all other aspects of their lives, setting in motion a happiness cycle for their marriage.

There are many reputable diet and exercise programs that can help. Dr. Don Colbert has devoted his medical career to helping Christians care for their bodies. Two helpful books he has written are *The Bible Cure for Weight Loss and Muscle Gain* and his great nutritional book called *What Would Jesus Eat?*, which shows the biblical plan for health.[4] Without promoting fad diets, drugs or surgery, Dr. Colbert has helped people across the nation lose up to 150 pounds.

Scriptural beauty

Without wanting to contradict the apostle Paul, who seemingly advocated the beauty of good deeds over external beauty treatments (1 Tim. 2:9–10), I think there is still validity to the argument that there are reputable hairstylists and cosmetologists who can help you look your best for your husband. Take advantage of their help so you can resemble the woman he fell in love with at the beginning—and add your good deeds as well.

Some well-meaning Christians have also argued that the virtuous woman described in the book of Proverbs 31 (sometimes called the "Proverbs 31 woman") was not praised for her beauty, but for her fear of the Lord and for the numerous ways she cared for her family and her home. To confirm their point, they quote verse 30: "Charm is deceptive, and beauty is fleeting; but a woman who fears the LORD is to be praised."

So, does the Scripture really teach women that it is an either/or proposition—either be beautiful or have character? I don't think so. Of course, fine character is vital to a relationship—every man wants to be able to trust his wife (v. 11). But that is not meant to substitute for his enjoyment of her physical beauty. Even in this passage of Scripture we read that this virtuous woman is clothed in fine linen and purple (v. 22)—meaning she dresses attractively. And in verse 17 we read that her arms are strong for her tasks—in other words, she keeps herself physically fit.

Other passages of Scripture point to the beauty of the bride in a very positive way as well. In the Book of Esther, chapter 2, we learn that Esther spent twelve months in beauty treatments and eating special food before she was chosen to be queen. When a wife was chosen for Isaac, she was both beautiful and had a body fit for hard work (Gen. 24). Isaac's son Jacob worked fourteen years just to marry Rachel, the beautiful girl that he loved (Gen. 29). And we have already read the physical description of the woman in the Song of Solomon:

> Your hair is like royal tapestry…How beautiful you are and how pleasing, O love, with your delights! Your stature is like that of the palm, and your breasts like clusters of fruit.
>
> —*Song of Solomon 7:5–7*

> I am a wall, and my breasts are like towers. Thus I have become in his eyes like one bringing contentment.
>
> —*Song of Solomon 8:10*

The key phrase in this verse is "in his eyes." If you are the woman he chose to marry, it was because you had the beauty he desired. While you don't have to become someone else during the course of marriage, you owe it to him and to yourself to be the *you* he married.

When plastic surgery makes sense

There are some things that are harder to repair than others, which brings us to the issue of plastic surgery. Over 13 million plastic surgery procedures were done in the United States in 2001.[5] This does not include laser eye surgery to eliminate the need for glasses, which certainly has cosmetic implications.

Because of our fallen state, we regularly deal with aging and disease of almost all of our organs at some point in our lives. We employ physicians, dentists, optometrists, chiropractors and other professionals to try to keep our bodies working as long and as efficiently as possible. Why, then, do some consider the visible organs to be off-limits for repair by the God-given medical knowledge we readily apply to internal organs? While this is only my opinion, I believe that plastic surgery has a legitimate role in correcting what damage and disease have wrought. It is not essential, by any means, but it is certainly a valid option if your finances and your spouse are in agreement.

The most common procedures my patients turn to are those that repair the damage that pregnancy, childbearing, and breast-feeding have brought. Breast augmentation is very popular with women who have experienced significant loss of fullness after breast-feeding. The cosmetic results can be very satisfying. This is not to be confused with what the younger women are doing to try to look like the models they see on television or in magazines.

Most models have also had breast augmentation; the result is a generation of women all chasing after the same illusion. It is here that a cautionary word about plastic surgery is needed; addressing one's expectations and motivation for the procedure is critical. Bigger breasts will not guarantee you a better husband or a happier life. While they may be necessary for certain career choices in this world, you must prayerfully evaluate your motives and desires. Ask yourself, *Is this where God is placing me, or is it what I am choosing for myself?*

On the other end of the spectrum is the difficulty many women have with being overly "blessed" with breast tissue. Breast reduction is a procedure that can greatly alleviate the back and shoulder pain experienced on a daily basis by those women whose breasts have gotten larger over time. Most insurance companies will pay for this procedure with the proper medical documentation. It can be argued whether or not this even constitutes *plastic surgery*, as defined in the minds of most people.

Certainly some women's faces age better than others. If there are upper eyelids that have fallen and now cover part of the opening of the eyes or there are large bags of skin under the eyes, surgery can be helpful, not just cosmetically, but to improve eyesight. Sagging cheeks and loose neck skin can be repaired as well.

A good facelift can take ten to fifteen years from your face, making you appear more healthy and refreshed. Before making your decision regarding this procedure, you must remember that its effects do not last forever and that it can be quite costly. Nevertheless, it is a procedure done to millions of women around the world each year. Again, a healthy dose of realism and prayer should guide these decisions, and they should always include the husband's complete agreement.

A newer procedure for handling wrinkles that has been introduced is Botox injections. These are injections made from a neurotoxin that causes paralysis. When injected under the skin, Botox paralyses the facial muscles that are necessary to cause the brow to wrinkle or the sides of the eyes to develop "crow's-feet." The FDA has recently approved Botox for use in the United States, and it is already the number one cosmetic procedure. Nearly two million people use Botox each year, according to the American Society of Aesthetic Plastic Surgery, accounting for $30 million in sales this past year. This number is expected to double by 2006.[6]

Botox has its side effects such as the occasional prolonged paralysis that can lead to temporary drooping of the eyelids or drooling from the mouth. This is almost always reversible with time. A reputable physician is needed to do these injections in an artistic way to avoid the appearance of a "frozen" face, one devoid of the ability to express emotion. Still, in places such as southern California, Botox parties are held for career women looking for a chemical facelift. Its visible effects last up to six months.

The final group of surgeries that may be helpful to women is gynecologic and is covered by all insurance companies. These surgeries are not considered plastic surgeries, but they function in a similar way. For many women, these gynecologic surgeries are also very crucial to their sexual self-esteem and even their ability to enjoy intercourse, since they repair damage done to the vagina by childbirth.

With our improvements in prenatal care, nutrition and antibiotics, along with smoking cessation, we are producing much larger babies as a nation than we did even a generation ago. It is now common for women to deliver eight- and nine-pound babies vaginally. While the number of children born per woman has decreased, it only takes one large baby or one poorly healed episiotomy to cause vaginal damage.

Every week I see women who suffer the prolapse (or falling) of their bladder, uterus or rectum. Many feel so "stretched out" that they receive no pleasure from vaginal penetration. Their attachments to the clitoris have been lengthened, and traction is no longer being applied. Many women suspect that their husbands are not satisfied because of this looseness, and this further diminishes their desire for sex and their sexual self-esteem.

Fortunately, all of these conditions are correctable if the woman musters the courage to consult with her gynecologist. Many also receive better bladder and bowel control after surgery, which makes them feel younger and more in control of their bodies.

Body image is crucial to a woman's sexual self-esteem and thus her sexual desire. The following story represents an example of how crucial this can be to a marriage. It is a composite of several people to protect the privacy of my patients.

Real Life

Susan is a thirty-two-year-old mother of four whose last pregnancy resulted in the birth of twins. Each twin weighed over seven pounds, which meant that she was "extremely" pregnant by the end. By the time the twins were two years old, Susan was in my office asking about a tubal ligation. When the decision had been made and we were selecting a date for surgery, Susan half-jokingly asked if I could put her back the way she was before she had the twins. It had been two years since delivery, and despite losing all of her pregnancy weight and exercising four times a week, she was unhappy with her body.

As Susan and I talked, she began to reveal the whole story. She had always been athletic but small-breasted. In a world full of bikini models, she was very content to be a B-cup with a rock-hard abdomen. Even after the first two children, she had been able to get back into her old clothes in just a few weeks after delivery. Susan breast-fed each of her children for almost a year, and, although her breasts were not exactly the same after two pregnancies, they returned close enough to "normal" that she was not unhappy. But the twins were a different story.

Susan was much larger with her twins' pregnancy as she carried nearly fifteen pounds of baby by the end. Breast-feeding two babies made her milk supply double, and her breasts became much larger than they had ever been before. The difficulty for Susan began after weaning her twins. She found that her breasts shrunk so dramatically from their larger size that they now drooped and seemed concave in certain sections. When not wearing a bra, Susan felt disfigured as they sagged downward.

Despite exercise and weight loss, Susan noticed that her lower abdomen "pooched" out over her pants. That had never happened before. She focused on abdominal exercises and could see her muscles toning on the sides. But she could not get them to come together in the middle. A woman at church even asked her if she was expecting another baby because of the prominence of her stomach compared to the rest of her body.

All of these changes left Susan with a poor self-image. She had always worked hard to be attractive to her husband, Mark, and had been comfortable with what God had given her. Even after two children, she was realistic about the changes that had occurred over time and still felt good about herself. But the twins had taken a toll on her from which she was unable to recover in her own power. Susan felt unattractive, especially when she was naked before Mark.

She no longer liked her breasts to be caressed or her stomach touched when they were making love; it drew her attention to those areas and made her self-conscious, limiting her ability to enjoy intercourse. As Susan limited the areas Mark could touch, the intimacy level decreased between them, and intercourse became a quick ejaculation with little foreplay. This was displeasing to both of them, as they had previously enjoyed a rich and fulfilling sex life.

When Susan finally admitted to Mark the things that she had been feeling, he tried his best to reassure her that those changes were not important to him. But he could see that they were important to Susan's self-esteem. Shortly after that conversation, Susan came to see me.

It seemed to Mark and Susan that while she was at the hospital and under anesthesia for the tubal ligation, she should get something done about the other areas of her body as well. Mark had arranged to take a week off from work, and Susan's mother was coming in to take care of the children. It was also financially better for them because the insurance would pay the hospital and anesthesia charges for the tubal ligation, and the out-of-pocket expenses would be limited to the extra procedures.

I arranged a consultation for Mark and Susan with a reputable plastic surgeon that was sensitive to the needs of mothers and not interested in making everyone look like an exotic dancer. Susan did not necessarily want bigger breasts; she just wanted them "lifted" back up and the concave areas filled in. The plastic surgeon explained to them that a small breast implant would be needed to fill in the spaces stretched out by breast-feeding, and because she had been larger at the peak of nursing the twins, a C-cup would be an appropriate cosmetic result for her.

The stomach would require a different approach. The twins had spread Susan's abdominal muscles so far apart that no amount of exercise would ever be able to bring them back together again. An incision would be made in the bikini line and the muscles sewn back together. In addition, the redundant skin that had once stretched to cover the overly pregnant uterus would be removed. While these procedures would cost almost ten thousand dollars, both Susan and Mark felt it would be worth it. They would not be going into debt to pay for it, and the results would last far longer than any vacation they could ever take.

I saw Susan several months after her procedures, and she was radiant. The results were very natural and reminded me of the woman I had first met several years, and several children, ago. Susan reported that her confidence level was high; she enjoyed her clothes again, and she liked how she looked in the mirror. Even Susan's friends, who had been skeptical of the need for plastic surgery, agreed that the results were exceptional. More importantly, Susan felt comfortable being naked with her husband again, and their sex life was wonderful. Mark commented that it was a great investment in their marriage.

Despite the pressures of work and raising four children, Susan and Mark are back on track and enjoying their married life together. Susan would be the first to tell you that plastic surgery is not for everyone, nor is it a cure for a bad marriage. But it can heal the effects of babies and time for those who find those effects difficult to live with. It has definitely made Susan feel that the sacrifices she made to give birth to, and nurse, four children have been worth it.

Chapter **Six**

MALE SEXUAL ISSUES

> So husbands ought to love their own wives as their own bodies; he who loves his wife loves himself.
>
> —*Ephesians 5:28*, NKJV

A s men, we tend to judge our success by how well we accomplish a given task (whether in business or personal life), how we perceive we compare with other men and how we measure up to our own standards. One of the most sensitive, yet fundamental areas of perceived success for all married men is the ability to have intercourse. This is directly related to achieving and maintaining an erection that is strong enough to allow vaginal penetration.

DO MEN HAVE SEXUAL CYCLES?

I was taught in medical school that men reach their sexual peak at age nineteen. Yet we live an average of eighty years. It is clear from the math that a larger portion of the male life span is lived in ever-diminishing sexual capability. Problems of sexual function manifest mostly in two common ways: *premature ejaculation* and *erectile dysfunction* (formerly called impotence). To treat these conditions it is important to understand the mechanics of the erection cycle.

There are four phases to the male sexual cycle: arousal, erection, ejaculation and latency. As discussed previously, the shaft and the head of the penis are comprised of three tubes that are filled with spaces that can hold blood. These spaces are surrounded by muscles. In the flaccid state, the muscles around the main arteries of the penis are contracted, allowing only a minimal amount of blood into the penis.

In the first phase of the cycle, called *arousal*, sexual stimulation causes relaxation of the muscles and increased blood flow into the penis. The stimulation can be physical, visual or mental. Even vibrations from the wheel of a bus can start the erection process without conscious mental desire.

Once blood flows into the vascular spaces of the shaft and head of the penis, it causes compression of the veins that let blood out, leading to the trapping of blood within the penis. As the penis becomes filled with more blood, it takes a rigid form called an *erection*. At its fullest, the arteries will be compressed and blood flow will cease. Several times each night during sleep, men experience erections brought on by signals from the brain that change penile blood flow, completely disconnected from anything the man may be dreaming about.

Continued sexual stimulation, especially to the head of the penis, causes semen mixed with sperm to be deposited at the back of the urethra. Increasing pressure in the urethra leads to an irreversible release called *ejaculation*. After ejaculation, the nerves send signals to tighten the muscles surrounding the vascular spaces, pushing blood back out of the penis and returning it to its flaccid state.

There is a period of time in which erection cannot be achieved while recovery from ejaculation is occurring. This period is called the *latency* phase, and it varies in length with each individual, getting progressively longer with age. Many men will be incapable of more than one ejaculation per night as they age.

ERECTILE DYSFUNCTION

Erectile dysfunction (ED), formerly called *impotence*, occurs in the following three main areas.[1] The first, failure to initiate erection, is a difficulty in the arousal phase. The cause of the problem may be hormonal, such as low testosterone levels. Neurological diseases such as multiple sclerosis, lumbar disc disease or spinal cord injuries can also cause this condition. However, the most common cause is psychological, in large part due to stress.

The second area is the erection phase, caused when the body fails to fill the penis with adequate amounts of blood. The result can range from no erection to a semi-erect state that is still incapable of sustaining intercourse. The cause is usually an inability to deliver blood through the arteries and can be a marker of a more serious medical condition. Diseases such as diabetes, hypertension, arteriosclerosis, high cholesterol and poor circulation in the extremities from a variety of causes all lead to decreased arterial blood flow. Aging is also a common factor.

The last area affects the ejaculation phase, due to failure to store the blood in the penis. This results in achieving an erection without being able to sustain it long enough to have satisfying intercourse and/or ejaculation. This difficulty may be due to problems with smooth muscle function in the penis.

Impact of lifestyle

In addition to the medical diseases already stated, lifestyle factors such as stress, cigarette smoking and alcohol consumption can impact erectile ability. Also, a variety of medications used to treat high blood pressure, diabetes, depression, high cholesterol, coronary artery disease and prostate cancer can affect the ability to have and maintain an erection. Previous surgeries, especially for prostate cancer, as well as pelvic trauma can lead to disruption of the normal nerve pathways necessary to achieve an erection.

Available treatment

There are a variety of options available to treat this disorder. Much of it lies with knowledge and communication. If a man is taking prescription medication that is hindering his sexual function, he needs to communicate this fact to his physician and seek alternative medications whenever possible. If aging is slowing the arousal response time, more stimulation is needed. Young men require almost no stimulation to achieve erection, but with age the requirement increases. Oral or manual stimulation by his spouse as well as more visual and mental input can help with achieving and maintaining an erection. A healthier lifestyle of reduced smoking and alcohol, along with increased exercise, can also improve blood flow to the pelvis.

The most significant breakthrough in treating ED is the development of sildenafil citrate, commonly sold under the brand name Viagra. It works to relax the muscles of the penis that allow blood to enter into it, thereby aiding the achieving and maintaining of erection. It comes in several strengths and has been highly successful, with millions of prescriptions written worldwide.[2]

Please observe the following serious caution: Because sildenafil citrate relaxes vascular muscles, it cannot be combined with certain medications that similarly relax muscles of the heart, such as nitroglycerin. Deaths have occurred in patients who have mixed these medications. For this reason, and because the right dose may need to be adjusted, it is important to seek medical advice before receiving this prescription. For many, seeking medical advice will require them to overcome male pride, ego and fear in order to take proper advantage of what I believe is one of the most significant and God-inspired discoveries of the past decade.

PREMATURE EJACULATION

While it may seem like the opposite end of the spectrum from ED, premature ejaculation, is, in fact, often closely related. Premature ejaculation is generally defined as "ejaculation that occurs before one or both partners desire." By definition, it becomes a subjective condition. The most obvious and undisputed problem is when ejaculation occurs before vaginal penetration as the result of mental and visual stimulation alone. Another scenario occurs after penetration but before the man is "ready." And lastly, this condition exists when ejaculation occurs before the spouse is "finished."

Premature ejaculation can become a problem in the following ways. Those men who struggle with ED, especially of the variety of failing to keep an erection, may become afraid they will lose their erection before ejaculation can occur. Therefore, they *train* themselves to reach ejaculation faster to avoid the embarrassment of ED, only to find they have frustrated their spouse in the process.

Another form of this faulty "training" occurs when young men grow up practicing masturbation as their sexual release. They often complete the process as quickly as possible to avoid discovery and to achieve the desired goal. This habit becomes subconsciously engrained in their minds and bodies, so that ejaculation continues to occur rapidly in intercourse, even when speed is no longer desirable.

Desirable solutions

Since ejaculation requires sufficient stimulation in order to deposit the semen, anything that disrupts that stimulation can help to prolong the act of intercourse. These distractions can include shifting mental stimulation to thoughts of something less desirable (such as baseball or politics).

However, I find no biblical precedent to encourage this behavior. Actually, it seems to be opposite from what God intended intercourse to be—the most intimate *knowing* of another person that is humanly possible. I do not believe it is God's best plan for a man to disconnect mentally from this experience of true intimacy.

Removing the penis from the vagina and starting again, or at least dramatically slowing the pace, can achieve far better results for the couple without interrupting their intimate communion. If the intensity still seems too great, the man or woman can firmly, but painlessly, squeeze the head of the penis between their thumb and index finger for several seconds. This will release chemicals that cause blood to flow out of the penis and help to diminish the erection.

The amount of erection loss will vary with the length of time this technique is applied; this technique is something a couple will become proficient in over time. As mentioned earlier, once the pressure builds up in the urethra past a certain point, ejaculation is inevitable and cannot be stopped. Learning what this point is and intervening before that time are critical to prolonging the experience of intercourse.

CALIBRATING YOUR EXPECTATIONS WITH YOUR SPOUSE

The subjective aspect of premature ejaculation is revealed by the individual desires of the man or woman, which can be sabotaged by unrealistic expectations. While the average man can ejaculate in two and a half minutes, the average time to female orgasm is between fifteen and forty minutes.[3] As mentioned in an earlier chapter, 70 percent of women will not achieve orgasm with vaginal intercourse alone, no matter how long her spouse "holds out."[4] Understanding this reality and using alternative methods for her stimulation can bring much needed balance to this situation.

Again, honest communication is the key to achieving a healthy balance that is mutually satisfying. If the wife does not really desire intercourse on a particular evening, but is simply meeting her husband's need, there is no obligation on his part, nor real desire on her part, for the encounter to last a long period of time.

If, however, a romantic evening has been planned and both parties have been looking forward to having intercourse, it is preferable if the experience is one that is lingered over and not rushed, giving the husband and wife time to explore and even experiment. Both will want satisfactory orgasms as part of this intimate act. As with so many other areas of marital life, knowledge and communication are the keys to a satisfying sex life. Developing those communication skills will be invaluable to the mutual satisfaction God intended you to enjoy.

HONEST COMMUNICATION IS THE KEY TO ACHIEVING A HEALTHY BALANCE THAT IS MUTUALLY SATISFYING.

Perhaps Peter's story (another composite example of my patients) will help to illustrate the realities that communication plays in our sexual satisfaction.

Real Life

I met forty-eight-year-old Peter at a men's conference where I had spoken. Outwardly, he seemed to have it all together: He was handsome, had a beautiful wife who adored him, two children and a successful career. But when the conference was over, he lingered in the back as I answered questions. When the last man was leaving, he stepped forward. I could tell that he wanted to ask me something, so I made the first move and introduced myself to him.

As we began to talk, Peter slowly unfolded his story. I was the first person he had ever felt comfortable enough to talk to, and he shared things even his wife, Tammy, did not know. Over the last two years, he had begun noticing that his erections were not as strong as they used to be. There were times when he had difficulty penetrating his wife's vagina, and there were other times when he lost his erection completely in the middle of intercourse.

At first this occurred only occasionally, but over the past few months it had become a problem every time he attempted to make love to his wife. The fear that he would lose his erection seemed to make things even worse, distracting him from the intimacy he desired because of his preoccupation with the strength of his erection.

Over the past six months, Peter had made love less and less. He stayed up late working on papers from the office, or he would find a movie on television that kept him busy. Tammy would invariably fall asleep before he came to bed, which is what he had hoped so that he could avoid intercourse. The one thing he used to desire from his wife more than anything else he now dreaded. He was gripped with the fear of failure. Then I discovered that, for Peter, his struggle with erectile dysfunction was a bitter irony.

When he was younger, sex was very important to him. He and his wife never seemed to be on the same page when the children were small. While Peter worked hard to build his business and provide for his family, intercourse with his wife was his stress release and his refuge at night from an outside world that had contended with him in the daylight. But during these years, Tammy was exhausted from working full time to supplement their income while his business was struggling. And she still did all of the cooking and cleaning at home.

Because she didn't want to add more pressure to Peter's life, Tammy also spent most of the evening with the children, finishing homework, bathing them and getting things ready for the next day. At the end of the evening, Tammy was rarely in the mood for intercourse, though she was willing to meet Peter's needs if he initiated sex.

As the children grew up and became less dependent, Tammy began having more time for herself. Peter's income was very good, and she no longer needed to work. When the last child left for college, Peter and Tammy were alone again in the house, as they were when they were first married. Tammy began to initiate intercourse more, and for a time, they felt like newlyweds again.

But what seemed like a curse descended upon Peter. Just when his wife wanted to make love more, he wanted it less and less. His erectile dysfunction was robbing him of what he had longed for most of his married life. Peter's pride kept him from telling anyone, especially Tammy. What kind of man would she think he was if he couldn't satisfy her in the bedroom? He felt that he was losing all that made him a man. He just couldn't tell anyone; it was too humiliating.

So when he heard me speak about erectile dysfunction at the conference, he realized that he was not alone. He understood that ED was a normal part of aging and that millions of men were having the same difficulty. As hard as it is to admit one is getting older, the body doesn't lie, and it was time for Peter to face this medical fact. The good news was that medical science had help for him. He just needed the courage to ask for it.

And courage was what I was able to help him gain that night—not only the courage to seek medical help, but also the courage to share his struggle with Tammy. One of the blessings the Lord intended when He declared "the two will become one flesh" was that when I am hurting, my wife feels the pain. When I struggle, my loving wife senses it in her spirit.

There are no issues in the life of a man that his spouse does not also share in some way. While Tammy did not know the reasons behind it, she was well aware that Peter was not whole. But she was patient enough to wait upon the Lord, interceding for her husband and trusting that all would be revealed to her in God's time. I have no doubt that had Tammy confronted Peter earlier about his decreasing libido, he would have covered up the truth with a lie. Instead, she was praying for a breakthrough for her husband when he attended the men's conference, and she was not disappointed.

I encouraged Peter to "get over" the male image he cherished so much, the ego and pride he felt for being a "man" in the bedroom, and to admit to his wife that his body was changing. The things he had taken for granted now needed nurturing and tender patience. I assured him that Tammy would be relieved to know his lack of sexual interest was not rooted in a decreased desire for her or a lust for someone else. Many wives come to those conclusions when their husbands withdraw from them sexually.

Peter's issues were rooted in fear, especially in the fear of failure. I reminded him that God had not given him a spirit of fear, but of power, love and a sound mind (2 Tim. 1:7, NKJV). I assured him that with the power of the Word and the help of medical science, he could overcome erectile dysfunction. And he could feel safe in the love of his wife.

In a biblical soundness of mind, Peter would not put undue pressure upon himself to perform to some standard he had set that did not reflect present reality. He began to understand that his manliness did not depend on his ability to have an erection; it was rooted in the person God made him to be and who he was in Christ. Even if he was never able to have intercourse again, Tammy would love him for who *he was as well as for all the things Peter brought to the marriage, all that he exemplified in his love for her and her children, his provision for their family and his service to God.*

As Peter began to discover the truth about his identity as a man, he realized that his ability to have intercourse was just one small slice of a very large pie. If he could get that slice back, all the better. But it was not the basis of his marriage nor the key to his wife's heart. When intercourse was placed in its proper perspective and he began to see his life and his marriage in the light of truth, the pressures he had placed upon himself through the years diminished greatly.

Peter had summoned the courage one night to confide in me, a brother in Christ. I gave him the courage to take the next step, armed with the truth. That night we witnessed the fulfillment of the scripture that says, "As iron sharpens iron, so one man sharpens another" (Prov. 27:17). When I saw him again several weeks later, he was beaming! His sexual life had never been better. But more importantly, he and Tammy discovered a new depth of intimacy they had never experienced before.

When Peter began to open up to Tammy about his erectile dysfunction, he discovered that intimacy was not experienced just through physical touch, but also in sharing the deep recesses of the soul, something most women know instinctively, but which many men never discover. Peter's deepest "secret" had been his most closely guarded fear. Once Peter opened that door and found love and acceptance instead of rejection, his worst fear melted in the warmth of Tammy's love. For Peter, there was no deeper level of intimacy that he could share. Having gone where he thought it impossible to go, every other thought or feeling seemed small. He didn't fear rejection of anything he wanted to share with Tammy because he had trusted her with his "big" issue.

Suddenly, Peter and Tammy were sharing other desires of their soul without fear of rejection. Because Peter was being honest about his struggles and fears, Tammy had permission to share with her husband the cares that she had carried all alone. This new depth of intimacy brought a closeness in their marriage they had never experienced before. And Peter found that emotional intimacy was a great aphrodisiac! He had experienced such love for Tammy that it cast out his fear (1 John 4:18).

Tammy also learned what she didn't know about male anatomy and physiology. I had given Peter some insight into the process of erection, and he was able to share with Tammy what he needed her to do. His erections might not spring up "automatically" as they did when he was younger. His mind might be turned on, but his penis needed a helping hand—literally! Caressing, kissing or oral stimulation could bring about the desired response and take Peter's mind off trying to "will" himself an erection.

I also gave him "permission" to stroke himself in her presence if he felt the erection begin to fade. For their first attempts at intercourse, I recommended Viagra. It was important that Peter succeed to build up his confidence. Viagra gives men a tingling sensation and warmth to the face when it reaches the bloodstream. It is like a signal that says you are ready to proceed with confidence; it will not let you down!

When Peter saw me several weeks later, he was excited as he shared the events of the past weeks with me. He discovered that after a few times of using Viagra, he regained his confidence. Tammy was attentive to his needs and helped him stay physically stimulated. Peter began trusting her with his erection and stopped placing all the responsibility on himself. This in turn stopped the fear that had been poisoning the erection in the first place.

Since Viagra needs about an hour to start working, those first few sessions were "planned" by him. Peter was the initiator when he felt the medication begin to work in his body. But there were other times when Tammy initiated sex and he was not premedicated. To his surprise, he discovered that he could often perform without Viagra.

Peter was grateful for my advice, but I was quick to remind him that it was he who had summoned the courage to open up to me, a stranger, and risk feeling like a fool. The love that Peter had for Tammy drove him to overcome his fear of being thought of as less than a man. He fulfilled his biblical duty, as we have cited:

> The husband should fulfill his marital duty to his wife, and likewise the wife to her husband. The wife's body does not belong to her alone but also to her husband. In the same way, the husband's body does not belong to him alone but also to his wife. Do not deprive each other except by mutual consent.
>
> —1 Corinthians 7:3–5

Peter was willing to reach out for help, and the Lord rewarded him beyond his wildest dreams.

Chapter **Seven**

SEXUALITY
AND SINGLES

Don't allow love to turn into lust, setting off a
downhill slide into sexual promiscuity...
—*Ephesians 5:3, THE MESSAGE*

Almost every person spends at least *some* adult years as a single person.
Yet, if there is one area with which the church (and all of Christendom)
struggles, it is the issue of sex and the single person. Each generation has
tackled this issue differently, with the result of placing progressively less sexual restraint on the single person in modern society (and in the church).

WHY ABSTINENCE
BEFORE MARRIAGE

In today's society, it seems that only a minority believe in living a lifestyle
of sexual abstinence until marriage, which the Bible teaches as the righteous
way to live. (See 1 Corinthians 7.) The pope regularly admonishes the millions of Catholics he leads to abstain from premarital intercourse, avoid
birth control and reject abortion as a choice for unwanted pregnancy. Yet
polls consistently show that only a minority of the world's Catholics obey
these instructions.[1] Protestants lack this kind of central voice for morality,
but even the most conservative churches led by fundamentalists still find
only a minority of their unmarried parishioners living a sexually pure
lifestyle according to biblical standards.

A common response to this discrepancy between the teaching of the
Bible and the sexual lifestyle of single Christians is that the biblical view of
sex outside of marriage is outdated and based on cultural constraints,
which were appropriate for that day but not necessary for the new millen-
nium. The argument goes that the value of virginity in biblical cultures,
especially for women, was based more on their status as "a possession" or
"property." A man's offspring were highly prized, with the passage of family land and possessions based on inheritance through an accurate bloodline. Only a virgin wife could assure this proper bloodline. For this reason

also, the penalty for adultery seemed to weigh heavily on the female offender.[2]

SEX IS MORE THAN JUST A PHYSICAL EXPERIENCE

Our society today is not based on the patriarchal bloodline for inheritance of agricultural land or livestock. And our blended families of "his" children, "her" children and "our" children seem to prove that virginity is not necessary for a successful marriage. Abstinence until marriage is now viewed as an outdated and unnecessary prohibition to a very pleasurable and natural activity.

Even our government decries attempts of abstinence-based education for our youth as ineffective and unrealistic, despite the evidence that programs such as *Worth the Wait* by Dr. Patricia Sulak and materials by Dr. Joe McIlhaney of the Medical Institute for Sexual Health have consistently led to a decline in teen sexual activity when they are used as curriculum for high school students.[3]

So what is the Christian single person to do? Our culture prizes education and achievement more than any previous culture. Our technological age demands years of advanced education for people to be viable in today's workplace. For this reason, many young people delay marriage until their late twenties or thirties in order to pursue graduate degrees or job promotions. They enjoy the freedom to move around the country, and even the world, as they work to achieve "the American dream." While their grandparents may have married their high school sweethearts at age eighteen, young singles of today may delay marriage for two more decades. Is it realistic to expect them to remain virgins for the duration?

Even our children's biological clocks seem pitted against the notion of abstinence in this new reality we are living. Young boys and girls enter puberty at earlier ages with each passing generation. In the 1800s, the average woman began menstruation at age seventeen.[4] By 1960, that age had fallen to thirteen. Today, it is not uncommon to see full sexual development of girls in this country by age fourteen.

Dramatic increases in sex hormones that accompany puberty also flood the mind with sexual thoughts and feelings. The media of today celebrate the emerging sexuality of teens as never before. Marketing gurus have targeted the teen years with aggressive, sexually oriented advertising. One needs look no further than Abercrombie & Fitch to see catalogues filled with nude and half-nude youth. The exploitation of these young people is sending sales to record highs.[5] Manufacturers have developed cosmetic and clothing lines specifically aimed at today's teenage girl to enhance her sexual attractiveness.

It seems our culture *expects* sexual activity from them, which in turn creates peer pressure to conform.

The natural reasoning seems to be: *How can young teens be required to avoid sexual intercourse while they are peaking sexually? And what, if any, are the advantages of abstinence until marriage?*

A more difficult situation may exist for the widowed or divorced, who have been sexually active in a previous marriage. They are now left without a sexual partner. After years of being sexually active and having an outlet for their sexual desires, they are suddenly cut off and alone. Not only are they left to grieve the loss of the relationship as a whole, but they mourn the loss of sexual intimacy as well. What do these older adults do when they are suddenly without a sexual partner after years of marriage?

ADVANTAGES OF ABSTINENCE

From a purely medical standpoint, abstinence outside of marriage has many advantages for the single man or woman. Though our society winks at these advantages, the serious person would do well to consider them.

Unwanted pregnancy

Unwanted pregnancy is a major concern of those contemplating intercourse. In generations past, the fear of pregnancy was a strong deterrent to premarital sex. The social taboos were much stronger and the consequences far steeper than they are today. A girl who became pregnant in high school was often whisked away to a more secluded setting until the birth happened, and the baby was placed for adoption. Or the families would press the expectant parents into a hurried wedding to cover the offense from society's prying eyes, lest the family name be tarnished.

But in today's culture, high schools have accommodated the all-too-common pregnant teenager with mainstream classes, childbirth and parenting instructions, and even home visitation, all in an attempt to reduce school dropout rates. It is no longer socially unacceptable to be pregnant in high school; it is unfortunately quite common.

The government also plays a leading role in aiding unwed mothers with a variety of public assistance. Some have argued that a girl who is unhappy at home can get food stamps, an apartment and free healthcare for the small price of getting pregnant outside of marriage.[6]

Even for the more financially established single female, motherhood is celebrated in the media. Many successful Hollywood "stars," such as Jodie Foster and Calista Flockhart, have abandoned their quest for the perfect mate and have purposely conceived a child to be raised alone. Today's career-oriented woman may find her biological clock ticking louder than her prospects for marriage. Many are seeking artificial insemination just to have a child before it is too late.

Against this backdrop, the single person no longer finds unexpected pregnancy to be the deterrent it once was. And with readily available, private and "safe" abortion as an alternative, unexpected pregnancy is even less feared than a generation ago. We are also experiencing a growth in contraceptive options that past generations could not access. Convenient daily, weekly, monthly, quarterly, five-year and ten-year reversible birth control makes pregnancy much less likely for the "responsible" single adult.

Sexually transmitted diseases

If fear of pregnancy is no longer a roadblock to sexual intercourse outside of marriage, the prevalence of sexually transmitted diseases certainly should be. I have dedicated two chapters to the terrible aspects of these diseases because of their awful impact on our society today. (See chapters eight and nine.) The scientific and statistical facts about STDs should restrain even the most daring in our society. But it does not.

Emotional trauma

If premarital sex is not deterred by the risks of physical harm, the possibility of emotional pain should restrain us. Especially for women, the act of intercourse means something more than a mere release of sexual tension.[7] It signifies a new level of intimacy and the expectation of a deepening commitment to the relationship. Many women would be reluctant to have intercourse if they knew the potential emotional pain that would result if their partner were unwilling to fulfill the relational expectations that intercourse brings.

While conventional wisdom states that intercourse will deepen a relationship and make it stronger, the reality is that intercourse outside of marriage more often than not weakens the relationship. One or the other partner is not ready for the level of commitment expected from them once the relationship becomes sexual. The woman's expectation that this relationship is heading toward marriage may frighten away the male partner who only wants to have fun and fulfill his sexual needs.

Both men and women may also use sex as a way to boost their self-esteem. The fact that someone finds them attractive and is willing to be joined with them sexually seems to validate their worth as a person. Unfortunately, the single man or woman may discover that their sexual partner was simply fulfilling a physical need and not looking for an ever-deepening relationship. This leaves the single person more alone and degraded than before, ripe for the next person who will offer the promise of acceptance and love. A pattern of sexual addiction can develop from this basic need to be loved and understood at that most intimate level. Each relational breakdown becomes the seed for beginning the next affair, hoping against all hope that this partner will be "the one."

Bible warnings

If the fear of pregnancy, sexually transmitted diseases or emotional pain does not deter premarital sex, the Bible offers cautions that should be considered, especially by Christians. The apostle Paul has much to say on the subject of fornication, premarital sex, adultery and homosexuality:

> But since there is so much immorality, each man should have his own wife, and each woman her own husband…they should marry, for it is better to marry than to burn with passion.
>
> —*1 Corinthians 7:2, 9*

> But among you there must not be even a hint of sexual immorality.
>
> —*Ephesians 5:3*

> It is God's will that you should be sanctified: that you should avoid sexual immorality; that each of you should learn to control his own body in a way that is holy and honorable, not in passionate lust like the heathen, who do not know God.
>
> —*1 Thessalonians 4:3–5*

> Do you not know that the wicked will not inherit the kingdom of God? Do not be deceived: Neither the sexually immoral nor idolaters nor adulterers nor male prostitutes nor homosexual offenders …will inherit the kingdom of God.
>
> —*1 Corinthians 6:9–10*

Is Paul just a religious fanatic, out of step with today's culture? Or does he know something about sexual intercourse that lurks beneath the surface act? He reveals the key to God's prohibition of sexual intercourse outside of marriage:

> The body is not meant for sexual immorality, but for the Lord, and the Lord for the body…Do you not know that your bodies are members of Christ himself? Shall I then take the members of Christ and unite them with a prostitute? Never! Do you not know that he who unites himself with a prostitute is one with her in body? For it is said, "The two will become one flesh."…
>
> Flee from sexual immorality. All other sins a man commits are outside his body, but he who sins sexually sins against his own body. Do you not know that your body is a temple of the Holy Spirit, who is in you, whom you have received from God? You are not your own; you were bought at a price. Therefore honor God with your body.
>
> —*1 Corinthians 6:13, 15–16, 18–20*

According to Lewis Smedes, the apostle Paul's main problem with sexual intercourse outside of marriage is that it is a "life-uniting" act.[8] Just as it is a spiritual reality that, for Christians, the Holy Spirit lives inside of our bodies—our temples—it is also a reality that the act of intercourse unites two people in a deeply spiritual union.

Even if the people involved do not intend for it to carry such weight, the act of intercourse does change them spiritually. In ways that penetrate the many levels of their soul, those two people who have joined themselves physically will never be the same. Sexual intercourse involves a powerful spiritual bonding that God intended for the strengthening and deepening of the marriage covenant. God created this reality for our good; however, people in relationship outside of this covenant are playing with spiritual fire.

Some Christians in the Charismatic movement believe that not only do we become "one flesh" through intercourse, but it is also possible to exchange demonic forces during the union as well. The practice of prayer for *deliverance* from these dark spiritual forces commonly breaks the *soul ties* that were created through past illicit sexual activity. As the apostle Paul states, "He who sins sexually sins against his own body" (1 Cor. 6:18). Intercourse outside of marriage hurts you physically, emotionally and spiritually.

SETTING BOUNDARIES

Suppose you accept the scriptural premise that premarital sex is not right. What about other sexual activity that falls short of vaginal penetration? Where should you draw the line between kissing and near-intercourse? The fear of pregnancy and sexually transmitted diseases has developed many "experts" who advise safe alternatives for releasing sexual energies.

Among those alternatives, they recommend a practice referred to as *outercourse*, which involves mutual masturbation. It is foreplay taken to the extreme. Before deciding on this as a viable option, you need to consider what the motivations are of the people involved. Will this activity leave the relationship stronger than it was, or will one of the parties feel used (especially the women who are more often than not the "givers" rather than the "receivers")? Will the couple feel the same pressures to move the relationship forward, even if one or both of them are not ready?

Simply avoiding vaginal penetration is not what the Bible advocates for living in sexual purity. Sexual activity of all dimensions has many pitfalls and dangers we may not realize until it is too late. While I do not know the precise line that should be drawn by any particular couple, I do advise that caution and consideration are paramount.

If we are Christians, we carry Christ with us in all activities of life.

Examine your motives, and ask Him to guide you into appropriate intimacy and enjoyment during the dating years. I would like to recommend the book _I Kissed Dating Goodbye_ by Joshua Harris, a helpful resource that addresses these issues.[9]

MY VIEWS ON MASTURBATION

A final word in addressing these sexual issues for singles who are not in a relationship and who desire to remain sexually abstinent until marriage: I am often asked what my views are regarding masturbation. The vast majority of Christians feel tremendous guilt over this practice that the secular media treats with celebration.

If a single person is sexually alive from puberty, what are their options for the decade or two they may live before marriage? Is masturbation a legitimate option, and if so, why does one feel so guilty about doing it? I realize as I tackle this issue that ministers with far greater theological credentials than mine may disagree with my views. That is OK. This is just the opinion of one Christian physician who is willing to venture where few dare tread.

There is little to go by in Scripture that is specific to the act. In the Book of Genesis there is a story that is often used to condemn masturbation (Gen. 38:8–10). In this story Onan is commanded to have sex with his brother's widow to produce an heir and continue the lineage of his brother. But Onan knew that if his brother died without an heir, the inheritance would come to him. So Onan "spilled his semen on the ground to keep from producing offspring for his brother" (v. 9).

This act was not performed for sexual self-gratification, but in disobedience to the laws of that day, refusing his duty as a brother. It was not even masturbation but _coitus interruptus,_ a method of birth control used around the world.

In a more specific passage of Scripture, there is a list of bodily discharges that cause a man to be "unclean" and unable to enter the presence of the Lord until cleansed (Lev. 15). It includes ways to be made clean again:

> When a man has an emission of semen, he must bathe his whole
> body in water, and he will be unclean till evening.

> —_Leviticus 15:16_

In verse 18, the Lord continues: "When a man lies with a woman and there is an emission of semen, both must bathe with water, and they will be unclean till evening." It appears that the Lord is listing two separate occasions when a discharge of semen would contaminate and render the man "unclean." If the second occasion is when the man has intercourse with a woman (presumably his wife), then what is happening in the first situation when he is alone? Is this masturbation? If so, there is no condemnation of this emission, simply instruction by God on how he was to be made "clean" again with respect to participating in the worship of God.

Young children explore their bodies and masturbate with freedom before someone tells them it is "wrong." I have even observed male fetuses fondling their genitals during an ultrasonic examination. They carry no moral or sexual baggage with it.

Adults, however, may employ fantasies of past relationships or more commonly, pornography, to visualize an ideal sexual partner during masturbation. In their mind, they are having intercourse with that person even if it is only on paper, television or a computer screen. If one can masturbate without these entanglements, it is certainly preferable.

The other problem with masturbation is that it is often a form of stress relief and can become addictive. Just as alcohol, cigarette smoking or pharmaceuticals can be misused to relieve stress, so can the release brought on by orgasm or ejaculation. Again, the apostle Paul writes, concerning living a life of liberty and purity:

> Everything is permissible for me—but not everything is beneficial. Everything is permissible for me—but I will not be mastered by anything.
>
> —*1 Corinthians 6:12*

Of course, some people use food or other substances and activities as stress relief, with serious physical consequences. The bottom line is that addictive masturbation leads a person to see themselves as their source of stress relief instead of their heavenly Father, who declares, "Cast all your anxiety on [me] because [I care] for you" (1 Pet. 5:7). If it is a shortcut that makes man the source instead of God, in that regard it is sin.

Even in its "purest" form, masturbation will never feel completely right. That may be from needless self-condemnation, or it may reflect the reality that we are never really whole as sexual beings until we are united in marriage with that person who completes us and with whom the one-flesh union is all that God created it to be. Masturbation pales in comparison to that reality, and it is, at best, a temporary remedy for a soul that longs for union with another.

That "other" may be in the form of a spouse or, in its highest expression, a union with our Creator. As Jesus and the apostle Paul were able to experience, there is no greater union of the soul than with the One who made them. Jesus taught His disciples: "I and the Father are one...Know and understand that the Father is in me, and I in the Father" (John 10:30, 38). The apostle Paul discovered this truth as well, declaring, "He who unites himself with the Lord is one with him in spirit" (1 Cor. 6:17).

Whether you are single for a season or a lifetime, the Lord is calling you to unite with Him and taste the riches of His comfort and love, a sweet union found in no other. Not only is masturbation a cheap substitute, but it is also a distraction that competes with the true Lover of your soul. "'Though the mountains be shaken and the hills be removed, yet my unfailing love for you will not be shaken nor my covenant of peace be removed' says the LORD, who has compassion on you" (Isa. 54:10).

RAISING SEXUALLY PURE TEENS

As the father of two teenagers, a boy and a girl, I am acutely aware of the dilemma parents face in raising sexually pure teens. For those whose children attend public schools, the frightening reality is that your teens spend the majority of each day under the influence of an educational system determined to influence their sexual behavior. Nearly every school district offers sex education. And the goals of their curriculum may be far different from what you teach at home.

What does your school teach about sex?

A national organization called SIECUS (Sexuality Information and Education Council of the United States) has as its goal the sexual education of every child from preschool to twelfth grade. Their view is that sexual activity should be "consensual, non-exploitative, honest, pleasurable, and protected."[10] There are no references to age for sexual activity, nor are there guidelines regarding commitment, moral guidance or even heterosexual orientation. In fact, some sections of their curriculum offer advice on same-sex interactions.

Their materials contain over 344 specific teachings on various sexual activities, from touching to intercourse in different positions. The past and present board members of SIECUS have supported pedophilia, homosexuality, pornography, condoms in school and abortion on demand.[11] In case you think this is just a "fringe" group with extreme ideas, let me explain that it has aligned itself with the CDC (Centers for Disease Control and Prevention), Planned Parenthood and the NEA (National Education Association), which is the leading educational force in this nation.[12] Much of their curriculum has been adapted to the public school sex education program.

I encourage every parent to review the curriculum of their school and be active in bringing your voice to the local school board. Expose those elements of the program with which you disagree, and rally as many parents as you can to your cause. It is quite possible that the school board will not be familiar with the curriculum. Even if they do not agree to make changes, many schools allow parents to exempt their children from material they oppose.

Parents' influence is still greatest

On a personal level, there is much you can do at home. The mother and father still influence their child's sexual development more than any other source. Two recent studies by the National Campaign to Prevent Teen Pregnancy (NCPTP) revealed that more teens named their parents as having the biggest influence on their sexual behavior. Stronger than friends, siblings, school or even church, the advice of the parents had the strongest impact on whether teens became sexually active.[13]

Researchers at the University of Minnesota found that teenage girls who had a close relationship with their mothers were more likely to remain virgins. They also discovered that while the vast majority of mothers strongly disapproved of their teenagers having sex, a large percentage of the teens did not know of their mother's convictions.[14]

Dr. Grace Kellerman lists five rules that I have found helpful in teaching children about sex:[15]

1. Never exploit another person for your own sexual excitement. Have respect for the bodies of your same-sex friends growing up, and later, for the bodies of the opposite sex.

2. Sexual activity must be saved for marriage. Teen pregnancy and STDs alone warrant this from a medical perspective.

3. Teach young girls how to dress appropriately. Preteen and teen girls should not dress in a provocative manner designed to "turn on" the opposite sex. Parents should guide them in dressing attractively but not seductively.

4. Sons need to protect women, not exploit them.

5. Teens need to know where to draw the line when dating and how to refuse anyone's attempt to cross that line.

Facts about teen sexual activity

Parents and teens should consider the following facts about teen sexual activity, which will be helpful to guiding you through these challenging years:

- Sex never improves a teenage relationship. It almost always overwhelms it because there is not the strength of commitment necessary to bear the weight of emotion that sexual activity brings. Sexual activity usually leads to a rapid end of teen romance.[16]

- Sexual activity at a young age usually leaves a strong feeling of being used, violated and devalued.

- Alcohol and drug use decreases the resistance to sexual activity.

- Sexual activity is greatest when a steady dating relationship occurs, especially if the boy is two or more years older than the girl. In a University of Utah study that compared the age teens began dating with the age they became sexually active, 91 percent of those who began dating at age twelve were sexually active by graduation from high school. Over 50 percent who began dating at age fourteen were sexually active over the same period. Only 20 percent of those teens who waited to begin steady dating until age sixteen had lost their virginity by graduation.[17]

- Sexual activity increases when there is little parental supervision. A report by the researchers at *Child Trends* reveals this truth. A national teen survey tracked eight thousand teens from 1997 until 2000. Of those teens who became sexually active during the year 2000, 56 percent had their first sexual experience at the home of their parents or their partner's parents. This highlights the responsibility of the parent to monitor their teens, checking on them frequently instead of letting them have "privacy," not allowing the bedroom door to be fully closed when the opposite sex is in the room, etc.[18]

- For those parents who both work and are afraid their teens will have sex after school lets out, the researchers offered these statistics: Only 15 percent of teens had intercourse between the hours of 3 P.M. and 6 P.M. The majority had intercourse after 10 P.M., with the rest having sex between 6 P.M. and 10 P.M. These are the hours when parental supervision is not only possible but necessary.[19]

How to decrease risk of your teen becoming sexually active

Because parents exert the greatest influence over their teens regarding their perspective on sexuality, concerned parents can help their teen make proper decisions that will protect them from painful sexual experiences. The following list includes some important ways parents can help their teens:[20]

1. Instill a religious commitment in your child. Those children who grow up with a personal religious conviction are less likely to engage in adolescent sexual behavior.

2. Teens who are committed to an educational goal or are involved in extracurricular activities have a decreased risk of teen sex.

3. If a teenager has a friend who is committed to remaining abstinent

until marriage, it will increase their own commitment to do the same.

4. A positive relationship with their father is key. Boys who see their fathers treat their mothers with respect will respect young women. Girls who are respected and affirmed by their fathers won't search for other male affection through sexual relationships.

There is evidence that these strategies are working. In the past decade, abstinence has been on the rise. In a report by the Youth Risk Surveillance System, the percentage of those teens in grades nine through twelve that were abstinent rose from 46 percent in 1990 to 54 percent in 2001.[21] In response to this trend, *Newsweek* magazine even devoted a cover story to what they called "The New Virginity."[22]

The rate of teen pregnancy has also steadily declined over the past decade. It decreased 17 percent from 1990 to 1996, and another 20 percent from 1996 to 1999.[23] Despite this trend, however, our nation continues to have the highest teenage pregnancy rate in the industrialized world.

While many in Washington believe the answer lies in sex education in the classroom and condom giveaway programs after school, the truth is that God has given the power to parents to influence our nation's teens. The Bible reinforces this fact, teaching parents to instruct their children continually in the ways of God:

> These commandments that I give you today are to be upon your hearts. Impress them on your children. Talk about them when you sit at home and when you walk along the road, when you lie down and when you get up.
>
> —*Deuteronomy 6:6–7*

In other words, talk about what God has taught in His Word and what you expect from your teens when you sit down to eat dinner, when you work on homework with them, when you tuck them into bed at night and when you prepare to send them off to school in the morning. The Scriptures give parents this wonderful promise:

> Train a child in the way he should go, and when he is old[er] he will not turn from it.
>
> —*Proverbs 22:6*

It really is up to you.

Real Life

Twenty-two-year-old Melinda is a member of a nondenominational church. She has been a Christian since she was a child and has always been involved in ministry activities of the church. She has also always been a very bright student.

Melinda's mother divorced her husband when Melinda was a young child; she later remarried a very loving Christian man. Melinda has three half-siblings. Her relationship with her biological father is nonexistent, and despite a good relationship with her stepfather, Melinda's need for male love and acceptance became stronger as she grew older. A real void developed that seemed to intensify as she entered puberty.

Melinda blossomed into a very beautiful girl in her mid-teens, and by her senior year of high school she was very popular with her peers. She met a boy named Ryan that she had seen both at school and at church. He was new to town and seemed like a nice Christian boy. Her parents liked him, and Melinda and Ryan began dating steadily. Ryan accompanied her to youth services and to church almost every Sunday. His affection for her began to fill the void for male love she had sensed since she was a child.

After a few months of dating and as the school year drew to a close, they began to talk about marriage. Both were becoming more physically involved, and there was a desire to continue to advance their sexual exploration. Because Melinda had been raised to prize her virginity, she knew that it could not be given away casually. It must be saved for the man she would marry. But that was exactly what Ryan was promising—to marry her. So did they really have to wait until the actual day of their wedding to consummate their love? Wouldn't having intercourse deepen their commitment to their promised marriage?

About two months before graduation, Melinda and Ryan found themselves alone at his parents' house, and, without fear of adult intrusion, they had intercourse. For those last two months of school, it seemed to Melinda that they were enjoying a level of intimacy they had never had before. She felt that she had made the right decision, but she was careful to hide this from her parents.

Shortly after graduation, Melinda realized she was pregnant. She was initially shocked because they had used condoms most of the time. But because they had already been talking about someday getting married, she felt it would be an easy thing simply to move up their plans.

When she told Ryan she was pregnant, he became angry. He had wanted her to use birth control pills, but she had resisted for fear that her mother would find out. Now, the blame for the pregnancy was being shifted back to her, even though it was Ryan who had failed to use condoms consistently. Melinda was unprepared for his angry reaction, which became even worse when she suggested they move up the wedding date.

Ryan countered that he was going to be leaving in a couple of months for college and that he had chosen a school out of state. He hadn't told Melinda because he wanted to enjoy his time with her before he left. He knew she would be upset that his plans had changed, but he considered the change because his parents wanted him to attend their alma mater. It was their money, and he felt he needed to abide by their decision.

Over the next several days, Melinda and Ryan fought almost constantly. It was as if a veil had been lifted, and Melinda was seeing a side of Ryan that she had not known existed. When she told her parents that she was pregnant, they immediately called Ryan's parents to arrange the wedding they had all thought would happen some day. But his parents informed them that their son would be moving away for college and could not be hampered by a pregnant wife. Ryan had reconsidered his feelings for Melinda and realized that he didn't really love her after all. The relationship was over.

Two weeks after this awful revelation, Melinda's mother brought her to me to evaluate some vaginal spotting that was occurring. My ultrasound examination confirmed that Melinda was beginning to miscarry. The complicated ordeal of the previous few months was about to come to an end.

The end of her relationship to Ryan only made the void in her heart more painful, which prompted Melinda to begin a series of short-term relationships that each lasted only a few months. Each partner offered her the promise of true love, and each relationship ended within a few months after beginning sexual activity.

Chapter **Eight**

SEXUALLY TRANSMITTED DISEASES

> For these commands are a lamp...keeping you
> from the immoral woman...for the prostitute
> reduces you to a loaf of bread, and the
> adulteress preys upon your very life.
> —*Proverbs 6:23–26*

From a purely medical standpoint, abstinence until marriage is sound advice because of the prevalence of so many sexually transmitted diseases (STDs). They are among the most common infectious diseases in the United States, with experts estimating that at least 50 percent of the population will acquire a sexually transmitted disease in their lifetime.[1]

Currently, sixty-five million Americans are carrying a sexually transmitted disease.[2] Fifteen million new cases are diagnosed each year with an annual cost for treatment of nearly $10 billion, excluding the $7 billion it takes to treat those infected with HIV.[3]

Two-thirds of all STDs are infecting people under the age of twenty-five, with 25 percent occurring in teenagers. The number of cases is believed to be rising due to an earlier average age for beginning sexual activity along with waiting to a later age for marriage. This cultural trend translates into more sexual partners in a lifetime than ever before. In addition, the nearly 50 percent divorce rate in this country means that many people will reenter the dating scene and add additional sexual partners to their life's experience.[4]

SERIOUS CONSEQUENCES

The promiscuous society in which we live celebrates sexual activity but does not prepare unsuspecting individuals for the realities of the consequences they must suffer for breaking moral laws.

Physical

Because many STDs are asymptomatic (or silent) in women, often women do not seek early treatment and thus suffer more frequent and more severe health problems than do men. Some STDs can spread into the pelvis and cause infections called PID (pelvic inflammatory disease), which can scar the fallopian tubes. These scarred tubes can lead to tubal (or ectopic) pregnancies, the leading cause of death in women due to pregnancy. STDs are also the leading cause of cervical cancer and can lead to disability or even death in newborns who acquire them from their mothers at birth.

Emotional

Of course, STDs are more than a physical health problem. The long-term consequences can be infertility, which is at nearly epidemic rates in this country. The majority of assisted reproductive technologies, formerly called "test-tube babies," are used to help women bear children who have been made infertile by STDs. The emotional and financial toll infertility places on a marriage is very great. I have seen many marriages end in divorce under the strain of infertility alone. Even without the reproductive issues, sexually transmitted diseases bring tremendous feelings of guilt, shame, anger, violation and betrayal. The once joyous act of intercourse now carries a heavy price tag that some may pay for a lifetime.

I see cases of STDs in my private practice almost every day. They shatter the fantasy world so many people live in when it comes to sexual activity. No one in television or movies, romance novels or contemporary music, seems to pay a price for their sexual conduct. So I guess it should not surprise me that the average person is in shock when they are given the diagnosis of an STD. No one prepared them for the real world as it exists today—a world where sexually transmitted diseases run rampant.

CATEGORIES OF STDS

Sexually transmitted diseases can be divided into several categories:

- Bacterial
- Viral
- Acquired by skin contact
- Acquired from bodily fluids

STDs that are bacterial can be eliminated with antibiotics; those that are viral have no cure at the present time. Certain diseases can be transmitted simply through contact with the skin of another individual. The diseases that are acquired through bodily fluids require transmission by blood, semen or vaginal secretions to become infected.

BACTERIAL STDS

While bacterial STDs can be cured with the use of antibiotics, there are real dangers that they can go undiagnosed until permanent damage is done to the body.

Chlamydia

Chlamydia is the most common bacterial STD in the United States with four to eight million new cases reported each year.[5] It is transmitted through oral, vaginal or anal intercourse. Symptoms include pus or discharge from the penis or vagina, and in men it may result in painful urination. These symptoms present within one to three weeks after exposure to the bacteria.

If chlamydia is left untreated in women, they can experience pelvic inflammatory disease (PID), with the infection spreading from the cervix into the uterus, through the fallopian tubes and into the pelvic cavity, where it circulates throughout the abdomen. This intense infection causes tremendous pain, fever, chills, nausea and vomiting; many women require hospitalization to receive intravenous antibiotics and pain medication. PID occurs in one million women each year, with half of all cases due to chlamydia. It is estimated that one hundred thousand women per year become infertile due to PID.[6] This is the chief cause of ectopic pregnancy, where the embryo gets *stuck* in the fallopian tube. The placenta then penetrates the wall of the tube, frequently causing it to rupture. The hemorrhage caused by this rupture can be substantial, making ectopic pregnancy the leading cause of death in women due to pregnancy.[7]

Some women who develop PID in the first trimester of pregnancy will experience miscarriage because of this STD. Newborn babies born to women with chlamydia can contract it in their eyes, which causes blindness, or into their lungs, which leads to pneumonia. There is a strong recommendation that every pregnant woman be tested for chlamydia at her first prenatal visit to eliminate this disease before she gives birth.

Men infected with chlamydia can experience inflammation of the testicles and prostate gland. The urethra can be a source of pain with urination, a symptom that often leads men to seek medical attention. Both sexes can acquire *conjunctivitis,* an infection of the lining of the eye often called "pinkeye," from touching their eyes after genital contact with themselves or an infected partner. After oral sex, chlamydia can lead to pharyngitis, or throat infections. People who believe they are practicing "safe sex" by mutually masturbating each other or by oral sex are quite surprised to discover that contact with these bodily fluids can give them a sexually transmitted disease.

Unfortunately, 85 percent of women and 40 percent of men have no symptoms from a chlamydial infection.[8] A recent study published in the *New England Journal of Medicine* found that 10 to 12 percent of military recruits had undiagnosed chlamydial infections at the time of enlistment.[9] In many areas of the country, chlamydia is present in 24 percent of the sexually active girls ages fifteen to nineteen.

The Centers for Disease Control (CDC) estimates that 92 percent of all chlamydial infections in females occur in those under the age of twenty-five. This has led them to recommend yearly screening for chlamydia in all sexually active patients under the age of twenty-five.[10] I have been amazed at the number of my patients who have tested positive for chlamydia at their yearly visit since this recommendation was put forth. These were all young women, with no symptoms, carrying a ticking time bomb for PID and infertility. It is estimated that 20 to 40 percent of untreated women progress to PID.[11] While chlamydial infections can be cured with appropriate antibiotics, the damage done to the body may last a lifetime.

Gonorrhea

Another bacterium that people commonly associate with sexually transmitted diseases is gonorrhea. It causes infections in the genital tract, mouth and rectum—anywhere that bodily fluids are exchanged. Several years ago it seemed that medical science was on the verge of eliminating gonorrhea as a sexually transmitted disease, but it has rebounded, especially among teenagers. There are just under one million cases in the United States each year.[12] It is often diagnosed in the same individual who has chlamydia, prompting laboratories to include gonorrhea testing whenever chlamydia testing is also sought.

TEENAGERS EXPERIENCE THE HIGHEST RATE OF PID.

Symptoms of the disease usually manifest within seven to ten days after exposure. For women, the disease can be silent, or it can include bleeding after intercourse, painful urination, vaginal discharge and PID. Except for AIDS, the most common and serious complication of STDs in women is PID.

Teenagers experience the highest rate of PID because the lining of the cervix is still immature and less able to protect them. Cervical mucus prevents the spread of STDs inward except during ovulation, when the organism may be carried on the backs of sperm, and during menses, when the cervix opens to let menstrual blood escape. In fact, symptoms of PID often begin shortly after menstruation. One-fourth of all women with PID require hospitalization for intravenous antibiotics at a cost of $7 billion per year.[13]

Approximately 50 percent of women experience very few symptoms, which causes them to miss the opportunity to prevent complications through aggressive use of antibiotics. The body is left to heal on its own, commonly with the creation of scar tissue as a way of trapping the offending organism. Scar tissue can form anywhere in the abdomen and pelvis. Some women may develop a condition called Fitz-Hugh-Curtis syndrome, where the normal circulation of abdominal fluids carries the bacteria upward, trapping it between the liver and diaphragm. The resulting scar tissue formed in this location sticks the liver and diaphragm together, causing upper abdominal pain under the right rib cage and transmitting pain sensations to the right shoulder.

Scar tissue formed in the pelvis can also cause pelvic pain on either side as various organs become stuck to each other or to the pelvic walls. There is a 20 percent chance of chronic, potentially lifelong, pelvic pain with each episode of PID. There is also a 20 percent chance that PID will lead to infertility due to damage in the fallopian tubes.[14] This is the leading cause of tubal or ectopic pregnancy, with seventy thousand cases in the United States each year. As mentioned earlier, this is also the leading cause of pregnancy-related deaths in the United States.[15]

Men infected with gonorrhea experience painful urination and pus draining from the urethra. Infants exposed to gonorrhea at birth can develop eye infections, which are now routinely prevented by giving antibiotic ointments at birth in most states in this country. While gonorrhea is easily treated with antibiotics, it is asymptomatic in 50 percent of patients. Prolonged exposure to gonorrhea can lead to arthritis, damage to heart valves and inflammation of the brain.

Syphilis

Syphilis is another bacterial STD that has been on this earth for at least a thousand years. It has been called the "great imitator" because it resembles so many other diseases. Syphilis is caused by a form of bacterium that infects through skin-to-skin contact and is poorly prevented by condom use.[16] Syphilis initially leaves an ulcer on the skin, then moves into and throughout the body, eventually damaging internal organs if left untreated. While it is fairly easy to treat with antibiotics if caught early, it is often not diagnosed.

There are three stages of syphilis. The first stage, called *primary* syphilis, presents as an ulcer on the skin approximately ten days to three months after exposure. This ulcer may be painless and go unnoticed. It can appear anywhere there has been skin-to-skin contact with an infected individual, either externally or internally. The ulcer will disappear within a few weeks even if untreated. The infected individual may misinterpret this as complete healing, but one-third will progress to the next stage.

The second stage, or *secondary* syphilis, occurs three to six weeks after the original ulcer has appeared. It manifests itself as a brownish skin rash. This rash can cover the entire body or just a few areas. A telltale sign of secondary syphilis is a rash on the palms of the hands or the soles of the feet, a most unusual location for any other type of rash. Any contact with this rash can spread the disease, even if it is nonsexual. This rash heals by itself over a period of weeks or months if not treated by antibiotics. Some untreated individuals will move into a dormant phase that has no symptoms and is not contagious. One-third of those untreated in the second stage will progress to the next level.

In the third stage, *tertiary* syphilis occurs, which means the disease has now become an internal disease. It begins to damage organs such as the heart and causing injury to the valves, which can be very serious. Tertiary syphilis can attack the bones and joints, leading to crippling arthritis. If it spreads to the eyes, it causes blindness. When affecting the nervous system, syphilis leads to a demented mind, difficulty with brain functions such as walking and eventually death. This stage of syphilis can last for decades and is usually incurable.

Pregnancy is an especially vulnerable time to contract syphilis. Twenty-five percent of infected pregnant women will experience stillbirth or neonatal death shortly after birth. Of those babies who survive birth, 40 to 70 percent will be infected with syphilis. For this reason, most states mandate prenatal testing of all pregnant women for syphilis at their first office visit. Women are again tested when in labor to detect those who may have contracted the disease during the course of their pregnancies. These tests are run to quickly identify and treat those mothers in the hope of preventing complications to their newborns.[17]

> **ROUGHLY ONE OUT OF FOUR PEOPLE IN THE UNITED STATES HAS HERPES.**

VIRAL STDS

Viral STDs are a critical problem because there is no known cure for them at present.

HSV (herpes)

The most common viral STD in the United States is herpes (HSV). There are two types of herpes. Type 1 has traditionally been called *oral herpes* and is associated with lesions around the mouth called *cold sores*. This form of herpes is not typically thought of as a sexually transmitted disease

(STD). Type 2 herpes is the genital variety that has historically been called an STD. However, these clear distinctions between Type 1 and Type 2 are beginning to blur due to oral sex, which can result in the transmission of Type 1 from mouth to genitals and Type 2 from genitals to mouth.

There are currently sixty million Americans with herpes, with one million new cases diagnosed each year.[18] That means roughly one out of every four people in the United States has herpes! This is certainly a shocking and sobering statistic and may explain the tremendous amount of research that is ongoing to develop a herpes vaccine. The progress has been difficult as the current experimental vaccine is only effective in women, and it is still several years from being available to the public.[19]

Herpes causes open sores or blisters in and around the vaginal opening, penis, anus, buttocks and thighs. These are the locations that infected semen would touch as it spills out of the vagina. The sores can lead to burning and itching, often confused with yeast infections in women. With the ability to purchase over-the-counter yeast remedies, it is quite possible that thousands of women are treating their herpes infections with the wrong medication and are never being diagnosed with this STD.

> **FOR WOMEN, THE FIRST OUTBREAK OF HERPES CAN BE VERY DIFFICULT.**

Herpes lesions are also painful when urine touches them, causing people of both sexes to mistake this for a urinary tract infection. And as mentioned earlier, herpes can present as *cold sores* after oral sex with an infected person or as a throat infection, mimicking strep throat.

For women, the first outbreak of herpes can be very difficult. They can experience symptoms similar to a viral flu with fever, chills, body aches, sensitivity to light and swelling of the lymph nodes. If there are many blisters near the site of urination, the nerves can temporarily malfunction, causing inability to urinate or have a bowel movement. I have personally admitted women to the hospital who could not urinate and required a catheter for several days. The lesions can last for two or three weeks at a time.

Symptoms usually present within two to ten days after contracting the disease. The virus resides in the nerve cells that lead to the skin. The lesion begins as a bump on the skin that tingles, turning into a blister that becomes an open sore. This sore eventually crusts over as a scab and heals, occasionally leaving a scar. The lesion is infectious from the time the skin begins to tingle until the lesion has been covered with a scab.

Once healed, the virus travels into the inner nerve cell and becomes inactive until the next recurrence. Forty percent of patients will have six or more recurrences during the first two years after the initial infection; 20 percent have more than ten recurrences each year. The recurrences are almost always in the same location each time, unless new sites develop from autoinoculation, which is the process of transferring the virus from the fingernails to new skin sites during scratching of existing lesions. There they will reside for life, just like the original lesion.[20]

Occasionally, women can have HSV infections and show no symptoms because the virus resides inside the vagina or cervix. This is perhaps why HSV continues to be spread so frequently, because women may not know they are infected.

There have been reports of death due to herpes infections in women who have weakened immune systems. There have been at least twenty-five cases of women who contracted herpes during the last trimester of their pregnancy, causing the virus to spread throughout the body and to all the major organs; 40 percent of the fetuses died. This condition carries a 50 percent mortality rate.[21] Acts of infidelity by a husband or boyfriend in the third trimester can result in the death of the mother and fetus.

The most devastating aspect of HSV is in its transmission to the newborn by an unsuspecting mother. Herpes acquired in the birth canal can be deadly in 50 percent of the newborns. Of those who do not die, serious and lifelong neurological difficulties are highly likely.[22] Because of this, women who are found to have a herpes lesion at the time of labor

HERPES IS A LIFELONG DISEASE.

are strongly advised to undergo a cesarean section to reduce the risk of infecting their newborn baby with this devastating disease.

Herpes can be treated with antiviral medications that are somewhat effective in preventing recurrences or in shortening the duration of outbreaks. But they are treatments, not cures. Herpes is a lifelong disease.

Long after the lesions have cleared, the emotional and psychological stress remains. I see many women in my office for whom the diagnosis of HSV hangs like a scarlet letter around their necks. They wonder if they are obligated to disclose this history to future sexual partners and if this knowledge will hinder that new relationship. Once married, they bear the burden of preventing transmission to their newborns and struggle to explain why a cesarean section is needed while trying to hide their secret shame. Often the diagnosis of HSV reveals to many women that their husband or boyfriend has not been faithful to them, with all the emotional damage that revelation brings. There are even herpes support groups to help women deal with the stress this diagnosis has added to their lives.[23]

HPV (human papillomavirus)

One of the most common STDs in the world today is the human papillomavirus, or HPV. It is estimated that twenty million Americans are currently infected, with five million new cases diagnosed each year.[24] HPV is the cause of genital warts, with approximately one million new cases of genital warts each year.[25] There are one hundred types of this virus, with a smaller number responsible for the majority of the STDs associated with HPV. Certain high-risk types can cause cervical, vulvar, vaginal and penile cancers.[26] It is estimated that 80 to 90 percent of all cervical cancer in the world is caused by HPV.[27] There is currently an experimental vaccine in clinical trials that blocks the acquisition of HPV-16, a type of HPV responsible for the majority of cervical cancers.[28]

While visible genital warts are the most easily recognizable form of the disease, half of all women and the majority of men have no symptoms. Most women are diagnosed at their annual gynecologic examination when their Pap smear returns abnormal. HPV is highly contagious by oral, genital or anal sex, and two-thirds of those who are exposed to it will develop the disease within three months of contact. For women, the common sites of HPV infection are the cervix, the vaginal opening and the anus. Men can experience lesions at the penis, scrotum and anus.[29]

Two main complications of HPV in adults can occur. The first is cancer of the genital organs of both male and female. Precancerous lesions, called *dysplasia*, can be detected in women by a Pap smear of the cells lining the cervix. Other lesions may be diagnosed on the genitals of both men and women through a biopsy. There are effective treatments for dysplasia, but they require diligent adherence to the recommended physical examinations offered in our current healthcare systems. Unfortunately, poorer communities may not have such access; they suffer the majority of genital cancers today.

The other main result of HPV infection is the development of genital warts. These warts are biologically and genetically similar to warts often seen on the hand. It is the reaction to the virus in infected skin cells that causes them to pile up into a wart. Genital warts can be very small or quite large, making urination or defecation difficult. In pregnant women, the weakened immune system can allow these warts to grow to such an extent that the opening to the vagina is obstructed, blocking the passage of the baby at birth and requiring a cesarean delivery.

Infants born to women with genital warts can occasionally become infected themselves, most commonly from swallowing vaginal secretion during birth. This brings the virus in contact with the infant's throat, and the development of warts on the pharynx can occur. If these warts grow, they can obstruct the passage of air to the lungs and become life threatening. Repeated laser treatments may be needed to keep the airway open.[30]

The treatments for HPV depend on the location and whether it is microscopic disease, such as with an abnormal Pap smear, or has developed into a wart. Some HPV infections may heal spontaneously through the body's own immune system. We see this commonly after pregnancy is completed. Other lesions can be treated with topical agents, freezing, electrocautery or laser. These treatments can be very painful and expensive. They are designed to rid the body of the visible warts but not the invisible virus.

HPV can persist in the body for a lifetime with recurrences being quite common. Unfortunately, even the best prevention strategies have fallen short. Research studies have been unable to confirm that condom use prevents the transmission of HPV, as we will discuss later on. In fact, many have been pressuring the government to require condom manufacturers to include warning labels alerting consumers that condom use may not protect them from acquiring HPV. A measure in the 2001 HHS (Health and Human Services) appropriations bill approved by Congress requires the FDA to evaluate whether the labels on condoms are medically accurate in addressing their effectiveness in preventing STDs, including HPV.[31] The promise of an HPV vaccine against the more serious subtypes remains the only medical hope.

Hepatitis

There are five known types of hepatitis virus, three of which are contracted sexually: types B, C and D. Hepatitis B is the most common of these types in the United States. Approximately 300 thousand new cases occur each year, with 50 percent of these transmitted through sexual intercourse. The rest of the cases are spread through exposure to infected blood or blood products. There are currently one million Americans who are chronically infected with hepatitis B.[32]

Despite the creation of a vaccine against hepatitis B in 1986, the rate of new infection continues to increase. Homosexual and bisexual males, intravenous drug users and their sexual partners make up the majority of new cases. With more effective screening of donated blood, this avenue of transmission has been virtually eliminated. While healthcare workers could contract hepatitis B from being stuck with an infected syringe or instrument, almost all have been immunized with the vaccine as part of the requirements of working in the healthcare field.

But as the data shows, those most at risk do not receive the vaccine. It is actually a series of three injections spread over several months. Because of the difficulty in reaching those most at risk, many states are taking steps in their legislatures that would require that all children be vaccinated as part of the public school requirements, just as they now must be vaccinated for other diseases such as mumps or measles. But until that generation is of age, the current generation will most likely continue to suffer increasing infection rates.

One of the reasons for the increase of infection is that sexual intercourse is a highly efficient way of transmitting the virus to others. While most people heal from the disease, some become chronic carriers and are at risk of developing liver disease. Each year in the United States, six thousand people die from cirrhosis and liver cancer.[33] It is increasingly common among recent immigrants to the United States from the Far East, where hepatitis B is present in the majority of the population from birth.

To prevent the disease from infecting newborns, most states now require testing for hepatitis B at the first prenatal visit and upon admission to the hospital once labor has begun. If the mothers are found to be carriers of the disease, newborns can be given powerful gamma globulin injections as well as the vaccine shortly after birth. Unfortunately, there is no cure for those who become carriers.

Hepatitis C is the most dangerous form of the virus. It is transmitted in the same way as hepatitis B and can remain silent for many years. Contact with infected blood or genital secretions can transmit the virus to adults as well as to the infant at birth. Most cases occur in people between the ages of twenty-five and forty-six, with at least one hundred thousand new cases diagnosed in this country each year. Only 15 percent of patients clear the virus from their systems. The majority become chronically infected, comprising the three million carriers of this disease currently living in the United States. Of those with chronic infection, many will develop severe liver disease, leading to cirrhosis and liver cancer. Hepatitis C is the leading cause of liver transplants in the United States. There is currently no vaccine against hepatitis C.[34]

HIV virus

The STD that has gotten the most publicity is the HIV virus, the agent responsible for AIDS. The HIV virus damages the immune system, rendering its victims unable to defend themselves against infectious diseases or cancer. There are currently one million people in the United States living with HIV. Half of all those who have been infected with HIV since its arrival to the United States in the early 1980s have already died.[35] This number of deaths represents more than the number of Americans who died in World War II.

Worldwide, the epidemic of AIDS threatens to rival the plagues of past centuries, which swept the earth before the medical advances of today. Unfortunately, just as in times past, medical science has been unable to keep pace with the devastation of AIDS worldwide. While in the United States HIV infection has primarily been confined to the homosexual and intravenous drug populations, the rate of increase among women is faster than any other group in the past decade. In the developing world, HIV is primarily spread through heterosexual contact.

According to the United Nations and National Institutes of Health (NIH), there are over 33 million people worldwide infected with HIV/AIDS, spread equally between men and women. Fourteen million people have already died from AIDS in the past twenty years with a current death rate of 2.5 million per year. Heterosexual transmission is responsible for 75 percent of all HIV cases worldwide. More than 90 percent of HIV-infected people live in developing countries, with every country on the face of the earth impacted by this disease. Half of all infections occur in people between the ages of fifteen and twenty-four—the next generation.[36]

The largest concentration of HIV-infected adults is in Africa, with the number reaching over thirteen million people. More women than men are infected, and millions of children have already died from AIDS they acquired at childbirth. But as large as this problem is, the next major wave of infection is occurring in Southeast Asia. The spread of HIV in this region has been very rapid among the heterosexual population. In one study, 44 percent of the men in Thailand had their first sexual experience with a prostitute, leading to rampant STD infections and the spreading of HIV virus to the rest of the population.[37]

The nation with the largest population in the world is China, and it is bracing for an explosion of HIV infection. It is estimated that approximately one million Chinese currently are infected. Due to the inability of the government to educate such a vast population of poor and illiterate, China could have ten million HIV-infected people by the end of this decade. Once a certain number is reached, the exponential growth could sweep the entire nation.

A practice peculiar to that region is the blood-buying industry. Poor, rural villagers sell their blood, which is then pooled together with other donations and the various components extracted from it. The remainder is then injected back into the donors to minimize their blood loss and enable them to be frequent donors. It only takes one infected person selling their blood to infect many as this tainted blood is mixed with others and then injected back into the donors, with the most concentrated portions going to the cities for sale to hospitals. This practice accounts for 10 percent of the HIV cases in China.

The vast drug trade is responsible for 68 percent of HIV cases, due to intravenous drug use. Once a certain percentage of the population is infected, heterosexual and homosexual intercourse will become the dominant route, as it has in all other developing nations.[38]

Since people can be infected with the HIV virus for many years, the true devastation of this disease will only be known as the most productive and vital segment of the world's population dies—our youth. As we have cited, in the United States alone, AIDS is the leading cause of death for people between the ages of twenty-five and forty-four, despite the best advances of modern medicine. As countless millions worldwide die in the prime of their lives, leaving behind their infected children to succumb soon after, the words of Leviticus 26:25 take on a new meaning:

> And I will bring the sword upon you to avenge the breaking of the covenant. When you withdraw into your cities, I will send a plague among you.

SAFE SEX?

The proverbs of Solomon, the wisest man who ever lived, warned young men not to sleep with a harlot. That warning is as appropriate in today's dangerous sexual world as it was when he wrote it:

> "Come, let's drink deep of love till morning, let's enjoy ourselves with love!"… With persuasive words she led him astray; she seduced him with her smooth talk. All at once he followed her like an ox going to the slaughter, like a deer stepping into a noose till an arrow pierces his liver, like a bird darting into a snare, little knowing it will cost him his life.

> —*Proverbs 7:18, 21–23*

In the past decade, we have been bombarded on an almost daily basis by the government about the use of condoms. Media celebrities and sports figures have been recruited to spread the "good news" that condoms make sexual activity safe. This hard-sell evangelism began in earnest in response to the epidemic of HIV/AIDS seen in the homosexual community in this nation. Because many in the artistic community are homosexual, high-profile figures in art, fashion design, theater, film, figure skating, ballet and dance became victims of this deadly disease.

Most of us remember the disclosures of famous people such as Rock Hudson, Liberace and Robert Reed (Mr. Brady of *The Brady Bunch*) who died with AIDS. And heterosexual sports stars such as Arthur Ashe and Magic Johnson made us aware that HIV/AIDS was not confined to the homosexual community; it could be acquired through blood or heterosexual sex.

While our nation's blood supply is the safest in the world, the problem of assuring safe sex is more difficult. Sex is a behavior, and behaviors are very difficult to change. Multiplied millions of dollars have been spent to do just that. But instead of responsibly teaching the public that sexual intercourse outside of marriage is dangerous, that anal intercourse between men is extremely risky and that multiple sexual partners may kill you, the government has promised its own standard for safety—the condom.

Setting a standard

The initial thrust of condom education was based on the fear of AIDS. But with the rising STD epidemic, the condom is now the government's primary weapon to protect our young people. The promise of "safe sex" is not by practicing monogamy in marriage, as God intended. It is the promise of the condom. And virtually every child in the public school will be taught this message of "safe sex" through the virtues of condoms. The only debate that remains is how early to begin teaching, with advocates reaching down into the elementary schools, suggesting they illustrate the lesson by placing condoms on bananas—all with our tax dollars.

Condoms have become a lightning rod, dividing many in this country. Many fear that this overt condom education sets a standard, sending a message to our youth that we expect them to be sexually active teenagers and that this is the "correct" way to do it. For those parents who believe in abstinence until marriage and those religious institutions that support them, condom education in public schools threatens their ability to raise their children according to biblical standards. Many fear that condom education will encourage their children to become sexually active through peer pressure magnified by the consent of the school system.

But those who have watched the skyrocketing teenage pregnancy, STD and AIDS rates among teenagers believe that teaching abstinence is unrealistic and even dangerous. Those leaders look at statistics showing that 60 percent of our nation's young people have become sexually active before they graduate high school.[39] They doubt that promoting abstinence will change these behaviors and fear that, without condoms, these children will fail.

In some ways, they are right. Abstinence was never meant to be an isolated teaching regarding a safe option for sexual behavior; it is a part of our personal relationship with God. Only as we acknowledge God's superior wisdom and receive His empowering through personal relationship with Him, which fills us with desire to please and obey Him, will the teaching of abstinence truly be effective. This divine answer to healthy sexual relationships will be difficult for those who do not know God.

Another fig leaf

Even from a strictly scientific perspective, are condoms the answer for a generation far from God? The answer is a resounding *no*. Man's rebellion against God did not begin yesterday. Ever since the Garden of Eden, he has attempted to cover his sin. You may recall that after Adam and Eve disobeyed God's command, they realized they were naked and tried to cover themselves with fig leaves. The condom is simply another fig leaf.

In its earliest form the condom has been around for three thousand years. It can be traced back to ancient Egypt in 1000 B.C., when it was made of linen and designed specifically to stop the spread of sexually transmitted diseases. The first medical trials of condom use for disease prevention occurred in the 1500s by a man named Fallopius of Italy. He recruited eleven hundred men and tested the linen condom against syphilis, the dominant STD at that time. None of his subjects became infected as far as he was able to diagnose.[40]

In the 1700s, condoms began to be made from animal intestines, but they were expensive; the result was that they were often reused with poor results.[41] The "natural" condoms available today are also made from animal intestines. They are prized for their thinness but discouraged in their use due to higher breakage rates. The larger pore size in these condoms also allows viral particles to penetrate, and, because of the HIV virus, their use has fallen dramatically.

In 1844 vulcanization made natural rubber more elastic and strong. With the same material used for tires, Goodyear and Hancock began the mass production of condoms. In the 1880s the first latex condom was created, and by 1935, 1.5 million condoms were being produced each day in the United States. The latex condom now accounts for over 90 percent of all condoms made worldwide. By 1993, the annual production of natural latex condoms had reached 8.5 billion.[42]

There are some men and women who are allergic to latex and could not use latex condoms. But a new condom became available during the 1990s that is made of polyurethane and, while more expensive, is designed for those allergic to latex.[43]

Condoms come in a variety of colors, shapes and sizes. There are dark-colored condoms for men of African descent who complained about placing a light-colored product on their skin. There are "snug" condoms for smaller men and "extra-large" condoms for those who think they need it! Condoms can be purchased that glow in the dark for those who like a bit of humor in their foreplay. In 2002, the heavy-metal band K.I.S.S. announced they would license their likeness to be imprinted upon condoms. This trend seems like only the beginning of a wave of celebrity entrepreneurs. Condoms are also made with a variety of designs such as ribbed condoms, projections designed to contact the clitoris and improve orgasm. It is hoped that these various differences will encourage condom use in the general public, but especially by the trend-conscious teenagers of America.

Do they work?

The bottom line is, do they work? Before the epidemic of AIDS, the main focus of condom use was for pregnancy prevention. As a contraceptive, studies have been done and statistics kept of the effectiveness of latex condoms. Professionals whose interests lie in family planning have calculated what they call *perfect use* and *typical use* to rate contraceptive effectiveness. The percentages of women who would become pregnant using a particular product over a one-year period of time is calculated for all available birth control options on the market today.

Perfect use reflects the number of pregnancies, or "failures," that would be expected to occur for one hundred women using a particular form of birth control, *in the exact manner it was prescribed,* for every single act of intercourse from beginning to end in the course of one year. *Typical use* describes the number of pregnancies that actually occur in the general population using that particular product. This takes into account the additional human factors such as inconsistencies of use or improper techniques. The *typical use* is what will happen to the average couple that chooses that particular form of birth control.

For example, in the *perfect use* of latex condoms, 3 percent of couples would get pregnant, or "fail," using this product perfectly for one year. In *typical use* for one hundred couples who use latex condoms for one year, 12 percent would become pregnant.[44] To keep this in perspective, remember that pregnancy can only occur between three to five days per month due to the life span of sperm and egg. Of the one hundred couples per year studied, statistics tell us that 10 percent are infertile and would not conceive even if no methods of contraception were used. So of the ninety couples left, twelve would get pregnant using latex condoms. This fact raises the failure rate of condoms to over 13 percent for an event that can only occur a few times each month. And remember, an STD can be acquired every day of every month! Based on this pregnancy data alone, one has to wonder how reliable this method of protection really is.

Why do condoms fail?

A significant reason condoms fail is that they fail to be used. Many couples dislike condoms and feel they are disruptive to lovemaking. It is not as easy as it might seem to put a condom on correctly, which is why there has been such an emphasis on condom education in our public schools. The following information may help you understand what even the most motivated couple must overcome to achieve condom effectiveness.

The product comes tightly rolled in a pouch. There is an expiration date that must be checked. It has a shelf life of only three to five years. Latex is susceptible to heat, so the condom must be stored at room temperature and away from sunlight. The glove compartment of your car is a dangerous place for a condom, as is your back pocket. The package must be opened carefully to avoid damage. This is especially important if the woman is handling the condom, as jewelry or fingernails can tear the condom.

Most condoms come with a reservoir at the tip that is designed to receive the semen. It must remain free and not pulled up against the head of the penis. It is necessary to pinch off the head of the condom while placing it on the penis to ensure that the reservoir remains. The other benefit of pinching the end is that if the air is not kept out of the reservoir, the act of intercourse might push a pocket of air against the latex shell and cause breakage at the very place designed to collect the semen.

The condom must be unrolled correctly onto the erect penis. It must not be placed inside out or pulled up after being unrolled ahead of time in order to prevent breakage. The condom must be placed on the fully erect penis to ensure fit and before the penis has any contact with the partner's skin. Upon erection, a small amount of lubricating fluid is released that not only contains a high concentration of sperm but also can harbor STDs. If vaginal penetration is begun and then the penis is withdrawn for condom application, the damage may have already been done.

> **CONDOMS ARE AMONG THE *LEAST* EFFECTIVE METHODS OF BIRTH CONTROL AVAILABLE IN THE UNITED STATES.**

Some of the failure of condoms can occur in breaks or tears that result because of friction during intercourse. It is recommended that commercial lubrication be added to help the condom glide freely. But it must be a water-based product, as oil-based lubricants such as massage oil, baby oil, lotions or petroleum jelly will rapidly begin to decompose the latex. The most recommended lubricant is K-Y Jelly.[45]

Condom manufacturers have only recommended their product for penile-vaginal intercourse. It is not recommended for penile-anal intercourse due to the tightness of the anal opening. Yet condoms have been proposed by every major governmental agency as their primary HIV/AIDS prevention strategy, beginning with the homosexual population.

Once ejaculation has occurred, the penis will immediately begin to soften and shrink. It is critical to condom effectiveness that the condom be held at its base and withdrawn immediately after ejaculation to prevent spilling semen out of the opening of the condom or leaving the condom behind in the vagina upon withdrawal.

It is easy to see why many couples dislike this method of protection. In a national survey of heterosexual adults with multiple sexual partners, only

17 percent reported using condoms with every act of intercourse. Many concurred that sex felt better without condoms.[46]

Effective for HIV?

In an article in *Family Planning Perspectives,* Karen Davis and Susan Weller concluded, "Condom efficacy may be higher for pregnancy than for HIV since HIV particles are smaller than sperm cells and may actually leak through condoms."[47] Have you heard this on the nightly news? Is this what is being taught in our public schools as part of understanding "safe sex"? The fact is that condoms are among the *least* effective methods of birth control available in the United States, yet this is our government's primary weapon against HIV/AIDS.

C. M. Roland and M. J. Schroeder of the U.S. Naval Academy tested samples of latex from two condom-manufacturing facilities. Latex condoms have very tiny, intrinsic holes called "voids." But the HIV virus is fifty times smaller than these holes. In one square centimeter of latex, one million particles the size of the HIV virus passed through the condom within thirty minutes. Roland and Schroeder went on to state, "The ability of a condom or surgical glove to prevent transmission of viral particles is problematic."[48] Problematic indeed! (Please see Appendix B for more discussion on the use of condoms.)

Real Life

Jennifer was nineteen years old when I met her in the emergency room of our local hospital. I was asked by her mother to evaluate her daughter's sudden abdominal pain. When I arrived, I spoke with the emergency room physician and discovered some details about Jennifer that even her mother did not know.

Jennifer had begun having intercourse with a new boyfriend she had known for about two months. She noticed a heavy vaginal discharge about a month prior to coming to the emergency room and bought an over-the-counter fungal cream for what she thought was a yeast infection. It initially seemed to help, until she stopped using the cream, and then the discharge returned. A few days after beginning her period, Jennifer began experiencing abdominal pain and fever. She thought it was intestinal flu and told her mother so. After a few days, the symptoms resolved, and she was able to resume intercourse with her boyfriend. They did not use any birth control.

For the past five days, Jennifer had noticed a light menstrual flow. It was not as heavy as her usual monthly flow, and it began five days late. She was going to do a pregnancy test, but when she began bleeding, she decided that she could not be pregnant. On this day, she awoke with dizziness and severe pain on her right side. Her mother brought her to the emergency room when Jennifer almost passed out in her bathroom.

The emergency room had done a pregnancy test, which had returned positive. A pelvic ultrasound revealed a mass near Jennifer's right ovary. There was fluid behind the uterus, signifying internal bleeding. Both the ER physician and I were concerned that this represented an ectopic pregnancy.

When I spoke to Jennifer, I asked her if she wanted her mother to wait outside of the room so we could speak privately. She declined and stated that she wanted her mother to stay with her. I told them that we suspected an ectopic pregnancy and would need to operate to remove the mass and save the fallopian tube as well as her life.

In that awful moment, Jennifer's mother had to come face to face with the reality that her daughter was sexually active, was pregnant, was losing the baby and was in serious danger. It was a lot to handle in a short period of time, but there was no time to waste. Jennifer was taken immediately to the operating room where I discovered that the right fallopian tube had already ruptured beyond repair and would require removal to stop the blood loss. Inspection of the rest of the pelvis revealed significant scar tissue involving the rest of Jennifer's female organs.

When I returned to the waiting room to meet with her mother and father, I had the unhappy task of telling them that she had lost one fallopian tube and might have difficulty getting pregnant again because of the damage that had been done by the infection that she thought had been the "flu." It had, in fact, been PID that had been untreated and would likely lead to infertility.

Jennifer would pay a high price for her choices that summer, a price that would be felt into her adult years when she would find the man of her dreams but struggle to bear him a child. When she did marry, tens of thousands of dollars in expensive fertility surgery and IVF procedures did not work, and she and her husband adopted a child several years later.

Chapter **Nine**

UNDERSTANDING AIDS

> My son, do not forget my teaching, but keep my
> commands in your heart, for they will prolong
> your life many years and bring you prosperity.
> —*Proverbs 3:1–2*

The ultimate consequence of sexual sin is when it costs the person his life. This has been dramatically illustrated in the worldwide plague of AIDS. While HIV/AIDS in this country has predominately been caused by homosexual acts, the majority of people worldwide have been affected through heterosexual intercourse. The sins of one have affected the lives of many, often innocent, victims, reaching apocalyptic proportions.

As we attempt to remain "safe" in North America, the rest of the world is rapidly being consumed by a plague that seems unstoppable, the primary result of sexual activity outside the covenant of marriage. In many ways, HIV/AIDS is changing human civilization on this planet. The magnitude of these changes will affect the generations to come in a profound way.

DEFINING THE PLAGUE

AIDS is a condition caused by the human immunodeficiency virus, or HIV. This virus becomes incorporated into the genetic makeup of the human cell, preferring the lymphocyte above all other cells. These cells are a major part of our immune system, protecting us against infection and cancer. The virus progressively destroys the immune system, leaving its victim vulnerable to unusual infections and rare cancers that a healthy person would not encounter.

The infected person develops what is called acquired immunodeficiency syndrome, or AIDS. The diagnosis is based on the development of certain infections in the presence of the HIV virus that signals a critical loss of the immune system. A person does not die directly from HIV itself, but from the infections and tumors against which his destroyed immune system cannot defend itself.[1]

Origin

It is believed that HIV originated in Africa, where it is similar to viruses found in monkeys. Many of the world's most deadly viruses reside in Africa. From time to time there are reports of an outbreak of the Ebola virus, for example, that has wiped out a village somewhere in the heart of the jungle. These deadly viruses are also the most rapid in causing death. While there is little that medical science can do against such a swift and powerful attack as Ebola, the spread of these viruses is generally contained to a small area. The host of the virus dies so quickly that he cannot make contact with many people before all those around him can see the obvious devastation of his illness. Terror sweeps through the village, and those infected are quickly isolated from the rest of the community. This is not the case with the HIV virus, which lives long and silently.

Infectious characteristics

While HIV is a deadly virus, its actions are slow and silent. Many of its victims are without symptoms for months or even years, outwardly appearing completely normal to everyone else. Unaware themselves of their infectious state, and free to mingle with the uninfected, the virus is silently passed from one unsuspecting person to another.

But unlike the Ebola virus, mere casual contact is not enough to infect with HIV. HIV is actually difficult to contract. As compared with the virus that causes the common cold, this virus dies when exposed to the air; it cannot be left behind on toilet seats or telephone receivers, nor passed by shaking hands with someone. It requires an almost immediate connection from the giver to the receiver, and it must travel inside bodily fluids such as semen, blood, vaginal secretions or, in some cases, saliva. It is often not contracted even by those exposed directly to it.

The fact that a person infected with HIV lives many years and progressively becomes more contagious means that over the course of that person's lifetime, many people could contract the disease from a single individual. In every country where its origins have been traced, the virus is concentrated first in homosexual men and intravenous drug users. These people frequently share blood-tinged needles or have sex with multiple partners over a short period of time.

It is not uncommon for homosexuals uneducated about the risks of HIV/AIDS to sleep with dozens of other men in a single day. As this occurs day after day in a particular segment of society, the concentration of infected people becomes higher. Soon, the girlfriend of the IV-drug user contracts it from heterosexual sex or the bisexual male brings it home to his suburban wife, and the virus has entered a new arena. Statistically, once the virus reaches a certain percentage of the population, it will rapidly consume the rest.

EPIDEMIC PROPORTIONS

In the United States, there are currently one million people infected with HIV/AIDS, and 70 percent are homosexual. But the fastest growing population of new cases is in women, particularly black and Hispanic. Even though less than 0.5 percent of our population is HIV-infected, it is still the leading cause of death in the United States for adults under age forty-five.[2] Imagine, if instead of recording every traffic fatality and every gunshot victim on the local nightly news, every person who died of AIDS that day was featured. Day after day after day, the relentless face of death would flash onto the television screens in every home in America. The typical citizen would no longer think of AIDS as something that only happens to someone else. He would see its deadly grip in every neighborhood in his city.

If we in North America are complacent about the AIDS epidemic, we need only look outside our borders to see a world being consumed with the virus. In a landmark publication presented at the 2002 International AIDS Conference in Barcelona, the Joint United Nations Program on HIV/AIDS (UNAIDS) released its figures on the extent of HIV/AIDS in the world today. In its *Report on the Global HIV/AIDS Epidemic*, eight United Nations agencies were brought together to issue statistics of HIV/AIDS incidence in each country as of 2001, the twentieth anniversary of AIDS as we know it. Peter Piot, executive director of UNAIDS, made several shocking statements in the Preface to the report. He noted the twentieth anniversary of AIDS as "an occasion to lament the fact that the epidemic has turned out to be far worse than predicted...We know the epidemic is still in its early stages." He continues by saying that "the report provides positive proof that HIV, if left to run its natural course, will cause devastation on an unprecedented scale."[3]

It was felt by many scientists that the percentage of the world population infected with HIV would plateau at some manageable level, as it appeared to have done in the homosexual communities in the United States. But lack of education and no access to medication have left vulnerable those practicing risky sexual activities or intravenous drug abuse, particularly in developing nations.

In 1994, twenty million people in the world were estimated to have HIV/AIDS. By 2001, the report showed estimates of forty million, with five million newly infected cases in the year 2001 alone. Three million people died of AIDS in 2001, and there are currently fourteen million children orphaned by the death of their parents to AIDS. It is estimated that in the next eight years, forty-five million more people will become infected.[4]

A decade from now, nearly one hundred million men, women and children infected with the AIDS virus will be living on this planet. The cost to treat these people, the economic loss of productivity these adult workers would have brought to the world, and the missing generation of young people lost to AIDS will be staggering realities of the twenty-first century. Not since the bubonic plagues of 1347–1351, when the Black Death swept through Europe killing seventy-five million, has the earth witnessed such devastation.[5]

As I read through this report, I was struck by the enormity of the disease. Every country on the face of the earth was listed and beside each name, the sobering statistics. Just as one observes an alcoholic lose his job and his family, yet continue to drink until he dies at a young age, so too do the sins of sexual immorality continue undeterred for a generation lost and without God. And, in contrast, the redemptive power of godly behavior can also be seen even in nations that practice a different religion from ours. In the northern part of Africa, where Islam is the driving force of the nations, HIV infection is almost nonexistent. Though on the same continent where AIDS is rampant, a different lifestyle keeps them free from disease.

For more information on the AIDS epidemic, please see Appendix A.

AMERICAN INGENUITY

While I hope these statistics are as shocking to you as they are to me, it is easy for some to discount the potential calamity that is coming upon the earth. As Americans, we have relied on our scientific advancements and wealth to solve nearly every problem we have ever encountered as a nation. It is one of our country's greatest strengths that we never give up; we never surrender to anyone or anything. As a nation, we believe that there is no problem so big that American ingenuity cannot solve it.

In past generations, that strength of spirit has been coupled with a reliance on almighty God to enable us to win the victory in whatever battle we faced. But today, in the face of an enemy created by our own sin, God is not the one we are turning to for answers. If anything, AIDS activists stand against those who suggest they take personal responsibility for their sexual behavior that promotes this epidemic. Instead, these activists are placing their hope for relief in the medical community and in condoms.

The results of study after study show that condoms will never be the solution to any STD. But no one has pushed condoms upon the American people as the AIDS activists have, with the full backing of the Clinton administration. The great tragedy is that in their zeal to save the world, many in government have actually harmed others in their misguided attempt to protect without demanding a change in behavior.

FALSE HOPES OF PREVENTION

In August 2000, the CDC issued a strong warning against using the spermicide nonoxynol-9.[6] This product is found in all spermicidal condoms (the bulk of all condoms produced) and in vaginal contraceptive foams, inserts and diaphragm jelly.

A study conducted in Africa from 1996 to 2000 asked one thousand female prostitutes who were HIV-negative to use a condom along with a vaginal jelly with every act of intercourse. One-half of those participating in the study received placebo jelly (with no additives in it), and the other one-half received jelly containing nonoxynal-9 spermicide. The thought was that if the condom broke or slipped off, as frequently happens, the spermicide would provide backup protection.

After four years, the CDC discovered that those women given the spermicide contracted HIV at a 50 percent higher rate than those given the placebo. The very people that the Centers for Disease Control and Prevention were trying to protect were given a death sentence by their treatment.[7]

In our country, Planned Parenthood and government agencies continue to pass out condoms containing spermicide as both contraception and STD prevention. But for women, the spermicide acts as an irritant, inflaming the vaginal tissues and cervical lining, leading to more tearing of the skin and giving entrance to the HIV virus. As more research has shown the ineffectiveness of spermicides in condoms and the dangers of spermicides for women, condom manufacturers are beginning to remove it from their products. The very product we thought would prevent disease actually makes it easier to acquire the disease. I am reminded of the words of the apostle Paul to the Romans: "Professing themselves to be wise, they became fools" (Rom. 1:22, KJV).

Pharmaceutical help?

In addition to condom prevention, the fight against AIDS is being waged in the pharmaceutical arena. There are powerful antiviral drugs that, in various combinations or "drug cocktails," can keep the amount of active virus or "viral load" to manageable levels, allowing HIV-infected people a significant prolongation of life and a slowing of the progression from infection to AIDS. These drugs are not a cure, and the eventual death from AIDS is not prevented but only postponed. The cost of such medication can be $20,000 a year or more and is only feasible in the affluent nations of the West.

For several years, the number of people dying from AIDS seemed to plateau, but this may be a short-lived victory. As people are becoming educated about the use of antiviral medications, and as they see seemingly healthy celebrities like Irwin "Magic" Johnson unchanged by time, the fear of HIV is lessening. It is now being talked about as a manageable disease, not a lethal disease, no different from diabetes or high blood pressure. One simply takes medication for the rest of his life just as millions of other Americans do for their illnesses. And the stigma of being HIV-positive has lessened as well.

As a consequence of these scientific developments, those at highest risk of acquiring HIV, homosexuals in urban areas, are beginning to abandon the condom message and are returning to their previous behaviors. And with the ease and privacy of Internet chat rooms, gay men are searching for anonymous encounters in their home towns and while traveling around the nation. Gay and bisexual men looking for sex through the Internet far outnumber their heterosexual counterparts.[8] The rate of HIV infection in the United States is once again on the rise according to the 2002 UN report. Hope for salvation from AIDS had turned from condoms to pharmaceuticals, but there has been no change in morality or behavior.

As mentioned earlier, few nations on earth can afford the tremendous expense of HIV treatment programs. The nations with the largest population of HIV/AIDS are struggling under civil and tribal wars, famine and starvation. Their populations migrate from one country to another in search of safety and food, nomadic refugees spreading their diseases wherever they go. Medical treatments will never reach those who need it the most.

A POWERFUL ENEMY

Even if all of the world's resources were spent on giving the most powerful antiviral medications we have to every HIV-infected man, woman and child on the face of the earth, we would not stop the spread of AIDS. HIV is a powerful enemy, and it is becoming resistant to the available medications we possess today.

In a study published in the *Journal of the American Medical Association*, 27 percent of newly infected men from the San Francisco area carried a form of HIV that was resistant to at least one of the three major classes of drugs available for treatment. This is becoming an increasing problem in such places as New York City where antiviral medications are widely used. Some patients carry a virus that is resistant to all available medications.[9] The complacency of the gay community in the United States could transform it into a breeding ground for a new form of virus for which we will have no medical treatments.

HOPE FOR A "SAVIOR": A VACCINE

The hope for a "savior" for AIDS is being placed on the development of an HIV vaccine. Millions of dollars are being spent by Western governments and pharmaceutical companies searching for the still elusive "magic bullet." But former Surgeon General C. Everett Koop believes there will never be a vaccine. And the reason is very simple: There is more than one type of HIV virus.[10]

In the United States, HIV-1 is the predominant variety, but in Africa, there are many types. HIV-2 was discovered in 1986. Because it is so rare in the United States, the CDC does not recommend HIV-2 testing, although most blood banks test for type 1 and 2 simultaneously. Those people currently asking to be tested for HIV are tested only for type 1.[11]

It is possible that with the influx of immigrants from other nations that carry HIV-2, the spread of this variety could remain undetected in the United States for some time. Not only is HIV-2 resistant to the available medications we have to fight it, but it is also not the focus of any vaccine strategy at this time.

Because the funds for vaccine research come from the West, the emphasis is on treating the paying customer! Once again, the populations most at risk will not receive the help they need. And as we have seen with the virus that causes hepatitis, new strains will most likely continue to be discovered. Twenty years ago, we did not know that there were more than two forms of the hepatitis virus, but now we have found several others. We have made a vaccine for only two of them so far. The viruses always seem to stay one step ahead of us. That does not strengthen hope for a "magic bullet" vaccine.

GOVERNMENT SUPPORT
FOR ABSTINENCE

President George W. Bush's administration has been a vocal supporter of abstinence-only educational programs. Secretary of Health and Human Services Tommy Thompson awarded an additional $17 million for such programs in 2001, now available in all fifty states. In the draft release that accompanied his department's report on condoms and STDs, he states, "Sexually transmitted disease is a serious health problem in America, but it is almost entirely preventable though behavioral changes, especially abstinence and commitment to a mutually monogamous relationship with an uninfected partner."[12] It is refreshing to see that the panel's report did not "spin" its leader.

Other leaders in healthcare have been bold enough to buck the politically correct emphasis on condom use. Dr. Harold Jaffee, chief of epidemiology of the CDC, says, "You just can't tell people it's all right to do whatever you want as long as you wear a condom. It [AIDS] is just too dangerous a disease to say that."[13] Dr. Robert Renfield, chief of retro-viral research at Walter Reed Army Institute, says bluntly, "Simply put, condoms fail. And condoms fail at a rate unacceptable for me as a physician to endorse them as a strategy to be promoted as meaningful AIDS protection."[14] Dr. Teresa Crenshaw, a member of the U.S. Presidential AIDS Commission, had this warning: "Saying that the use of condoms is 'safe sex' is in fact playing Russian roulette. A lot of people will die in this dangerous game."[15]

Even the World Health Organization, far from being a bastion of conservative thought or moral values, issued this surprising statement during World AIDS Day: "The most effective way to prevent sexual transmission of HIV is to abstain, or for two people who are not infected to be faithful to one another."[16]

GOD'S WAY WINS

Science is proving what God the Father knew all along. The only way to prevent serious, lifelong disease and death is for both partners to be virgins at marriage and to remain faithful to one another for life. Abstinence is not some outdated and archaic moral position; it is literally a matter of life and death.

It is worth hearing again what Moses proclaimed to the children of Israel:

> This day I call heaven and earth as witnesses against you that I have set before you life and death, blessings and curses. Now choose life, so that you and your children may live.
>
> —*Deuteronomy 30:19*

BIBLICAL INSIGHT

The purpose of this book is to provide medical information from a biblical foundation, and I cannot help but wonder what role the epidemic of AIDS will play in the End Times. The Scriptures speak of plagues coming to earth during the End-Times tribulation. While I am not an expert in End-Times prophecy, here are some verses from the Book of Revelation that stir my medical mind:

> When the Lamb opened the fourth seal, I heard the voice of the fourth living creature say, "Come!" I looked, and there before me was a pale horse! Its rider was named Death, and Hades was following close behind him. They were given power over a fourth of the earth to kill by sword, famine and plague.
>
> —*Revelation 6:7–8*

Chapter 9 of the Book of Revelation depicts a series of calamities, and then concludes:

> The rest of mankind that were not killed by these plagues still did not repent of the work of their hands...Nor did they repent of their murders, their magic arts, their sexual immorality or their thefts.
>
> —*Revelation 9:20–21*

If current projections hold true regarding the HIV/AIDS epidemic, and the Lord tarries in His return for another decade or so, the exponential spread of AIDS over the face of the earth will be in the hundreds of millions, robbing every nation of an entire generation. Black leaders wonder aloud if their race will be wiped off the face of the earth. Could the economic and political shifts caused by such a devastating plague as this be part of the End Times prophesied so long ago?

Divine protection

As a physician who practices in a specialty that can be highly exposed to HIV, I take great comfort in the Scriptures as my defense against this epidemic. I am not looking for a vaccine to protect me. My trust is in the Lord! Psalm 91 is one of my favorite promises, and I pray it whenever I am exposed to someone else's blood:

> He who dwells in the shelter of the Most High
>   will rest in the shadow of the Almighty.
> I will say of the LORD, "He is my refuge and my fortress,
>   my God, in whom I trust."
> Surely he will save you from the fowler's snare
>   and from the deadly pestilence.
> He will cover you with his feathers
>   and under his wings you will find refuge:
>   his faithfulness will be your shield and rampart.
> You will not fear the terror of night,
>   nor the arrow that flies by day,
> nor the pestilence that stalks in the darkness,
>   nor the plague that destroys at midday.
> A thousand may fall at your side,
>   ten thousand at your right hand,
>   but it will not come near you.
> You will only observe with your eyes
>   and see the punishment of the wicked.
>
> —*Psalm 91:1–8*

To the community of believers who may fear the statistics I have given you or who tremble at the nightly news reports, let me remind you of another of God's promises:

When I shut up the heavens so that there is no rain, or command locusts to devour the land or send a plague among my people, if my people, who are called by my name, will humble themselves and pray and seek my face and turn from their wicked ways, then will I hear from heaven and will forgive their sin and will heal their land.

—2 Chronicles 7:13–14

Real Life

Angela, a thirty-four-year-old mother of two, came to my office in her first trimester for prenatal care. It was an unplanned but wanted pregnancy. Angela and her husband, Rafael, had been married for six years. This would be their first child together.

As required by the laws of my home state, Angela underwent prenatal blood work to screen for STDs (including syphilis, hepatitis B and HIV) that could be passed to the fetus. I was shocked when her blood results revealed that she was HIV-positive.

Angela would be my first pregnant HIV-infected patient. She was not a prostitute or an intravenous drug user, or even a promiscuous woman. She was a mother of two, soon to be three, living faithfully with her husband of six years.

The State Health Department receives copies of all test results that show the presence of an STD for the purpose of contacting the patient to determine what other sexual partners might need to be tested. It is hoped that this method will decrease the transmission of STDs by asymptomatic and unsuspecting carriers.

The Health Department contacted me about Angela's HIV status and received the name of her husband. When they scanned his name into their database, a surprising result appeared. Rafael had been treated three years earlier for chlamydia at a community clinic. At that time, he told health officials that he was single and had contracted the disease from a prostitute. Angela never knew about his infection.

I had the unpleasant task of calling Angela and informing her that I needed her and her husband to come to the office to discuss her test results. I could not have this kind of communication over the phone. When they arrived, Angela's first concern was that I had detected some abnormality with her baby. I assured her that the fetus was developing normally. The test results showed a problem with her.

What I told her next shocked her beyond words. As I reported that she was HIV-positive, her face became white and she was speechless. Rafael turned his face away. He could not make eye contact with Angela. Their body language said it all as she turned to see him retreat from her. He was not recoiling in fear or disgust; his own guilt was pulling him away.

Angela grappled with this news as any wife would. How could she be HIV-positive when she had no risk factors? Didn't you have to be gay or use drugs to get AIDS? She had not slept with anyone but her husband for the past six years. She had never had a transfusion. How did this happen to her? It became quite apparent that Rafael was the source.

For the past four years of their marriage, Rafael had returned to the prostitutes he used to frequent when he was single. He had thought that his addiction to sex would disappear when he got married. And for two years he stayed away. But as the routines of marriage, family and job began to set in, Rafael felt new levels of stress he had not previously known. When he was single, life was simpler, albeit lonely. But with his marriage to Angela, he was instantly a husband, a father to her two children and a provider. He needed a release from all this stress. The familiar fix of sexual gratification pulled at his soul. His old "friends" were still where he had left them.

When Rafael had contracted chlamydia, he took a few doses of antibiotics and was cured. He figured if he ever contracted another STD, it would be a simple problem to solve. He didn't have any symptoms. He didn't feel any differently. How could he have a life-threatening virus like HIV?

And now he had given it to Angela. If she died from AIDS, it would be his fault. That was something he had never thought of when he slept with those other women. What about the baby? Would he be born with HIV? Would he die? Rafael had no children of his own. This baby, although unplanned, represented his future, his seed upon the earth. Had he destroyed future generations with his sin?

Both Angela and Rafael began treatments to suppress their HIV-viral load. Medical studies indicate that pregnant women who take antiviral medication and decrease their viral load dramatically reduce the risk of passing HIV to their newborn during delivery.

Because she would require the care of infectious disease specialists and a hospital with an intensive care nursery, Angela transferred her care to the University Hospital. I never saw her again. This devoted mother and faithful wife never imagined she would be the victim of the deadly HIV virus.

Chapter Ten

THE WEDDING NIGHT: BASICS YOU SHOULD KNOW

As a bridegroom rejoices over his bride, so will
your God rejoice over you.
—Isaiah 62:5

From time to time, couples who are both virgins ask for advice regarding their wedding night. I wish this situation was more common, but on those rare occasions when both partners have saved their virginity until marriage, one or both may be nervous about their first sexual experience. Sometimes the bride-to-be has heard "horror stories" from other women about their wedding nights, and this only adds to the fear and anxiety. The groom-to-be may be concerned that he doesn't know male and female anatomy very well and might appear clumsy and feeble.

Again, there are resources available with diagrams and drawings as well as instruction on sexual techniques that may be of great value. Sitting down before the wedding and reviewing these materials together can be a way to open up a dialogue about whatever fears or reservations each person might have. Gaining knowledge about the male and female anatomy can give the opposite partner more confidence when approaching intercourse for the first time. Knowing in advance some general principles of pleasure can make a world of difference.

GETTING STARTED

Hopefully, the earlier chapters in this book have been a place of beginning for some of you as you learned about each gender from an anatomical, biological and hormonal perspective. We also discussed some differences in the ways the male and female think and act. These are all broad brush strokes to get you started. Only time and attention will fill in the details for each person; after several years an accurate portrait of their likes and dislikes, and their strengths and weaknesses, will have been made.

If you ask people who have been happily married awhile, they will tell you that sex gets better over a period of time. Honeymoon sex is often not that great. Although it is an important rite of passage, it is not the benchmark by which all other encounters will be measured. There are several reasons for this. Usually, the bride and groom are exhausted from the rehearsal, wedding ceremony, reception and other activities that precede the event. By the time they arrive at their hotel room that night, neither is in peak physical condition.

Both bride and groom will have worn uncomfortable clothing and shoes, smiled endlessly until their cheeks hurt and eaten sporadically, if at all. This is not the ideal preparation for a night of great sex! While your wedding day may indeed be the happiest day of your life, I am suggesting that you need to be realistic in your expectations of each other on your wedding night. Realize that false expectations of the consummation that you can't fulfill were based in fantasy in the first place.

Before the wedding

Hopefully before the wedding night, you have both talked about contraception and whether or not you wanted to use any. If you chose hormonal birth control (pill, patch, ring or injectable), you would have needed to be on your second month to have adequate protection for your wedding night. If you were fitted for a diaphragm or decided upon condoms, these need to have been brought with you.

It is a good idea to have any barrier methods you are going to use readily accessible before initiating intercourse so that the flow will not be interrupted. As we will discuss in the chapter on contraception, a diaphragm must be inserted ahead of time, while a condom can be placed as part of foreplay. Review in your mind the proper technique for whichever method you choose, if you are going to use contraception at all.

Relieving fears

For women, the greatest fear (besides pregnancy) is that intercourse will hurt. Most women are familiar with the hymen, a band of skin that encircles the opening to the vagina. It is a seal upon virginity that, once opened, will never be resealed.

In the Old Testament, the breaking of the hymen and the resultant bleeding that occurred were proof that a husband had been given a virgin as a bride. The bed sheets were inspected for the presence of blood the following morning. A bride who was found not to be a virgin could be stoned to death (Deut. 22:13–21). So proving one's virginity by bleeding on the wedding night was a major event in the culture of the Bible, one that held life-or-death consequences.

But in our day, the rupturing of the hymen and the resultant bleeding are not a celebrated event. In fact, the thought of it causes fear among many a virgin bride. Since such evidence is not necessary under the New Covenant, it is preferable to many of the couples I counsel to avoid such physical trauma.

Part of the counsel to betrothed virgins is about the stretching of the hymen before the wedding night. If they have been tampon users, some stretching of the hymen has undoubtedly occurred. If they have not used tampons, I instruct the women to take a lubricant, such as K-Y Jelly, and place it on their index finger. Gently inserting the index finger to the second knuckle will begin the process of stretching the hymen. An intermediary step is the insertion of two fingers crossed over each other. The goal is to eventually be able to insert comfortably two lubricated fingers side by side into the vagina. While the erect penis is still wider than this, it will be a good starting point for the evening.

Some women will not want to do these things and prefer to experience their wedding night without any prior preparation. That is, of course, completely acceptable. These suggestions are for those who fear the tearing of the hymen and would like to reduce that risk, providing for a more pleasant beginning to their sexual life.

Preparing for intercourse

Of course, the conduct of the groom is equally important if this preparation is to be successful. While the hymen is a bridge of skin that can be stretched, the vagina is a tunnel of circular muscle that can be contracted to a very small opening prior to childbearing. A frightened bride can squeeze the opening so tightly that the groom cannot gain access. So the conduct of the man must be slow, gentle and as relaxed as possible.

I suggest wine or champagne for both partners, either during the reception or at the hotel. The goal is to be as relaxed as possible, but not drunk! Both should change into clothing that is appropriate for the evening and is easy to remove. Try to avoid complicated bra fasteners or belts that can interfere with romance and cause the other person embarrassment or feelings of insecurity from struggling to remove an article of clothing. Save those daring maneuvers for a later time. The point is to have everything go as smoothly and as confidently as possible.

When both are ready, slowly undress each other, taking time to admire how God has created the other. Don't be in a rush to reach the genitals. Take time to explore other areas of the body and build excitement. This will increase the woman's natural lubricating fluids and prepare the vagina for later entry. After several minutes of foreplay, and when both partners feel ready, it is up to the groom to enter his bride. She can facilitate this by taking the penis and guiding it slowly into herself.

This accomplishes two things. First, it relieves a common fear (and mistake) that men have of missing the vaginal opening and ending up at the anus. It is an easy thing to do since the two openings are only an inch apart. Second, by guiding the penis, the woman can feel in control of the speed of entry and give herself time to get accustomed to the stretching as the penis is progressively inserted.

As mentioned in an earlier chapter, every vagina can accommodate a penis. But the penis does come in different lengths and widths when erect. The bride and groom will form a perfect fit no matter what the size if they are both gentle and patient. Sometimes the addition of a lubricant, such as K-Y Jelly, is helpful, especially if the woman does not feel she is well lubricated on her own. This will reduce friction as a source of tearing of the vaginal skin.

Most of the discussion so far has centered on the hymen, which is an issue of width or girth of the penis. The topic of length comes to bear in the back of the vagina. Once penetration has been achieved and the bride is comfortable with the penis fully inside of her, the groom will begin to withdraw it partially and thrust it back in again in a rhythmic motion. This is the basis of intercourse and what is necessary for the male to achieve ejaculation. Several facts mentioned in earlier chapters now come into play.

If the woman is sufficiently aroused, the muscles of the deep vagina will pull the cervix inward and cause the vagina to elongate, accommodating almost any length of penis. But this is not universal. Sometimes the arousal phase will not be complete, either from pain or fear, and the vagina will not reach its maximum elongation. Some men have longer penises than others and are able to reach the back of the vagina, hitting the cervix. Since the cervix is attached to the uterus, which is attached to the ovaries, rhythmically bumping the cervix can transmit pressure waves to the ovaries. This can be quite an unpleasant sensation for the woman, akin to slapping the testicles repeatedly.

If during deep penetration the bride is uncomfortable, she must say so, as the groom will have no way of knowing otherwise. He should press inward to the depth that she finds comfortable, and she should let him know if he is going too deeply. Since the majority of the pleasure sensations for the penis are located in the upper third of the organ, the depth of entry makes no difference in the ability to achieve ejaculation. And since the clitoris is on the outside, pushing into the vagina too deeply can only cause pain. Communication is the key. A couple will discover the right "fit" both in the vertical and horizontal dimensions of the vagina.

If after ejaculation the woman has not achieved orgasm (roughly 70 percent will not have), then the groom should begin to stimulate the clitoris directly to bring this about.[1] Again, communication is the key. The bride must tell her husband where to rub, how hard or soft, how quickly or slowly, depending on what she needs to achieve orgasm. It takes far longer for the woman to achieve this experience than the man, especially in the beginning when neither is well skilled. And the woman is capable of several orgasms in a row if allowed to continue to the end. In general, the female orgasm is a process of many minutes, while the male orgasm can be measured in seconds![2]

Don't be disappointed

This reminds me to caution those who may be disappointed with their first sexual experience. Intercourse, like most things in life, gets better with practice. We often feel that because it is "natural," we should automatically be good at it. But no activity we do in life is excellent without instruction and practice. Several years into your marriage you should be able to look back on those first few months of lovemaking and see the great progress you have made. This comes from "knowing" each other in all the ways God intended when He created marriage. The more we get to know one another, the greater the intimacy and the sweeter the lovemaking.

Preventing complications

One final note of instruction for newlyweds is in the area of prevention of early difficulties. There is a medical condition nicknamed "honeymoon cystitis." It is a bladder infection that is caused by intercourse, especially in virgins or those remarrying after several years of abstinence. The female urethra is short, and bacteria from the vagina can be pushed into the urethra by the thrusting penis, especially if the vagina is not well lubricated. Within twenty-four to forty-eight hours, the woman will experience burning with urination and a tremendous urge to void, even though there is no urine there. The infection can be treated effectively with antibiotics. However, if one is on a honeymoon far away from the family physician, antibiotics can be difficult to obtain.

One preventative measure is for the woman to void after she is finished with lovemaking. This will flush the urethra of any bacteria that may have entered during intercourse. Another consideration would be to ask your family physician or gynecologist for a prescription of antibiotics that treat urinary tract infections and to fill the prescription before the wedding.

If the bride is taking birth control pills, some antibiotics can interfere with the absorption of these hormones and reduce the effectiveness of the contraception. Ask for one specifically designed for the bladder. Nitrofurantoin is an excellent choice, as it will not kill the normal vaginal bacteria that are necessary to prevent yeast infections. Take one tablet at bedtime each night of the honeymoon. In about a week, the woman's body should have adapted, and antibiotics will no longer be necessary.

It is my hope that these suggestions will make your wedding night a pleasant experience and lay a foundation for a lifetime of marital happiness. Everything in life that you will ever excel in will come about through practice and study. Sex is no different. This night is only the beginning of marital satisfaction.

Chapter Eleven

BIRTH CONTROL: WHAT ARE YOUR OPTIONS?

> Like arrows in the hands of a warrior are sons born in one's youth. Blessed is the man whose quiver is full of them.
>
> *—Psalm 127:4–5*

I realize that I run the risk of offending Christians of differing denominations when I devote a chapter to contraception. There are those who believe that contraception is against the Word of God. Some people believe that the Lord will control how many children they have and that they should do nothing to hinder conception. There are many verses in the Old Testament that show the Lord as the One who opens and closes the womb. For example:

> When the LORD saw that Leah was not loved, he opened her womb, but Rachel was barren.
>
> *—Genesis 29:31*

> Then God remembered Rachel; he listened to her and opened her womb.
>
> *—Genesis 30:22*

These sincere Christians also quote other passages to show that God desires couples to be fruitful in reproducing children. They point to God's command to the first couple:

> Be fruitful and increase in number.
>
> *—Genesis 1:28*

And they reference the psalmist's commendation:

> Like arrows in the hands of a warrior are sons born in one's youth. Blessed is the man whose quiver is full of them.
>
> *—Psalm 127:4–5*

THE NATURAL ORDER OF LIFE

A classic study of potential human fertility is a sect in South Dakota called the Hutterites. This is a religious order originally from Switzerland. Contraception is condemned, and all women breast-feed. The communal living arrangements and shared resources encourage all families to have as many children as the Lord gives them. The average age of marriage is twenty-two, and the average age of last pregnancy is forty-one.

Breast-feeding without artificial supplementation of formula or baby food results in an absence of the menstrual cycle until the child is twelve to eighteen months of age. This naturally spaces children every two years. Given this interval, the average couple would have eleven children during their marriage. Those who married younger or breast-fed for shorter intervals could potentially have fifteen children.[1]

I have personally cared for women with ten to twelve children who have done well physically and are very happy with their large family. There are other Christian families who reason practically that they can only afford to take care of a certain number of children, given the increasing cost of living, expenses of college and so forth. They see scriptural truths about being able to support one's family and rule over them in a way that brings God glory. Their conviction comes from verses such as:

> But if any provide not for his own, and specially for those of his own house, he hath denied the faith, and is worse than an infidel.
>
> —1 Timothy 5:8, KJV

> If anyone does not know how to manage his own family, how can he take care of God's church?
>
> —1 Timothy 3:5

> A deacon must be the husband of but one wife and must manage his children and his household well.
>
> —1 Timothy 3:12

What glory does it bring God if a man cannot take care of what he has brought into this world and must depend upon the government to assist him? There are many in the body of Christ who feel that they can only properly handle a certain number of children. Others want to postpone having children until they are finished with their education or until they can afford a house or get out of debt.

Those couples who share the concerns mentioned ask me what their options are for contraception; they desire choices that fit their own spiritual convictions. For those who desire instruction on contraceptive options, I will examine the advantages and disadvantages of each method, letting the reader decide which method fits their need at a particular time in their lives.

NATURAL METHODS

A popular form of birth control that many Christian couples are comfortable using is *natural family planning*, also called *the rhythm method*. It was widely used by generations past when other contraceptives were not yet an option. It is the exact opposite of the method used to *enhance* fertility. Using the rhythm method, one attempts to discover when the most fertile times of a woman's cycle are and then avoids having intercourse on those days of the month.

This method requires no drugs or devices and is absolutely free. It does not interfere with the body's own reproductive cycle; it is merely an attempt to avoid having intercourse on days when conception would be more likely to occur. In this way, a measure of abstinence is included in every menstrual cycle.

Self-discipline is involved if one is to effectively use natural family planning (NFP). It may well require denying the marital rights of intercourse for ten to fourteen days each month, which may not be an easy task for many people, especially the newly married.

Principles of NFP

The principles of NFP are rooted in reproductive science. A woman ovulates, or produces and releases one egg from an ovary, every twenty-eight days on average. This generally occurs fourteen days from the beginning of the menstrual period if the woman has menses every four weeks. If her cycle is longer or shorter than twenty-eight days from the start of one period to the beginning of another, that will require modification of this rule.

The egg can be fertilized for only eighteen to twenty-four hours after ovulation. This seems like a narrow window of opportunity, and it is, except for one thing. God in His wisdom gave sperm the ability to live for three to seven days after ejaculation. In some women, the cervix has glands that form small inlets where sperm can be stored and nourished, gradually being released for up to one week. In practicality then, the fertile period is not the one day that the human egg can survive but the seven days that the sperm can still fertilize after intercourse.

The cervix also secretes mucus that enables the sperm to leave the vagina and enter the uterus. Once the egg has died, the mucus shrinks rapidly, and the pathway to further sperm migration is closed. The ovary begins producing progesterone to prepare the uterine lining to accept an embryo.

Progesterone thickens the mucus and raises the body temperature. These two signs signal the end of the fertile portion of the cycle.

Enhancing NFP

One way to enhance the efficacy of NFP is to monitor the changes in cervical mucus production throughout the menstrual cycle. As menstruation comes to a conclusion, the vagina is dry. After a few days, thick mucus will develop. As a woman gets closer to ovulating, the mucus will become thinner and more abundant. At its peak, the woman will notice a large amount of thin, sticky mucus that signals impending ovulation. For those trying to conceive, this is a helpful sign. After the days when fertilization of the egg should have occurred, the production of progesterone thickens the mucus again, and another "dry" spell will occur, leading to menstruation. For those practicing periodic abstinence using cervical mucus, the days from the start of mucus production until it dries up again would be considered the non-intercourse period.

Another way to enhance NFP involves measuring the basal body temperature (BBT). This is the body temperature that one has upon awakening. It requires measuring a woman's temperature as she awakens, before any bodily activity can raise the temperature level. A graph is made, and one can see that after ovulation has occurred, the BBT is about one degree warmer until menstruation, when it returns again to a lower level. Those practicing abstinence using the BBT do not have intercourse from the menstrual period until after the temperature has risen to its higher level.[2]

In using either of these methods, a significant number of days per month are off-limits to intercourse. This method requires diligence and self-sacrifice to be successful. Many do not achieve perfection with this method due to their lack of self-control, which is recorded by its 25 percent failure rate (or pregnancy rate) per year.[3] In other words, one couple in four who choose this method of birth control will get pregnant each year.

Variation of NFP

Because of the measure of abstinence required in NFP, a variation that is also "natural" is often used either in conjunction with NFP or by itself. It is the "withdrawal method," or *coitus interruptus*. This is the withdrawing of the penis during intercourse just before ejaculation occurs and experiencing ejaculation outside of the woman's body.

Withdrawal is the same method that Onan used to avoid fathering Tamar's child (Gen. 38:6–10). While God struck him dead for this practice, the motivations for his act were most likely the reason rather than the act itself. Onan was refusing to follow God's command to produce an heir who would continue his brother's name and cost Onan a larger share of the inheritance.

The withdrawal method allows for intercourse whenever a couple desires in the menstrual cycle, but it demands that the man have the discipline to pull out of the vagina at the very moment he is experiencing greatest pleasure. Because of the lack of self-control, this method has a failure rate of 20 percent per year.[4] There is also a small amount of sperm concentrated in the lubricant or pre-cum that is made at the beginning of the erection and is available to fertilize before ejaculation ever occurs.

BARRIER METHODS

The next class of contraceptives forms the *barrier method*. The barrier method involves blocking the entrance of sperm into the cervical canal to prevent fertilization of the egg. There are four types of products used in this method, all of which depend upon proper placement in advance of intercourse to be effective. Whether these devices can effectively become a part of foreplay or if they interrupt the natural flow of lovemaking determines how consistently a couple will use them. Of course, this in turn will alter the effectiveness of each device in preventing pregnancy.

There are two measures of contraceptive effectiveness used by researchers.[5] The first is called *perfect use*. This is the number of pregnancies per one hundred women during one year of using the product exactly as prescribed for every act of intercourse. This statistic is what is presented to the FDA to win approval as a contraceptive device. The second measure is called *typical use*; it is the percentage of women getting pregnant in one year who use the product as a typical couple would in real life. This combines the difficulty in using the product correctly, the motivation of the couple to use it every time and the failure that occurs even when the couple uses it correctly. Typical use is the statistic that is most important when counseling a couple about failure rates.

The average typical use for the barrier method shows a success rate of between 64 to 88 percent. In other words, between twelve and thirty-six couples out of one hundred will get pregnant using these products each year. The perfect use has a success rate in the 90 percent range, but this is rarely achieved in real life except by the most diligent and motivated couples.[6] As I describe each method, you will be able to see where the typical couple falls into trouble.

Spermicides

The first group of barriers is the spermicides. These include jellies, creams, foams, films and suppositories. They can be purchased without prescription and are inexpensive. The spermicide used in all of these products is nonoxynol-9, which can cause irritation in up to 25 percent of women. The spermicide kills sperm and must be placed in the back of the vagina before each act of intercourse. Some preparations must be inserted ten to thirty minutes prior to intercourse to be fully effective.

The diaphragm

The diaphragm is a round piece of rubber that covers the cervix and comes in a variety of sizes. It requires a prescription from trained medical staff who fit the woman with the appropriate size. It is roughly seven centimeters in diameter and is flexible, so that it is folded in half for insertion, opening up as it enters the back of the vagina.

At the patient's initial appointment for diaphragm fitting, the appropriate size is selected that will cover the cervix while lodging behind the public bone for support. If it is too large, pressure against the urethra can cause bladder infections. If it is too small, it may fall forward, allowing semen to pass around it. When properly fitted and placed in the vagina, neither the woman nor her partner will be able to feel the diaphragm during intercourse.

The diaphragm does require some practice to insert it correctly, and it requires the addition of spermicidal jelly. The outer ring of the diaphragm is coated with spermicidal jelly in the event that sperm try to pass around it. Squeezing this lubricated dome in half and pushing it into the vagina can be challenging initially. The diaphragm has been known to shoot across the bathroom during insertion!

The diaphragm must be properly inserted before intercourse; if this has not been done prior to the husband initiating sex, the wife must get up, find the diaphragm and the jelly, lubricate it and put it in. This is usually done in the privacy of the bathroom while the husband waits. This can be quite disruptive to the flow of intimacy.

Because great discipline is required on the part of both partners, it is not uncommon for the man to discourage his wife from using it "just this one time" rather than interrupt the flow and possibly his erection. Once intercourse is over, the diaphragm must remain in the vagina for at least six hours to allow all of the sperm to die.

Diaphragms should be replaced every two years to prevent holes from occurring in the rubber. If the woman has gained or lost significant weight, had vaginal surgery or delivered a baby since the diaphragm was prescribed, a new fitting should be done to ensure the size is still appropriate.

Cervical cap

The cervical cap is similar in concept to the diaphragm, only smaller. It is also made of rubber and fits over the cervix with a tight seal. It also requires a small amount of spermicide. While it may be easier to insert, some women find it difficult to manipulate the cap over the cervix to make a tight fit. One may feel like a contortionist, attempting to reach around and find the cervix while maintaining the sexual passion for lovemaking. The cap also must remain at least six hours after intercourse, but it can stay in place for up to thirty-six hours, allowing multiple acts of intercourse with one application. The longer it remains, however, the greater the chance of vaginal irritation or odor. It too requires a prescription after the correct size has been determined by a trained professional.

CONDOMS

The final barrier method is also the most popular. It is the condom. The condom may be easier to fit into foreplay than the other barrier methods, is inexpensive and can be purchased without a prescription.

The female condom

A newer variation is the female condom. This is a pouch that has a front and back section. It is inserted into the vagina by squeezing the inner ring between the fingers. When properly inserted, about one inch of the condom remains outside of the vagina and is held in place by the woman during intercourse.

Some women have complained that the condom makes noises during intercourse, and lubrication may be necessary to reduce friction. Just as with any latex product, the lubricant must be water-based, and not a petroleum product, to prevent melting the latex. After ejaculation, the outer ring is twisted closed and the condom removed. Most of my patients have found this product to be the least appealing of the barrier methods available. Sales of the female condom have been minimal and have appealed mostly to women whose partners refuse to use the male condom.[7]

THE "PILL"

The remaining contraceptives I will discuss have typical use rates between 95 to 99 percent, but they are also the most controversial within the Christian community.[8] There have even been conflicting safety data in the medical literature on most of these products. They all have some expense to them and require the expertise of medical personnel. I will discuss their mode of action, letting you and your spouse decide which, if any, of these methods you might choose.

A breakthrough in contraception occurred in the 1960s with the development and widespread distribution of the birth control pill. It has been credited with spawning the "sexual revolution" of the same decade, as women were "freed" from the fear of unwanted pregnancy. The "pill," as it is referred to, is a combination of estrogen and progesterone that mimics pregnancy, preventing ovulation of the egg through signals sent to the brain. If there is no egg present, pregnancy cannot occur. To keep the ovaries in a dormant state, at least twenty-one consecutive days of hormone ingestion are required.

Most birth control pills come in four-week packets that contain three consecutive weeks of hormones, followed by one week of placebo or "sugar" pills that signal the uterus to menstruate. When that menstrual week is over, a new round of pills begins again. The effectiveness of the pill depends upon maintaining a consistent level of female hormones in the bloodstream. If the woman forgets to take them at the same time each day, variations in blood levels could allow natural ovulation to occur, which opens the possibility of conception.

Two secondary mechanisms of action are known to take place in addition to preventing ovulation. First, the progesterone component of the pill simulates the "dry" part of the cycle and tightens the cervical mucus, preventing migration of the sperm into the cervix. Second, the lining of the uterus is also thinned, making it more difficult for implantation to occur should fertilization take place.

It is the latter mechanism of the pill that has some concerned that the pill may be an abortifacient, meaning that it is a product that causes abortion of an embryo. I can tell you from both a scientific and medical perspective that this is not the case when the pill is used in the standard fashion. If the pill has not stopped ovulation, it is highly unlikely it will stop implantation at the doses commonly prescribed. In fact, I see dozens of pregnancies each year that occurred despite patients faithfully taking their pills, even through the first two months of an unsuspected pregnancy, with no ill effects to the baby.

There is a form of birth control that is called the "morning-after pill" (known as emergency contraception in the medical community). It is specifically designed for cases where the condom breaks or a woman has not used contraception prior to intercourse and desires pregnancy prevention after the fact. It is a two-day dose-pack that is twice as strong as the regular pill. It can postpone ovulation by a few days, allowing any sperm that exist time to die. It also shrinks the lining of the uterus dramatically to prevent implantation if ovulation has already occurred.

The morning-after pill could be considered an abortifacient if one believes that life begins at conception. If one holds that life begins with implantation into the mother's womb, it is not. From a medical perspective, *pregnancy* is not defined as conception but as attachment of the embryo to the mother's uterine lining and the development of a placental connection between the two. It is only then that the pregnancy hormone is made and a woman can be diagnosed as pregnant by blood or urine tests.

When life begins

The union of egg and sperm is done every day in fertility clinics around the world, but these unions can be frozen for years awaiting implantation into the woman. Life begins for the embryo when it is accepted by the uterus and nourished. As many as 50 percent of all conceptions that occur naturally fail to develop into pregnancies because the embryo does not attach to the lining and is washed out of the womb.[9]

There are biblical passages that describe life within the womb.

> The babies jostled each other within her [Rebekah], and she said, "Why is this happening to me?" So she went to inquire of the LORD. The LORD said to her, "Two nations are in your womb, and two peoples from within you will be separated; one people will be stronger than the other, and the older will serve the younger."
>
> —*Genesis 25:22–23*

> From birth I was cast upon you; from my mother's womb you have been my God.
>
> —*Psalm 22:10*

> For you created my inmost being; you knit me together in my mother's womb.
>
> —*Psalm 139:13*

There are also numerous passages that speak to the "shedding of innocent blood," which are commonly applied to the abortion debate. The medical facts are that the embryo makes no blood until it implants in the womb approximately one week after conception, when it becomes a fetus. I am discussing this issue because it is an important consideration when it comes to choosing contraception, if one even chooses a method of contraception at all. I have great respect for those who believe that life begins at conception and understand that they may struggle with the issue of the birth control pill if indeed it prevents implantation.

My medical opinion is that at the lower doses used in 99 percent of all the pills on the market today, conception is not occurring very often. If it does, implantation seems to happen at the rate it would normally, as evidenced by the thousands of babies born each year in the United States to women taking the pill for contraception.

The "morning-after" pill is a separate issue, and one can make the case that its goal is to prevent implantation after fertilization has already occurred. This may or may not be a morally sound choice for you.

Dangers of the pill

From a medical standpoint, the pill is not without its potential dangers. Women older than thirty-five who smoke and take the pill are at greater risk of heart attack and stroke. There is a small risk of high blood pressure, blood clots in the legs, gallbladder disease and liver tumors in some women who take the pill, although these are rare complications. The jury is still out on whether taking the pill increases the risks of breast cancer.

There are also some benefits to taking the pill besides preventing pregnancy, which has a long list of potentially life-threatening complications of its own. Women who use birth control pills have fewer ovarian cysts and a reduced risk of ovarian and uterine cancers. There is less uterine bleeding and cramping, with fewer cases of anemia as a result. Some pills reduce acne and facial hair, and also control PMS.[10]

Since the introduction of the pill almost forty years ago, doses have been progressively reduced and the safety concerns have greatly diminished. In fact, current doses are just one-fourth what they were when the pill was first introduced.

A variation of the pill is the "mini-pill," a progesterone-only product that is used as contraception by breast-feeding women. Because it contains no estrogen, it is safe for nursing mothers. Other patients may wish to use it if they, for medical reasons, need to avoid estrogen. It does not cause a regular menstrual cycle and, unlike traditional pills, is taken without a placebo week. Many women stop menstruating on the "mini-pill." Because it contains no estrogen, it is a weaker formula and has a higher failure rate when not used as a supplement to breast-feeding.

OTHER METHODS

Because the pill must be taken daily, some women find it difficult to maintain consistency, therefore causing pregnancy to occur. It can also interact with other oral medications that reduce its absorption into the bloodstream. For these reasons, three formulations have been introduced that combine estrogen and progesterone into a vehicle that delivers it directly into the bloodstream.

- The first is called *Lunelle*, a monthly injectable that can be given at a doctor's office or at home by a trained assistant. Its hormones last three weeks and then fade to give a monthly period.

- The second innovation is a patch called *Ortho Evra*, which is changed once a week for three weeks followed by one week off to allow menstruation.

- The third innovation, *NuvaRing*, contains both hormones in a flexible plastic ring the size of a fifty-cent piece. It is inserted by the woman into the vagina and left there for three weeks. It is removed in the fourth week to allow menstruation. Neither the woman nor her partner can feel the ring when it is properly placed.

All of these variations still contain the same hormones as the pill, so the same benefits and risks apply. It is hoped that the newer delivery systems will make compliance easier and improve the typical use statistics.

There are two other hormonal contraceptives available at the present time that contain only progesterone and are delivered directly into the bloodstream. Both of these are suitable for breast-feeding patients.

- The first is the *Norplant*, a series of six small rods inserted under the skin of the upper arm that release progesterone over a five-year period. It is a highly effective contraceptive, but complications of irregular bleeding and ovarian cysts occur regularly. There has also been difficulty in training personnel to insert and remove the rods correctly. Together, these complications have resulted in a class-action lawsuit that has caused the product to no longer be sold in the United States.

- The other product is *Depo-Provera*, an injection of progesterone that is given every three months in the doctor's office. It has been especially popular in family planning clinics that see young women who are less likely to take the pill correctly. The Depo-Provera injection usually results in a cessation of menses after a few months and can be of great benefit to those women who suffer from heavy monthly bleeding, severe menstrual cramping or PMS.

The side effects of Depo-Provera are irregular bleeding in the first few months and weight gain that averages ten to fifteen pounds over a year. It is slightly less effective in the severely overweight woman. In general, however, Depo-Provera provides the most effective contraception available that is still reversible.[11] Because the injections last for up to six months but must be overlapped every three months, there are at least six to nine months from the last injection before a woman can conceive. This timeline must be accounted for in any contraceptive strategy a woman makes with her physician.

THE IUD

For those women who do not want to take, or cannot take, hormonal preparations and find the barrier methods undesirable, there is a final form of reversible contraception. It is the intrauterine device, or IUD.

The IUD has had a difficult history and is a choice that must be evaluated carefully. In its early development, several designs caused problems with infection and later infertility. Because it is a device that is inserted into the uterus, sexually transmitted diseases such as gonorrhea and chlamydia can migrate up the IUD and enter the fallopian tubes, causing infertility.

For this reason, the IUD is recommended only for faithfully monogamous couples and preferably those who have already had children. These couples are the least likely to be exposed to STDs. Should a complication arise that impacts future fertility, it would not be nearly as devastating as it would be for a woman who has no children. The IUD must be inserted by a trained healthcare professional, as improper insertion of the IUD can lead to perforation of the uterus. Another controversy of the IUD concerns whether or not it is an abortifacient. There are two types of IUDs in the United States: the *Mirena* and the *ParaGard:*

- The Mirena is a progesterone-containing device that releases the hormone locally. It does not cross into the bloodstream. The device causes the uterine lining to become thin, which does impede implantation. Because the lining is thin, most women will cease menstruating, which may make it a choice for women who have excessive periods as an alternative to a hysterectomy. The Mirena gives similar results as the Depo-Provera injection but without the side effects of weight gain. The Mirena is inserted in the physician's office through the cervix and can last for up to five years.

- The ParaGard is a T-shaped device that contains copper, a naturally occurring spermicide designed to kill any sperm that enter the uterus. It is effective for up to ten years. It does not change the uterine lining, but should the sperm live in spite of the spermicidal effect of the copper, implantation may be prevented by the T-shaped design blocking entrance of the embryo into the uterus.

If pregnancy does occur with the IUD, it is more likely to be tubal, or ectopic, which, of course, is a serious situation that demands immediate attention. Fortunately, it is also very uncommon. Should pregnancy occur in the womb, the IUD must be removed to prevent damage to the developing fetus. And removal of the IUD can carry a 25 percent miscarriage rate, depending on the proximity of the fetus to the IUD.[12] The IUD is marketed for married couples who think they may be finished with childbearing but do not want to make a permanent commitment to sterilization.

STERILIZATION

Finally, while some Christians do not feel couples should choose how many children they want to have, there are couples who have agreed upon the number they feel that they can raise. According to that decision, when they have reached the desired number, sterilization may be an option for them to consider. It is the most widely used method of birth control in the United States, but it is meant to be permanent. Attempts at reversal are expensive and often unsuccessful. This is a weighty decision that a couple must make after much discussion and, hopefully, sincere prayer.

For those who have made that choice, the options are tubal ligation for the woman or vasectomy for the man. From a purely medical standpoint, vasectomy is simpler and safer. It involves cutting the vas deferens and sealing off the ends, preventing the migration of sperm from the testes to the urethra. The procedure is done under local anesthesia in the doctor's office. The skin of the scrotum is numbed and a small incision is made on each side to locate the vas deferens and then tying off and removing a small piece. It is mildly uncomfortable, but requires only a couple of days to recover at home.

One word of caution: A vasectomy does not become effective for several weeks. The sperm are like troops marching down the road. A vasectomy blows up the bridge so no further sperm can cross. But all of the "troops" who made it across before the vasectomy are still marching on. It takes a certain number of ejaculations to clear these sperm from the system.

Some men are fearful of the pain of vasectomy in a region of the body that men guard carefully. To voluntarily ask someone to operate there is a psychological leap for some. Others fear that sex will be different, that they will be "shooting blanks" and ejaculation will not feel the same. In truth, the sperm are a very small part of the ejaculate. The semen is mostly fluid from the seminal vesicles and prostate gland. Ejaculation will be exactly the same with the same volume of semen as before.

But because of these fears, and because women are the ones who get pregnant, tubal ligation is ten times more popular in the United States than vasectomy. Tubal ligation involves interrupting each fallopian tube and preventing the union of egg and sperm. The procedure can be done immediately after delivery and is called a postpartum tubal ligation. A small incision is made in the navel, and the tubes are pulled through the hole. A segment of each tube is cut out and the remaining ends tied off. It requires some form of anesthesia such as an epidural, spinal or general, where the woman goes to sleep.

The other form of tubal ligation that is popular is the laparoscopic version. This can be done anytime after the postpartum period. It involves inserting a laparoscope, which contains a small camera, through a navel incision and either burning, clipping or banding the tubes. This is an outpatient procedure done in a hospital setting and requires general anesthesia. If done correctly, only one out of two hundred women will get pregnant after tubal ligation.[13] Those who do have a high risk of tubal pregnancy and must seek immediate medical attention.

HANDLING THE CONTROVERSY

I know that this has been a controversial chapter for some believers and that I have risked angering others. But I see so many Christians who ask for help in making contraceptive choices that I felt the subject should be addressed. Appendix C summarizes the options available.

These decisions go hand in hand with the decision to have intercourse. The choices one makes can greatly influence sexual satisfaction, and contraception is an issue every newlywed and every "full-quiver" couple must eventually face, no matter what decision one ultimately makes.

Real Life

Newlyweds Janice and Todd came to my office to discuss contraception. Both were full-time students, and each worked a part-time job as well. While they desired children at some future date, they wanted to wait at least three years.

Janice was a junior in college, pursuing her teaching certificate. She was already being recruited by a local Christian elementary school. Janice had a strong calling to teach in a Christian setting, having herself been a product of Christian education.

Todd had worked full time since graduating from high school to save the money they would need to start their new life together. He was just beginning his freshman year at a local community college and was unsure about his future career plans. Since his parents had divorced when he was very young, Todd felt strongly about spending the time necessary to establish a firm marital foundation before beginning his own family. He too thought they were at least three years away from desiring a pregnancy.

I presented all of the available options to them. Janice and Todd wanted an effective birth control method for at least three years; the NFP and barrier methods, with a 20 percent failure rate per year, would give them a 60 percent chance of having an unplanned pregnancy in that time period. This was a level of risk far higher than they desired.

Since Janice had never had a child, the IUD was not an option for her. Hormonal birth control seemed to be the best fit for their particular situation. This put most of the responsibility and the burden on Janice. A review of her personal and family medical history did not reveal any contraindications to hormonal therapy. As a young woman who was very body-conscious, fear of weight gain was a major concern. Depo-Provera was definitely not an option for her.

While the patch or rings were intriguing ideas, neither spouse had prescription drug benefits on their health insurance plan. Because Janice was already in the habit of taking daily vitamin supplements, the category of oral contraception was an obvious choice. There were generics available that brought the cost down for a couple on a tight budget.

We did discuss the need for consistent use to achieve contraceptive effectiveness of 3 percent failure per year for a typical married couple.[14] This would give them less than a 10 percent chance of unexpected pregnancy over three years, a level that was acceptable to them.

I continued to see Janice at regular intervals, and she did very well with the pill. At age twenty-five, she discontinued the pill, and she conceived their first child three months later.

Chapter **Twelve**

LOVE HAS
THREE NAMES

The entire law is summed up in a single
command: "Love your neighbor as yourself."
—Galatians 5:14

Many of you reading this book are about to be married or already are married. You believe that God wants you to have a fulfilling sexual life, but you may not know exactly how to achieve that goal. This chapter will give you some guidance and insight into the beauty of God's plan for marital sex.

This is not a "how-to" chapter. There will be no diagrams or drawings of people making love. I am not against that; it is just that those resources already exist. You can find them at most Christian bookstores. Clifford and Joyce Penner, a husband and wife team, have written several excellent books on this subject.

Instead, I want to talk about some of the foundations for marital sex from God's perspective. If those are not solidly established first, all of the how-to books in the world won't help you. Sexual relations will only be truly successful when you follow God's way, and if you are married or about to be married, you qualify for His guidance. He places His blessing on the covenant of marital love. (See Hebrews 13:4; 1 Corinthians 7:2–5.)

> **SEX IS NOT LOVE—
> THEY ARE TWO
> DIFFERENT THINGS.**

The most important foundation for a fulfilling sexual life is to realize that sex is not love—they are two different things. Sex is an act between two people who may *be in love*, but it is not love itself. Intercourse is the most powerful expression of intimacy, but it is not intimacy itself. Love and intimacy are huge concepts of which sex is only one part—a large part, but only a part.

CONFUSION OF TERMS

Many people confuse love, intimacy and sex. If you consider sex to be your only way of expressing love, that view lends itself to the belief that when you are in love, you must have sex to express it. Not only does this view of love lead to promiscuous sex outside of marriage, which is biblically wrong, but it also puts undue pressure on intercourse as your only expression of love. And it follows that if one spouse isn't in the mood for sex, it can be interpreted as not being in love with you.

Intimacy is the deep longing to know another and to be fully known by them. It implies profound friendship, emotional nakedness and a vulnerability that knows no limits. Intimacy removes the masks we wear when we face the world. It invites another to experience who we are at every level of our soul. If sex is your only avenue for intimacy with your spouse, you are missing out on so many other aspects of your marriage. When intercourse isn't happening as often as you like, you stop being intimate with one another, not expressing your deepest feelings, thoughts and aspirations apart from the act of intercourse.

It is important to understand that there are seasons in marriage where intercourse is not the top priority for one of the partners. If the other partner equates sex with love or can only experience intimacy when having intercourse, that person is headed for trouble. He or she will seek to have those powerful needs for intimacy met somewhere else.

We all crave love and intimacy, to know and be known by another. If we are not having that need for intimacy met by our spouse, over time we will seek it illegitimately. Men will seek false intimacy from pornography, while women seek it from romance novels or soap operas. Since intimacy, by definition, involves another living being, these substitutes will never be *true* intimacy. Eventually, either the husband or wife may turn to a sympathetic neighbor or coworker for these relational needs to be met, and the seeds of an affair are sown.

DEFINING LOVE

To understand love, we need to realize how imprecise our use of this English word really is. We say we "love" chocolate, or we "love" football. But that usage defines love as a *preference*, which is not the biblical definition of love.

The New Testament uses three different Greek words for love, each defining a special quality of love. Translators of the Scriptures into English use the word *love* for all three different forms of love taught in the Bible. We need to understand and possess all three to fully function as a spouse.[1]

Eros = love

The first Greek word the Bible uses for *love* is *eros*, from which we get the word *erotic*. Though the world has corrupted that word, God designed the beauty of a love that is erotic. *Eros* love is not sinful. It can become sinful if it takes place outside of the boundaries of marriage, but it is part of God's design for love.

Eros is the fire, the passion and the drive God made to give physical expression to love. Though using equivalent language in Hebrew, the Old Testament records beautiful instructions regarding *eros* love, as we have mentioned. For example, Ecclesiastes 9:9 says, "Enjoy life with your wife, whom you love." Proverbs 5:18–19 states, "May you rejoice in the wife of your youth. A loving doe, a graceful deer—may her breasts satisfy you always, may you ever be captivated by her love." And the entire book of the Song of Solomon is dedicated to the erotic love of two people. God has designed us to experience and enjoy erotic love.

Unfortunately, much of today's culture has made erotic love all there is. When erotic love fails, that is the end of all love, according to the world's standard. Many marriages end because of a lack of knowledge of what true love involves. Erotic love, as powerful as it is, is only one aspect of marital love. When it falters or fails, there are still two more pillars of love that are strong enough to hold up the marriage, as we will discuss.

Eros love is especially important to men. We have referred to *His Needs, Her Needs: Building an Affair-Proof Marriage*, written by Willard Harley.[2] In this helpful book, Harley lists the top five needs of men and the top five needs of women. As you might imagine, they are completely different!

The number one need of men is *sexual fulfillment*. Men are very responsive to erotic love. Though it has contributed to our downfall since sin entered the world, it is still our most basic need in marriage. When men get married, they are making a vow that they will not seek sexual fulfillment, their number one need, with any other woman besides their wife for as long as they live.

This vow creates a huge responsibility for the wife toward her husband, because if she denies her husband intercourse and erotic love, he has nowhere else to turn if he is to remain faithful to his vows. And his number one need cries out to be satisfied. Unfortunately, many women mistakenly think husbands are sex-crazed perverts because sexual fulfillment is not high on the woman's need list. That is simply because men and women are different.

If the man's need for erotic love is not met by his wife, he will often seek fulfillment through pornography, masturbation or an affair. You could look at it this way: Not being able to have sex for a man is like not being able to go shopping for a woman!

Because erotic love is such a strong aspect of defining love for a man, having his wife deny him sex can be interpreted as denying her love for him. The truth is, she may just not want sex, which is an activity to her. But to her husband, it seems she is saying she doesn't love him, even if this was not her intent.

When his wife rejects sex, a husband may feel that he has been personally rejected as a man. The pain of this rejection, especially if it happens repeatedly, leads a man to stop seeking intercourse with his wife. Unconsciously he reasons, *It is better not to have sex than to suffer the pain of rejection when I am refused.* But I will guarantee you that most men will not go very long without seeking sexual fulfillment. It is simply a matter of who, what, when and where.

It is a sad reality that, in my medical practice, I have learned of many husbands who have had brief sexual affairs during times of prolonged sexual neglect. These times of neglect can be as innocent as the legitimate needs of pregnancy and childbirth. Sometimes a man will separate his need for sexual fulfillment in his mind from his love for his wife, which leads him to gratify his sexual needs elsewhere when they are not being met at home.

Dr. Gary Chapman, in his book *The Five Love Languages*, lists *physical touch* as a primary love language.[3] This love language seems very important to many of the men with whom I counsel. When a wife has intercourse with her husband, it speaks *love* to him in ways that other things she does may not.

For some men, keeping the house clean or fixing dinner each night is important. But it is the language of physical touch that many men crave. Even if intercourse doesn't always happen because of monthly conflicts such as work schedule or menses, there are other ways to communicate this love language, such as oral sex or masturbation of your partner. If it is done with the right spirit as an act of love, these substitutes can go a long way in telling your spouse that you love him. As I mentioned before, when you reject sexual expressions with a person who views sex as the primary way of showing love, you have rejected that person, even if that was never your intention.

Phileo = love

The second word that is translated *love* in English is the Greek word *phileo*, which means "brotherly love or friendship." Paul instructs us to cultivate this kind of love:

> Love must be sincere. Hate what is evil; cling to what is good. Be devoted to one another in brotherly love. Honor one another above yourselves. Never be lacking in zeal, but keep your spiritual fervor, serving the Lord. Be joyful in hope, patient in affliction, faithful in prayer. Share with God's people who are in need. Practice hospitality.
>
> —*Romans 12:9–13*

It is through *phileo* love that husbands and wives learn to become each other's best friends. It is the love of companionship. Your spouse should be the person with whom you most want to spend time. You should prefer his or her company above any other. You should cultivate the intimacy of sharing with your spouse your innermost thoughts, dreams, visions, fears and heartaches as you would with no one else.

Phileo love brings true intimacy, of which intercourse is only a part. Intercourse is erotic by its very nature, but *eros* love is not fully expressed unless it also involves an act of service to your spouse. In marriage, *phileo* love comprehends fully and desires to serve our mate by relating to that person through an understanding of that person's likes, dislikes, preferences, fantasies and fears. Intercourse, when expressed in *phileo* love, is what the King James Version of the Bible translates as "knowing."

For example, we read, "And Adam *knew* Eve his wife; and she conceived, and bare Cain, and said, I have gotten a man from the LORD" (Gen. 4:1, KJV, emphasis added). The Hebrew word for *knew* is *yada*, which is a primitive root that contains the concepts of familiar friend, advice, respect, tell, understand, comprehend, instruct—all meaningful relational words.[4]

Before Adam and Eve disobeyed God and were cast out of the Garden of Eden, they were *intimate and unashamed.* The Scripture declares clearly: "The man and his wife were both naked, and they felt no shame" (Gen. 2:25). Nothing was hidden from the other. Since they were the only two people on earth at the time, they were each other's *only* friend and companion, besides God.

When Adam had intercourse with Eve, it was not just erotic. Their sexual expression was built on a foundation of his ever-increasing knowledge of her. The intimacy they shared was deeper than just a sexual act. *Phileo* love has the advantage of limitless exploration. There will never be an end to the pursuit of knowledge and the delight of discovery of the other person. Each new discovery can be revealed through an endless display of intimacy for those who are willing to know—and be known.

In the New Testament, Peter instructs men of the church concerning their wives:

> Likewise, ye husbands, dwell with them according to knowledge, giving honour unto the wife.
>
> —*1 Peter 3:7, KJV*

Peter is describing companionship—the sharing of your time, your hobbies and your activities of daily life as husbands and wives living together in ever-increasing knowledge, forming your own family as well as sharing within the family of God.

Phileo love is what women need most. For a woman, having her man's attention is very important. And it is not sexual attention she seeks primarily, but his affection, conversation and companionship. In his book *His Needs, Her Needs*, Willard Harley identifies *affection* and *conversation* as the top two needs of women.[5] A woman desires hugs, holding hands and having the car door opened for her. She likes to cuddle, sometimes consenting to sex just to get to the end when she can be held in her husband's arms for a few precious minutes before he falls asleep.

A wife likes to call her husband at work just to talk to him. When he comes home, she asks, "How was your day?" She expects a conversation, not a one-word answer like "Fine." When a man engages in conversation and listens attentively as his wife relates the details of her day, he speaks volumes about his love for her. When a man holds his wife's hand as they walk in public, he is announcing to the world (and reassuring her) that she belongs to him, that he wants to be seen with her and that he is protecting her from the danger that may be around the next corner.

For women, doing what you say you will do is not only right; it is *an act of love*. If, as a husband, you promised to take out the trash or help with the dishes and you don't, you are telling her by your actions that she is not important, causing her to feel rejected by you. But when you serve her, she feels loved. In *The Five Love Languages*, Dr. Chapman calls this language "acts of service."[6] Erotic love is not her focus; it is *phileo* love that she craves. Wives watch what you *do* as a husband, not what you *say*. Telling your wife you love her, but not doing what she asks is, in her mind, making what you said a lie. As a man, if you expect her to meet your need for sex that night (erotic love), you need to have something invested on her side of the scale (*phileo* love), or you will be disappointed.

Of course, husbands also have a need for *phileo* love. The second greatest need for men, according to Harley, is *recreational companionship,* which is their need for *phileo* love.[7] Often during the dating period, a woman will spend time doing the things her boyfriend likes to do. She will go to football games, watch sports with him on television, hike, fish or any number of other recreational things, simply to spend time with him.

But once she is married, often that same woman no longer wants to participate in the activities with her husband that she once did. Her husband feels abandoned and seeks out other men for companionship, while the wife sits home alone (or with the kids, which is worse) and resents the time he spends away from her. His number two need is often not met by the same woman who was faithfully by his side before marriage.

I am not saying that men shouldn't have male friendships or spend time with other men for companionship. Enjoying friendship with another man is a wonderful thing. In the Scriptures, an example of such a friendship is David (later King David) and Jonathan, King Saul's son. When Jonathan was killed in battle, David declared of his friend: "I grieve for you, Jonathan my brother; you were very dear to me. Your love for me was wonderful, more wonderful than that of women" (2 Sam. 1:26).

There are things that men can share with each other that women will never understand, because they are not men. But a man would never seek to have his friendships with other men be stronger than his relationship with his wife. Even if he is playing sports with the guys, having his wife watch him from the stands is a very important way that he perceives her love for him.

Again, we can listen to the instructions of the apostle Paul: "Be devoted to one another in brotherly love. Honor one another above yourself...Be *joyful* in hope, *patient* in affliction, *faithful* in prayer" (Rom. 12:10, 12, emphasis added). When you are fulfilling those godly instructions in your relationship with your spouse, you are serving the Lord. *Phileo* love seeks to meet the other person's needs; it is not self-seeking.

Consider what a different kind of marriage we could experience if we were devoted to one another, if we honored the other above ourselves. A love that is *joyful* while still hoping for something better, *patient* in the midst of not having things go our way, and *faithful* to lift our spouse up to the Lord in prayer is the kind of love Paul was recommending to us all. This wonderful goal leads us to the last pillar of love, which is *agape* love—the kind of love that only comes from God.

Agape = love

Agape, the third Greek word the New Testament Scriptures use for love, is the word that describes God where we read: "God is love" (1 John 4:16). It is the God-kind of love that gives unreservedly, not expecting anything in return. *Agape* love gives even when the person doesn't deserve it. The apostle Paul gives us a portrait of godly love in 1 Corinthians 13. The word he uses to describe this love is translated from the Greek word *agape*:

> Love is patient, love is kind. It does not envy, it does not boast, it is not proud. It is not rude, it is not self-seeking, it is not easily angered, it keeps no record of wrongs. Love does not delight in evil but rejoices with the truth. It always protects, always trusts, always hopes, always perseveres. Love never fails.
>
> —*1 Corinthians 13:4–8*

Agape love, as you might imagine, can only be expressed in the lives of those who are plugged in to God's love. It flows from Him to them, and they overflow that godly love to others from their own experience of God's love in their lives.

Agape love should be the foundation for every Christian marriage. While men seek *eros* love as their primary need, and women seek *phileo* love to satisfy their deepest desire, *agape* love should undergird both of these valid kinds of love. Only by receiving from God the power of *agape* love can each spouse make a commitment to God (and to one another) that they will meet the other's needs, even when they feel they don't deserve it.

It is from our own experience of receiving God's love toward us, totally undeserved, that we can be filled with desire to meet each other's needs in an unselfish way. *Agape* love is sacrificial. The Bible declares, "But God demonstrates his own love for us in this: While we were still sinners, Christ died for us" (Rom. 5:8). Pastor Chip Ingram states in his sermon series Love, Sex and Lasting Relationships that *agape* love is "giving the other person what they need the most when they least deserve it, because God has given it to me."[8]

When all three kinds of love—*eros, phileo* and *agape*—operate in a marriage, it is very uncommon for that marriage to fail. Ecclesiastes 4:12 states, "Though one may be overpowered, two can defend themselves. A cord of three strands is not quickly broken." Though I am aware that the context of this passage does not relate to three kinds of love, it may be a fair analogy to consider that if your marriage includes all three "cords" of love, nothing can easily destroy it.

Many marriages today have come into existence because a couple had a great premarital sex life. They interpreted that relationship as "love" and formed the basis of their marriage on sexual gratification. Their philosophy goes something like: *No matter what goes wrong, no matter how much we fight, if we can have great sex afterward everything will be all right.* That is an especially powerful myth for men. But when one strand of love fails (is "overpowered" by difficulties), the whole marriage fails, if that is all it was built upon.

If a couple has been wise enough to make each other their best friends and faithful companions by adding *phileo* love to their marriage, when difficulties come they will find that "two can defend themselves." But without God, even these two strands of love can fail. When *agape* love enters the marriage, each partner is motivated by divine love to meet the erotic and companionship requirements of the other as a sacrifice unto God, persevering even when it seems easier to give up, and extending grace when the other deserves nothing of the kind. This three-strand cord is not easily broken.

The sad state of affairs in the average church is that the divorce rate of couples that claim to be "Christian" is the same as those who make no such claim. George Barna remarks, "It is unfortunate that so many people, regardless of their faith, experience divorce, but it is especially unsettling to find that the faith commitment of so many born-again individuals has not enabled them to strengthen and save their marriages."[9]

The good news is that for couples who regularly attend church, pray together and regularly spend personal time with God, the divorce rate is in the single digits.[10] The difference is *agape* love—and it will only come from spending time with God. The rewards from a sexual perspective are so great that to embark upon a discussion of marital sex without this foundation, I believe, is pointless.

A wife who expresses *agape* love will meet her husband's erotic love needs, not because she "feels" like it, but because doing so pleases God. A husband who experiences *agape* love will meet his wife's *phileo* love needs, not to manipulate her to get sex, but because God commands it as an act of service to Him.

The "by-product" of giving and receiving this divine love is that each spouse will have their own deepest love needs met and will desire to do the same for the other person. A husband "knows" his wife, and a wife "knows" her husband. And marriage becomes what God created it to be—the greatest institution on the face of the earth.

Chapter Thirteen

MARITAL SEX

Wives, submit to your husbands as to the Lord...
Husbands, love your wives, just as Christ loved
the church and gave himself up for her.
—Ephesians 5:22, 25

In the context of the three kinds of love we discussed in the previous chapter—*eros, phileo* and *agape*—assuming that *agape* love is our foundation for marriage, we can look specifically at what married couples can do to enjoy a fulfilling sex life. Remembering that men and women are different physically, hormonally and relationally, with different priorities in their "needs" scale, a husband and wife must approach each other in "knowledge." This understanding will help us to take the knowledge we have gained from the preceding chapters and apply it to everyday life.

ACCOMMODATING PHYSICAL ATTRACTION

Men are visual creatures; they are sexually attracted by what they see, especially in terms of particular areas of the body they equate with sex. These "areas" of the body have changed dramatically over the centuries, but history records many cultures' attempts to protect men from their visual lusts.

Women in some parts of the world have, from biblical times, been required to dress in layers of cloth that obscure any physical form they possess. We have witnessed this in the Islamic-controlled nations of the Arab world, where even the faces of women are hidden behind a thick hood. It is their culture's attempt to cover every aspect of a woman's body that might cause a man to lust. A woman's chastity brings honor to the family; thus, in order to be respected by men and protected from them, a woman should not flaunt her looks in public.[1]

In our own nation's history, in previous centuries, women were required to dress in such a modest fashion that the exposure of an ankle was enough to send men into flights of fantasy. How far we have come! Today's liberated woman is often barely dressed when she leaves her house, often exposing as much skin as she would on the beach. Visually stimulated men of today are bombarded by seductive images on every street corner, on magazine covers, in television commercials and in theaters. It is physically impossible to avoid all of the "body parts" that women flaunt.

It takes great commitment to God for a man to be able to keep his eyes from focusing on what the world has to offer his senses. With advancements in plastic surgery and computer enhancements, the images that are available to him can cause him to develop an unrealistic view of what a "normal" woman should look like, creating an "ideal" with which his wife could not possibly compete.

Yet man is a visual creature by divine design. In his book *His Needs, Her Needs*, Willard Harley lists "attractive spouse" as man's number three need in marriage.[2] It may seem odd that Christian men should place such a strong emphasis on "body image," but it is an honest assessment of how we are made. It has been so from the beginning of time. When God presented Eve to Adam, He did not dress her from head to toe in heavy cloth. She walked through the Garden of Eden to meet her husband naked—and unashamed. Man has been sexually stimulated by women's bodies ever since.

The point is that a major part of a man's attraction to his wife was physical before he decided to marry her. She may not have been the perfect "10" figure, but it is reasonable to think that whatever she possessed won the heart of that particular husband and will be just as important to him after marriage as it was before marriage. As we have mentioned, when the committed Christian man says, "I do," he is forsaking every other woman on the planet to have sex with this one woman for life. A contract has been made, and for the marriage bed to stay undefiled, both people will need to keep their commitments. For the woman, her physical attractiveness to her husband is a big part of the deal.

The wife's responsibility

I am not talking about a wife trying to maintain perpetual youth; that is unrealistic. Time takes its toll on all of us, and women are particularly vulnerable to dramatic changes in physical appearance. For example, each pregnancy takes its toll, naturally, and I find that a large number of women abandon their previous healthy lifestyle when they become pregnant. They eat differently and exercise less, often because of the dramatic hormonal changes occurring in their bodies that cause nausea, fatigue and discomfort. Because they are taking in more calories than they burn up, weight gain occurs at a level higher than is needed for a healthy pregnancy. The obesity that results, often continuing after the pregnancy has ended, is an example of dramatic change in physical appearance that can affect her relationship with her husband.

It is not uncommon for a woman to gain fifty to seventy pounds during a nine-month pregnancy, while the average postpartum weight loss is only twenty-five pounds. With greater time demands of each additional child, she has less time to spend on herself, causing her to neglect exercise and nutritional restraint. Three or four children later, this woman now weighs seventy to one hundred pounds more than she did when she got married.

While this may seem unfair, I have met many a man who is unhappy with the physical changes that have occurred in his wife. He may feel less sexually attracted to her, decreasing physical touch and other gestures of intimacy so important to his wife. She may feel rejected and experience decreased self-esteem, which sabotages her desire to be more attractive.

I am often amazed that the same man who complains about his wife's appearance has a large belly and less hair than when he first got married! But his wife loves him just the way he is. Thank God!

For both spouses, it would be helpful to consider that proper diet and exercise will improve stamina and self-esteem, which will in turn increase confidence and personal satisfaction. This will not only improve appearances of both husband and wife, but it will also enhance the efforts of a godly woman who seeks to help her husband resist the temptations surrounding him in the outside world and stay focused on the one to whom he has committed his life.

The husband's responsibility

Does the man have a part to play in a healthy sexual relationship? Absolutely! As we have discussed before, a woman places a strong emphasis on her man showing his love through works. When the husband helps at home and keeps his promises, the wife feels loved. This is especially critical for those women who work outside of the home. The husband must share the household duties if she is to have any energy left for sex at the end of the day.

A stay-at-home mom with preschoolers also needs a lot of help when her husband gets home, if she is to have dinner ready, the kids bathed and so on. If her husband has kept his promises to help her, she will be much more likely to feel like meeting his needs. A woman who is treated like a queen will, in turn, treat her husband like a king.

In truth, most husbands lavished their "beloved" with affection, attention, gifts and conversation when they were dating. When a man marries, his wife also makes a commitment to forsake every other man and be devoted only to him. She can feel equally "cheated" when he retreats behind his newspaper or his computer, when he no longer helps her with the mundane chores of life, when he doesn't share in conversation and listen to her attentively. For the husband who fails to relate to his wife in these ways, to expect great sex at the end of the day is an illusion—he has deposited nothing into her emotional needs during the day.

Another strong need women have is for financial security.[3] I have seen far too many lazy Christian men who are content to let their wives pull the load financially because they can't find anything they like in the workplace. They flit from job to job with long "rest" periods in between while their wives steadily work the same job.

A variation of this irresponsible behavior is the man who wants his hobby to be his job, despite the fact that it makes no money, is part time at best and is really more about fulfilling his desires than it is about the financial well-being of his family. That is not what she signed up for. I have even seen this financial irresponsibility happen under the guise of "ministry" where the husband decides he is "called" to the ministry and quits his job, leaving his wife to be the sole source of income while he dabbles with church work. I'm not sure God calls a man who has fathered several children to stop supporting his family so he can "minister" for Him.

An underlying resentment will build in the wife who has to place her children in day care, when she would rather be with them, and face the daily office grind, knowing that her husband is home pursuing his "dream." She may never feel she has the right to verbally question his pursuit, especially if it is being done in the name of God, but her resentment will speak volumes in the bedroom.

We have also talked about the differences in the way men and women experience pleasure in intercourse. A husband needs to understand that many women are satisfied to simply cuddle and be held safely in the arms of their man. A woman will often have intercourse just to get to the end where she can enjoy being held in her husband's arms. Unfortunately, a husband is not usually as comfortable in this "snuggling" arena as he is the penile penetration phase of intercourse. He may often roll over and fall asleep after ejaculation, completely satisfied himself but leaving his spouse feeling used and forgotten. This does little to encourage her participation in future lovemaking. The wise husband will hold his wife in his arms and share his heart with her. She, in turn, is invited to reveal her deepest thoughts and feelings in the shelter of his embrace, intimate and unashamed. If her husband would offer that place of refuge and safety, she would long to return to it again and again.

Another area of responsibility where a husband often fails is in his ignorance of the unique needs of a woman's body. As we discussed earlier, most men have received little instruction in the art of bringing a woman to orgasm. Unfortunately, most women do not know what they need either. If any good has come from the sexual "enlightenment" of our present day, it is that women, even Christian women, are learning to expect more from intercourse than facilitating their husband's ejaculations. They have a right to the same pleasurable release their husband enjoys. While most men are capable of only one or two orgasms in any lovemaking session, women can have a dozen! God has given women a fantastic gift, but many men do not know how to help them experience this fully.

As I mentioned previously, this is not meant to be a "how-to" book. There are many Christian and non-Christian resources available that can be invaluable in teaching both the man and woman what brings pleasure in marital sex. I would recommend avoiding those books with photographs, lest it become pornographic for some. Couples will pick and choose their expressions of love, based on their own preferences.

Of course, neither spouse should feel forced to do anything he or she doesn't want to do. But God has given us a lifetime together to explore each other and learn what pleases the other. Even without the benefit of a single resource or book, except for a desire to serve, each partner should discover what the other likes and what works for them. That is part of the enjoyment of married life.

It is logical that if the woman feels sexually fulfilled from the lovemaking experience, she is more likely to want to repeat that experience. The clitoris is often the key to such fulfillment, but it is not the only one. A woman who has never known the thrills of orgasm will still feel satisfaction in the embrace of a man who is having intercourse with all of her—body, soul and spirit—instead of just one part. If she feels loved and embraced, instead of used for his sexual pleasure, intercourse will be a fulfilling experience for both.

MARITAL BOUNDARIES

I am often asked about boundaries in marriage as men and women begin to explore the various avenues of pleasure available to them. Many couples were not Christians when they became sexually active. After finding Christ, they wonder what aspects of their sex life are "holy." Depending on our image of God, it can be difficult to picture God approving of intercourse itself, let alone any departure from the "missionary" position (man on top; woman underneath). Because intercourse is necessary for procreation, many Christians can easily accept that God wants them to have *that* kind of sex. But what about all the other things?

The Bible records very few boundaries regarding sexual activity for marriage. Obviously, adultery is forbidden, as is stated in the Ten Commandments (Exod. 20:14). Jesus expanded the definition of adultery to include what you see with your eyes: "But I tell you that anyone who looks at a woman lustfully has already committed adultery with her in his heart" (Matt. 5:28). What we focus on with our eyes, we take in through our imagination. We begin to fantasize about what it would be like to have sex with that person or that image. If that person or image is not our spouse, according to the Bible, we are committing adultery.

Some couples wonder if pornographic magazines or videos can be used as marital enhancements to "spice up" their sex lives. According to the teachings of Jesus, I would say *no*—this would not be acceptable. You are inviting those people into your bedroom when you do that. The focus then shifts from intimacy with your spouse to a "shared" intimacy with those images, which is adultery. Even when the pornographic material is not physically present in the bedroom but you bring it back to your mind to fantasize with a particular image or person when you are making love to your spouse, it is adultery.

In addition, you are missing the whole point of intercourse, which is to *know* your spouse in the most intimate fashion God created. If your mind is somewhere else, you are simply performing a sexual act; you are not "making love" to your spouse. As a result, even that will become old and stale because it lacks the spiritual power that a godly union would bring to the relationship; thus it is ultimately disappointing. Your spiritual man knows that there is more and will be dissatisfied with the mediocre.

The other boundaries for marital sex recorded in the Bible, besides the prohibition of premarital sex found in 1 Corinthians 6:18, are found in chapter 18 of the Book of Leviticus. A quick perusal will reveal a prohibition against incest, sexual relations with a variety of relatives, homosexuality and bestiality (or sex with animals). Most married couples will find few struggles in these areas.

Sexual exploration

This brings us to the major theme of sexual exploration in marriage. As a general rule, nothing should be asked for or done that is demeaning, painful, humiliating or a cause of bringing shame upon the other party. Everything must be mutually acceptable, or it will not further love and intimacy, which is the goal of sex.

Many Christians are surprised that God did not give specific instructions regarding sexual technique, positions or attire. He did not confine sexual relations to one particular room of the house, or say it must be inside the house at all! Adam and Eve didn't have a bedroom; they made love under the stars, or wherever else the urge struck them. If sex is discreet and private, it can be done anywhere and at anytime. A private beach or picnic spot can be an exciting departure from the same bedroom walls you've seen for years.

No one even says you have to wait until the evening to have sex. Sometimes a brief interlude in the afternoon when the kids are napping or otherwise preoccupied can be helpful for a wife who may be more tired in the evening than she is during the day. Sneaking home for a lunchtime rendezvous can be very exciting and romantic. People having affairs seem to master these concepts better than those who are faithfully married.

What about oral sex?

So what about oral sex? This is the most common question asked by both men and women at the seminars I hold. A close second behind vaginal intercourse, oral sex, or fellatio, is a highly desired sexual activity for men. Many men also like to give orally to their wives, stimulating the clitoris with their tongues instead of their fingers or a vibrator. Many women enjoy receiving oral sex. But more often when the question is asked, it relates to the wife *giving* oral sex to her husband. This involves taking the penis into her mouth and simulating intercourse there, often with a light suction. It may lead to orgasm in the mouth or outside of the mouth.

Surely there is some Bible verse for this one—but there is not. Oral sex is not listed as being prohibited, and God is never caught off guard. It falls within the broad freedoms we possess within marriage to explore each other and discover what pleases the other (1 Tim. 4:4). One reason that oral sex is so desired by men is that it feels good! Another reason lies in the fact that the penis is the symbol of manhood. When a woman acknowledges that organ and gives special attention to it, she is letting her man know that she appreciates him as a man.

It is common for a man to struggle secretly with insecurity regarding his ability to please a woman, wondering how he compares to any other man she could have had (or has had). Oral sex tells him that he is man enough for her and that she likes what he has to give. And it doesn't have to continue to climax, but it can be a part of foreplay alone. This is important, because some women do not enjoy oral sex for fear of the ejaculate.

There can be no coercion by either party to get the other to do something they do not want to do. But if both are willing, oral sex can be a wonderful enhancement to marital sex.

Novelty items

Some people ask me about vibrators and other sex toys that they see the world using. Vibrators can be used to help a woman reach orgasm if it is acceptable to each party. Other things that are novelty items may also add some fun to the encounter. I am not a fan of "bondage" items such as leashes, handcuffs, whips and so forth, because it may demean and demote the other person. But I would not interfere with what is honestly mutually acceptable to both spouses. There are those who even find various foods such as chocolate, whipped cream or strawberries an exciting addition to lovemaking. It might make a great excuse for your wife to break her diet!

Some couples ask if there is a role for fantasy in sexual intercourse. My opinion is that as long as it involves just those two people, they can pretend to be whatever role they wish. A man can pretend to be a fireman rescuing a woman in distress. He must still be *himself*, playing a role. A woman can pretend to be a nurse, giving her "patient" a sponge bath or massage—you get the idea. A word of warning concerning role-playing is that each person must stay true to his gender. The man should never dress up or pretend to be a woman and vice versa.

God knew that in the sixty to seventy years we might be married to the same person, there would be a lot to learn. Part of the excitement of marriage is the discovery of what makes the other person happy and what pleases them. As our bodies are constantly changing, we will never come to the end of our quest for knowledge and the delight of discovery, if we will only continue to pursue it.

In general, I find men more willing to experiment than women. A certain *Puritan* ideal, which conveys a false modesty, is prevalent in many Christian circles, even into the bedroom. Many women would never dream of wearing a Victoria's Secret garment to bed because, in their minds, it conveys the world's view of sex and women. The real problem with Victoria's Secret is that is has left the secret place of the bedroom and now appears on billboards and television sets across America. It is not wrong in the bedroom if the message you are trying to convey is an invitation to explore the sweet gift God gave your husband when He gave you to him.

Song of Solomon paints an intimate portrait of a wife who knows how to use the resources God had given her to both arouse and capture her man's attention:

> Why should I be like a veiled woman beside the flocks of your friends?…While the king was at his table, my perfume spread its fragrance. My lover is to me a sachet of myrrh resting between my breasts.
>
> *—Song of Solomon 1:7, 12–13*

And the man replies:

> You have stolen my heart, my sister, my bride; you have stolen my heart with one glance of your eyes, with one jewel of your necklace. How delightful is your love, my sister, my bride! How much more pleasing is your love than wine, and the fragrance of your perfume than any spice!…The fragrance of your garments is like that of Lebanon.
>
> *—Song of Solomon 4:9–11*

This is a biblical portrait of a sensual woman who has perfumed herself and worn garments that are pleasing to her lover. The sensual man makes wise use of those things the Lord has created that bring pleasure to a woman. God has covered the earth with beautiful flowers that display a rich palate of color and fragrance. Women are endowed with an ability to appreciate these gifts of love and affection. A bed sprinkled with rose petals is an invitation to drink deeply of love. The flickering of scented candles is but a prelude to the warm embrace that awaits her.

There are countless other examples I could give of questions I am asked from sincere Christians. The bottom line is that God desires sex to be fulfilling, pleasurable, intimate and lifelong. Sex is not the cure for all of life's problems, but it has the potential to be far more satisfying than most Christian couples allow it to be. It is not an activity, as men often see it, nor an obligation, as women may tend to view it.

Marital sex is an invitation God extends to a husband and wife through which He invites them to know one other person on this planet at a level and a depth that will not be found anywhere else this side of heaven.

In the union of man and wife, of two differing yet complementary strengths, God reveals Himself in His creation. As we experience the riches of marital love and intimacy, we are drawn to the One who is the source of it all. As a result of our loving marital union with our spouse, we can reflect to the world God's character, His love and His heart.

Chapter **Fourteen**

MARITAL SIN

> If we confess our sins, he is faithful and just
> and will forgive us our sins and purify us from
> all unrighteousness.
>
> —*1 John 1:9*

Into every marriage will come sin. For many of us, it will be sexual sin. It is inevitable; we are sinful creatures. Some of us will bring sins from the past into our new union, sins committed by us or done to us. All of us will sin against our spouse at some time, or multiple times, in our marriage. Not only do these sins—past, present and future—determine our ability to be intimate with one another, but the very survival of our marriage rests on how well we overcome these sins. Born-again Christians, who make their marriage vows before an almighty God, are abandoning them at the fastest rate this country has ever seen.[1] Much of this failure in marriage has to do with having wrong expectations, both of our spouse and of marriage.

A FALSE ILLUSION

Many people enter marriage believing it will be the source of ultimate fulfillment, enjoyment, stability, safety, companionship and love. When those expectations are not perfectly fulfilled by an imperfect spouse, we become disillusioned. To suffer "disillusionment" means we have suffered from an "illusion" to begin with. An unrealistic illusion is what our expectations of marriage were all along.

No human being was created to become all the other person needs him or her to be for complete fulfillment, or to do everything that person needs done to be happy. God purposely created us with a deeper need for relationship so we would seek Him as our primary source of love, prosperity, security, safety, fulfillment and fellowship. Often, God gives us spouses who can become "agents" to supply these things, but they are not the source of them. And they can never supply them perfectly because of their imperfections. The psalmist understood that God was the source of all satisfaction when he wrote:

> You open your hand and satisfy the desires of every living thing.
>
> —*Psalm 145:16*

His illusion

In his illusion, men enter marriage looking for a wife who is a combination of sexual goddess, cook, housekeeper, child-bearer, faithful companion, financial partner and friend. No woman can be all of those things simultaneously. When the sex is failing or work outside of the home causes the domestic duties to suffer, the husband is disappointed.

When having a baby means she wants to quit her job and forfeit half of their income, the financial pressures mount. When dragging the kids to soccer, ballet or birthday parties takes his wife away from the Saturday companionship he used to enjoy after a long workweek, the husband can feel abandoned. Progressively, all of these things he thought would be there when they married are dwindling. The "contract" of his illusion has been broken.

Her illusion

The woman also has unrealistic expectations of what marriage will be like. She is expecting a good provider, a strong father for her children, a repairman and a best friend with whom she can share the details of life. But then her "provider" gets laid off and sits at home in a fog, bruised and battered by corporate downsizing. She may discover that he is a lazy disciplinarian, leaving her to do the difficult tasks while he immerses himself in his own world. She finds herself constantly nagging him to mow the lawn, fix the disposal, take out the trash—all of the "man" things she thought she could count on him to do. Over time, the wife may find her husband withdrawing from her, uninterested in her daily life, unwilling to listen to the details of her day. Her partner has retreated, leaving her feeling very much alone in the relationship.

Andrew Comiskey, founder of Desert Stream Ministries, gave a wonderful illustration of how we get to this place in marriage at a seminar in Dallas-Fort Worth that I attended.[2] In Creation, God made Adam from the dust of the earth and gave him dominion over all things. Man is thus deeply connected to the earth, to achieving, conquering, building and advancing. All of these characteristics were in full force before Eve ever came into existence. Adam was naming all of the creatures God had made and was the manager of the universe, as far as he was concerned.

Eve was formed from Adam's rib, and from her, all other human life originated. Women are creatures of relationship, both to their husbands and to their children. Their worth and purpose are found, not so much in achievements outside of the home, but in the survival and advancement of her children. Her husband becomes the foundation for financial security and emotional safety upon which she will build the next generation.

OVERCOMING DISILLUSIONMENT

As Andrew Comiskey points out, a problem men have in succeeding in marriage is that they disconnect from the family as they focus on achieving their goals in the outside world. The pressure to succeed and the competition for advancement can consume them. Yet, gaining financial wealth or a successful career means nothing without being in relationship with a person with whom you can share it. Jesus alluded to this fact when He warned, "For what shall it profit a man, if he shall gain the whole world, and lose his own soul?" (Mark 8:36, KJV). Yet, after committing to a relationship, the man finds that the woman is imperfect and cannot provide everything he needs in life. In his disillusioned state, he often withdraws and begins to seek satisfaction elsewhere.

Understanding addiction

When men experience disappointment, stress, anger, fear or rejection as they make their way in the world, they often don't engage their spouses for support. And many don't seek God for the comfort, shelter or strength He has promised to give. Instead, men often try to fix things themselves. But the quick "fix" often turns into addiction.

The problem of addiction—which can be an addiction to anything—is rampant in our society. Most people are aware of addictions to alcohol, drugs or gambling. But just as devastating are addictions to food, work and sex. Because of the STD epidemic we have already discussed, many men are now turning to pornography for their "fix." While in the past they would have to drive to seedy bookstores or risk being seen buying magazines in a convenience store, most now have easy access to pornography, viewing it over the Internet.

Many men now have computer access at work or at home. Because either of these locations can be places of stress, when men feel the need, they can find their "fix" with just a few short clicks of a mouse. In its perverted way, pornography powerfully eases the pain of life, distracting people from their daily problems and opening them to a world of fantasy and excitement. If their voyeurism is coupled with masturbation, men can also achieve a physical and chemical release that temporarily relieves stress.

Because of these chemical changes, patterns form in the brain very similar to those seen in drug addicts. Those who have made a habit of getting stress relief from pornography have programmed their brain to respond to it—creating a habit that can be very difficult to break.

While Christian men may feel shame and regret over pornography, it is compartmentalized as a "problem" they need to deal with. They simply place it in its own "box." But as Andrew Comiskey teaches to thousands of couples all over the world, addiction is not an isolated problem.[3] It is a sin against the marriage; it is adultery.

When the wife discovers the Internet pornography (and she always does), her perfect world begins to collapse. The man she had placed all of her hopes upon has been found to be a fraud. She now sees him as a liar, an adulterer and a weak creature that would risk everything for momentary pleasure. That is not what she signed up for when she took her marriage vows. In a very real way, those vows now seem broken to her. What for her husband is a compartmentalized "problem" he needs to deal with is, for his wife, the crumbling of her whole world.

How can a wife who has made such a discovery possibly trust her husband again with her sexuality? She now believes he has lost all affection or sexual attraction he once had for her and has sought some "pretend" women in her place. Was he fantasizing about another woman the last time they made love? In his mind it may be just pictures on a computer screen, but to his wife they are real people. Without her knowledge or consent, other women have been in bed with her when she was the most exposed and vulnerable she could be.

There is a reality to this depth of betrayal perceived by a wife that few men understand. For the man, pornography is a problem to be conquered. For a woman, it is a huge hole in the very fabric of their relationship that calls into question everything she ever believed about her husband.

However, women also become addicted to "things" in an effort to escape the stress or even boredom of daily life. I know many wives who have difficulty understanding their husbands' pornography addiction, yet these same women overeat when they feel sad or lonely, succumbing to a food addiction. A close examination of our lives will reveal that we are all susceptible to some form of addiction that gives us a quick and reliable solution to our present emotional or spiritual need, even if the long-term consequences only cause us more pain.

The solution

The solution is God. He never intended husbands and wives to depend upon each other to meet all their needs. While their relationship would provide important avenues through which love, security, companionship, compassion and grace would flow, God is always the source. Without Him, we will always fail each other trying to live life in our own strength. And when we fail, the ones we disappointed often abandon us while they seek someone else to meet their needs.

When a man realizes he cannot handle the stress and pressures of the outside world, as well as the rejection and disappointments that come with daily life, he must seek a source of refuge and strength. While his wife can be a great resource of comfort and compassion, she cannot be everything. And the quick "fix" that man would give himself only leads to death, both physical and relational. Only God can truly affirm what He made that man to be. Only God can be Father, Mother, Protector and Friend.

> **ONLY GOD CAN BE FATHER, MOTHER, PROTECTOR AND FRIEND.**

When a woman discovers that her husband cannot be the firm foundation she needs for her life and that of her children, she must seek God as well—the One who is unshakable, immovable and unchanging, the same yesterday, today and forever (Heb. 13:8). And He really is the God of yesterday who can go back and forgive the sins of our past and help us to forgive each other in the present.

CONSEQUENCES OF SIN

When we realize that the person we married is no longer "perfect," we free each other to be imperfect in our past as well. Virtually all of us bring our past with us into our present marriage. Many that I see in the office are not just dealing with current sin, such as Internet pornography, but they are also facing the consequences of sins of the past, some of which they were not responsible for.

Because I am a gynecologist, I will approach this discussion from the woman's experience, though the same truths apply to men as well. On a monthly basis, I meet at least one woman who has contracted an STD from her husband. While STDs can result from adultery, most are a result of the husband's past. As we discovered in our study of STDs, a husband often silently carries disease for many years, unaware that his new bride may inherit the sins of his past sexual experiences.

I am confronted by couples who are seeking explanations to a sudden abnormal Pap smear. As I review the chart, I see several years of normal exams before marriage and an abnormal Pap smear the year following marriage. As the biopsies often document, HPV (human papillomavirus) is the culprit, which the new husband has brought to the marriage bed from his past. An outbreak of herpes is another common finding for a woman whose husband never knew what those small blisters on his penis meant.

In cases of infidelity, STDs are often the "smoking gun" that alerts the woman to her husband's affair. Many are hoping that this is a dormant infection he has carried for years instead of a new disease. A careful review of their history and the amount of time to infection will usually separate those two possible choices. It can be difficult for me to explain to one of my patients that the man she has been happily married to for several years has given her an STD that he acquired elsewhere.

While transmission of STDs from past premarital sex can be easier to deal with than current infidelity, both situations require forgiveness. Infidelity also requires repentance and recommitment, but in both cases, the victimized party feels betrayed. The person they thought was "safe" is not. A situation they never thought possible in a monogamous relationship, acquiring an STD, has occurred, and they are often unprepared for the shock of it.

Because a man is generally less emotional and more pragmatic, receiving an STD from his wife is not as devastating to his ability to be intimate as it is for a wife receiving it. Men tend to have fewer symptoms and are not as physically bothered by the STD as women. But the emotional attachments of sex are very vulnerable for women when an STD is acquired.

Even when the wife knew of her husband's past sexual experience, and even if she knows he has had a viral STD in the past, acquiring one from him causes great damage to her desire for sexual intimacy. Intercourse has now been defiled and is "dirty." For those STDs that recur and have no cure, each episode reminds her of his past and her future. She is also very aware of the woman who gave it to him, even if she doesn't know her name. The "competition" is out there somewhere.

All of these thoughts and feelings interplay with a woman's sexual desire and can greatly diminish libido. Even if she is the one who originally gave the STD, she is sensitive to her diseased state. It is difficult to feel attractive sexually and diseased at the same time.

Again, forgiveness is the key: forgiving your partner and forgiving yourself. When we take wedding vows that say "for better and for worse, in sickness and in health," that is exactly what they mean. When we take a spouse, we take the past as well as the future. Both may be uncertain, and neither can be controlled.

CHILDHOOD ABUSE

Perhaps the most difficult situation I see in the office is a woman (or man) who was sexually abused as a child. The innocence of life was torn away, and they were exposed to adult "things" before they were old enough to understand. Every one of the victims feels responsible and carries tremendous guilt and shame, despite the fact of being completely innocent. The sins perpetrated against them often cause them to see themselves as "damaged goods." Fearing abandonment and seeking love the only way they had ever seen it displayed, they often become sexually promiscuous. The virtue of virginity is no longer theirs to hold, and they mistake sex for love.

A woman who has suffered such abuse and finds Christ may discard her promiscuous lifestyle, but she still has no basis upon which to build a normal sexual relationship with her husband. Since sex first represented sin that was done to her, and then sin she later committed, holy marital sex can be a difficult concept to grasp. These women are often "frigid" and find intercourse very painful.

I have even known couples who were unable to consummate their marriage because the woman was unable to have intercourse. A husband may have no idea that his wife carries this secret shame. It is only after the marriage reaches a crisis that it comes to light. I strongly advise these couples to seek counseling and receive prayer for inner healing. Though they will find themselves on a fairly long journey to wholeness, recovery is achievable if this dark past is brought to light.

Other abuse

A similar sin committed against a woman is the crime of rape. It is really a crime of violence instead of sex, but the two become intertwined in the minds of the victims. Rape can be at the hands of a stranger or, as we are now discovering in a majority of cases, as a result of date rape. Because the women are older, rape doesn't injure the core of their being as much as childhood sexual abuse, but it can still cause tremendous damage to a woman's perception of men and sex.

If the rape happened during a date, it can be very difficult for a woman to trust the next man she meets. No matter what the circumstances, men are now tagged with suspicion and fear. Even a woman's own husband may have difficulty achieving the level of trust and intimacy that would have been theirs before this violation. Again, rape counseling is invaluable, even if it has been a number of years since the offense. Opening the past to your husband will allow him to understand your fears and will help him to know that he is not the source of your anger. That which is hidden can never experience the light of God's power and love.

Healing from sexual sin, whether in the past or in the present, is just one more beautiful promise of God's love and His grace toward us. As the church has been emerging from its silence about sex, organizations both within and without have sprung up in virtually every city in the United States to tackle these painful issues and offer help in the healing process. My favorite national organization is Desert Stream Ministries, which is a ministry to men and women who are sexually and relationally broken. Their website, www.desertstream.org, is a great place to begin seeking help, and they have chapters all over the country and are expanding worldwide.

I strongly encourage you to reach for all that God has for you in the realm of your sexuality. As you commit your life to the Lord, Jesus has promised you healing and wholeness. In Luke 4:18–21, He declared Himself to be the fulfillment of these wonderful words of the prophet Isaiah:

> The Spirit of the Sovereign LORD is on me, because the LORD has anointed me to preach good news to the poor. He has sent me to bind up the brokenhearted, to proclaim freedom for the captives and release from darkness for the prisoners, to proclaim the year of the LORD's favor and the day of vengeance of our God, to comfort all who mourn, and provide for those who grieve in Zion—to bestow on them a crown of beauty instead of ashes, the oil of gladness instead of mourning, and a garment of praise instead of a spirit of despair…Instead of their shame my people will receive a double portion, and instead of disgrace they will rejoice in their inheritance.
>
> —*Isaiah 61:1–3, 7*

Real Life

Thirty-year-old Marissa had been my patient for many years. She had faithfully guarded her virginity while she waited for God to bring her the "perfect" man. When she met Nick, she felt that her prayers were answered. Nick was a thirty-three-year-old successful businessman who had become a Christian at the age of twenty-seven. He made a radical change in lifestyle, quitting smoking, drinking and having premarital sex. By the time that Marissa met him at church, Nick had become a gifted leader and a man she admired even before they began dating.

They had dated about a year when he proposed to her. Although he was not a virgin, Nick was not aware of having ever contracted an STD. He had been faithful to use a condom every time. To put Marissa at ease, he even had an HIV test. When the wedding night came, Marissa was a bit nervous, fearing she would not compare well with the other women with whom Nick had slept. But Nick was gentle and devoted, quickly erasing any fears she had.

After several months of marriage, Marissa returned to the office for her annual examination and Pap smear. She discussed their desire to begin having children since she was already thirty. I prescribed prenatal vitamins and reviewed ovulation cycles as she made preparations to discontinue her birth control pills.

Several days later, her Pap smear returned with dysplasia, a pre-cancerous condition of the cervix, and evidence of HPV infection. Biopsies confirmed this, and a few weeks later, Marissa and Nick were in my office to discuss treatment options. Marissa was devastated. While most women are unhappy and a bit fearful of an abnormal Pap smear, Marissa felt betrayed. She had faithfully remained a virgin until she was thirty, partly out of religious conviction and partly to avoid STDs.

To acquire HPV and have cervical treatments not only meant delaying conception of a long-awaited pregnancy, but in some way she felt she had wasted her time being "good." Marissa struggled with the fact that Nick had experienced so many women before her while she had waited for the right man. Now, it was as if she too had slept with all of those people because someone from the past had sneaked into her honeymoon suite and deposited HPV in her cervix.

I explained to both of them that Nick had gotten HPV prior to his conversion to Christianity. While his past sin was forgiven, the consequences did not magically disappear. It was perhaps naive to think that Marissa was in no danger of acquiring an STD just because Nick had no symptoms. Because HPV is usually invisible to the naked eye, there was no way for Nick to know, nor was there a way of preventing transmission. For Marissa to get pregnant, Nick could not use condoms. But even with condoms, Nick had acquired the disease, a possibility that condom manufacturers are now required to disclose on every condom packet.

Marissa would have to accept Nick for who he was when she married him; he was not a knight in shining armor or a "perfect" gift from God, but a mortal man with a past. Despite this past, she had fallen in love with him, and everything about him that she originally loved was still there. But her illusion of him was now gone, and she would have to see him and their marriage through the eyes of the truth.

Marissa would also have to forgive him for what his past was now doing to her in the present. She could not afford to wallow in bitterness or resentment, nor could she see herself as a "victim." They were a partnership, and each brought various things into the marriage for the good and for the bad. She was no exception.

After a few months of allowing her cervix to heal from treatment, Marissa returned to the office and received a clean bill of health. She and Nick are now attempting to conceive. It is my prayer that the birth of their baby together will help ease the pain Marissa has felt over Nick's past. Only time will tell.

Chapter **Fifteen**

THE ABORTION ISSUE

I, even I, am he who blots out your
transgressions, for my own sake, and
remembers your sins no more.
—*Isaiah 43:25*

Each year, three million women become pregnant "accidentally."[1] Of these unintentional pregnancies, one million women will choose abortion as a solution. Since abortion became legal in 1976, over forty million babies have been aborted in this country.[2] That means that for hundreds of women sitting in church pews all across this land, abortion is part of their past. Many men also participated in these decisions, often with women who are not their current partners.

THE SIN PROBLEM

It is common for both men and women to hide this secret from their spouse. If they became Christians some time after the abortion took place, many times they come to believe they murdered an innocent life and are convicted of their sin. For many, it is difficult for them to conceive of a greater sin than that of abortion.

Many of us rank sin according to our perceptions of their degree of evil. We falsely believe that while Christ shed His blood to cleanse us from our sins, He couldn't possibly include abortion on the list. Surely abortion would rank too high to be covered by Christ's sacrifice. But even if we can believe God has forgiven us (because He has to), we doubt whether our spouses would. Why should they forgive us when we can't forgive ourselves?

Many of my patients who have had an abortion in the past have trouble coming to the office for their yearly physical examinations. The instruments remind them of the procedure that ended a life. Certain sounds can trigger anxiety. The clang of metal may bring flashbacks of a day they wish they could forget. The sound of suction may send shivers down their spine.

First trimester abortion

Ninety percent of those who had abortions did so in the first trimester of pregnancy where an office procedure using suction removed the developing fetus.[3] It was over quickly, even if it was painful, and did not seem to have any side effects. But the women left feeling "empty," knowing that life had just left their bodies. Many experienced a post-abortion depression that took time to lift. Some felt such loss that they purposely got pregnant again to replace what they had done. I see this quite often in my practice, especially with young women. It is not uncommon when taking a medical history to discover that my newly pregnant patient had an abortion just three months earlier.

Second trimester abortion

Approximately 10 percent of abortions, or one hundred thousand cases per year in the U.S., are done in the second trimester.[4] Several techniques are employed, depending on the training and expertise of the abortionist. Most will place a dilating device into the cervix to open it overnight, having the patient return the following day to continue the procedure. Then they may inject the uterus with a saline solution to kill the fetus and place the woman into labor.

Alternatively, and more commonly, the cervix may be further dilated under local anesthesia to admit a large suction device. This removes as much of the sac, placenta and fetal body parts as possible. Some prefer grabbing the fetus with an instrument and removing the body by hand. In either case, the various body parts must be accounted for to ensure that nothing has been left inside the uterus. This is a gruesome task for even the most cold-hearted of medical staffs.

I will never forget one night in medical school when I was assigned to the emergency room at the university hospital. A young woman came in crying hysterically. She had had an abortion earlier that day at an abortion clinic. That night, she felt something come out of her vagina, and she brought into the emergency room a small leg that had been left behind. Needless to say, the psychological trauma of that experience would stay with that young woman for many years to come. I can still picture it in my mind some twenty years later.

Because all abortion is the result of sex, intercourse now reminds these women of their sin, their guilt and their shame. Even if the pregnancy was the result of rape or incest, intercourse is now tainted. These women feel they have no freedom, no "right" to enjoy sex when intercourse led to the death of an innocent baby. They will have sex for the sake of their husbands or to have children, but not for pleasure—they don't deserve it.

KEY TO RELEASE

You can see how difficult it will be to attain any level of real intimacy with this secret wedged between a husband and wife. The husband who has no idea why his wife shies away from sex will misinterpret her distance as a rejection of him, when in truth she is rejecting herself.

In various women's seminars and retreats in which I have participated, the speakers have each presented the same key to the abortion issue: forgiveness. A woman must forgive herself and let go of the past. She must accept God's unconditional pardon, realizing His promises to her:

> I, even I, am he who blots out your transgressions, for my own sake, and remembers your sins no more.
>
> —*Isaiah 43:25*

> For I will forgive their wickedness and will remember their sins no more.
>
> —*Jeremiah 31:34*

Only after determining to receive God's promise of forgiveness will an intimate sexual relationship be possible for the woman who bears the guilt of abortion. The good news is that you *do* deserve to be happy and fulfilled, no matter what is in your past, because of what Christ has done for you on the cross.

This wonderful truth can be even more difficult to accept if you had more than one abortion, as if God puts a limit on His forgiveness. One sin is the same as many as far as He is concerned. To refuse to forgive yourself is to make Jesus' death less than sufficient for you. That is a lie that you cannot afford to believe if you want to live in the unmerited favor of God's grace and be the helpmate the Lord intended your spouse to have.

Once I have guided the woman into accepting God's forgiveness and forgiving herself, I encourage her to tell her husband about her abortion. We have all sinned in our lives, and the men are no exception. As I mentioned before, many men have also participated in the decision to choose abortion.

Often the men will have to receive forgiveness for the way they encouraged abortion or left a previous sexual partner to fend for herself, leading her to choose abortion because she was alone. A wife's confession gives her husband permission to share his own past with her. I have found these moments of truth to be universally a healing time for a couple as the light of truth shines onto the dark secrets of the past and destroys the power of fear and shame those secrets once possessed. It takes courage to trust God and your spouse, but the rewards are far greater than you can imagine.

Real Life

Twenty-four-year-old Beverly had an abortion at the age of seventeen. She and her high school sweetheart had become sexually active at age sixteen. He had promised to marry her when they graduated. When she became pregnant, she assumed that they would simply move the wedding date up and everything would be all right. But instead, he became hostile and distant. They fought constantly, and he looked for any excuse to be angry with her. Finally, in her fourth month of pregnancy, he broke up with her.

Without a commitment to marriage, Beverly's parents did not want her to continue the pregnancy. They had reluctantly supported marriage, but now they saw a chance for Beverly to start life over again and move on from this mistake. Although Beverly wanted to keep the baby, her father pressured her every morning before school and every evening at dinner to seek an abortion.

With the pressure from her parents and the feelings of rejection from her boyfriend, Beverly consented to an abortion. Because she was so far along in her pregnancy, her father drove her to a hospital to have the procedure. She remembered the male doctor who came to do the abortion. He didn't introduce himself or even explain what he was going to do or how she would feel during the procedure. After injecting her uterus with saline, he left the room. She would go through this alone.

After a few hours of painful cramps, Beverly felt a pressure sensation in the rectal area. Believing she needed to have a bowel movement, she went to the bathroom. As she pushed, she heard a loud splash in the toilet and felt a relief of the pressure. But when she wiped, there was only blood. As she stood up and looked down, there was her baby floating in the toilet.

She was shocked that it looked like a fully formed baby. She had pictured a blob of tissue that would be unrecognizable. But as she stared at it, Beverly could see the arms and legs, the hands and feet, and the innocent face. She knew in that moment that she had just killed her baby.

Beverly began to scream and cry loudly. The nurse who came to attend her told her to quiet down so as not to scare the other women. She was left alone with no counseling, no support and no shoulder to cry on. It was her responsibility to bear, her grief to suppress.

After a couple of hours, her father came to take her home. Neither spoke a word on the drive back. In fact, almost seven years later, Beverly cannot remember the last real conversation they have had.

Beverly left for college after graduation, choosing one that was out of state in her desire to leave her past behind her. She rarely dated in college, focusing on her studies to the exclusion of everything else. She had few friends and kept to herself. In her mind, if she developed deep relationships, she would have to share her past, and she knew she would be instantly rejected. Who would want to be friends with a baby killer? She didn't. And she was determined not to face the prospect of an unplanned pregnancy again.

After college, Beverly took a job even farther away from her family, coming to Texas, where she found my office. When I first met her, we would engage in small talk and proceed through the annual examinations routinely. She never had a question for me and was always in a hurry to leave. At first I thought she didn't like me as a physician, but she would faithfully return each year. I later realized that her aloofness was her fear that I would discover her past abortion and reject her for it. She had begun attending the same church that I attended, and she was afraid her secret would be revealed and she would be asked to leave the church.

During one office visit, Beverly announced that she had met a man at church who really loved her. Despite her reservations, she had begun dating again. Over time, she had let herself feel love for him as well. When he proposed, she said yes. But she subsequently began to have panic attacks. They would spring up with no warning and did not seem related to any particular stress. Her job was going well, and she was in love. When she asked for my advice, I was given permission to ask some difficult questions.

I began by telling Beverly that I had noticed on her office history form that she had had an abortion in the past. Her face froze and the color drained from it. As I shared with her how common this was in my patient population, even among women in the church, she began to relax a bit. When she saw that I was not going to judge her, she shared her story with me.

Several things came to light as she shared her experience. I explored each one to see if they might be triggers to her panic attacks. The first was a fear of rejection. The boy she thought she would marry at seventeen had rejected her. Could it be that she feared her current fiancé would reject her as well, especially if he knew the truth about her past? Beverly admitted that she was afraid to tell him about the abortion and that every time he tried to bring up the idea of children together, she would change the subject.

Secretly, Beverly feared that God had made her infertile because she had killed the first baby He had given to her. No matter how many years had passed, she could not erase the image of her baby floating in the toilet. She was convinced that when she was found to be infertile, she would have to confess her abortion and her husband would reject her. She would never be able to bear him a child.

Even if she let the idea of getting pregnant enter her mind, she knew she would miscarry and her husband would discover that her past was now seeking revenge on her future children. No matter how wonderful he seemed right now, he would leave her. How could she trust he would stay, and how could she really expect him to once he knew the truth?

The second trigger to her panic attacks involved her family. I pointed out to Beverly that she seemed to have moved farther away from home with each transition in her life. It had been years since she had seen her parents face to face, and they rarely spoke but a few minutes on the phone each month.

But with the plans for a wedding, she was again confronted by her past. Her parents insisted that she be married in the church she grew up in. Beverly would be facing the old demons of her youth. Everything she had run away from would be there when she returned for her wedding. The high school would be there as well as acquaintances that knew what she had done in her junior year. Maybe she would run into her old boyfriend. Maybe she would see the hospital where the abortion took place. What if someone her parents invited to the wedding had too much to drink and blurted out her sin to her new husband?

They seemed like such stupid thoughts to her intellectual mind, but her heart raced every time they sprang up. With every phone call from her mother to plan the wedding or the reception, panic would set in. Even the casual mention of the upcoming wedding by a coworker could prompt an attack. With her eyes open to the truth, Beverly began to see a pattern to her panic attacks. What she wanted was medication. But what she needed was courage—and forgiveness.

While Beverly believed that God had forgiven her for the abortion to the extent that He would not send her to hell when she died, she was still waiting for Him to spring her "punishment" on her. She cited the biblical story of King David. When he sinned with Bathsheba, God forgave him, but He took the life of their newborn son (2 Sam. 12:13–14). Beverly thought there was a payday someday; she just didn't know when it would happen.

I explained to Beverly that when Jesus died on the cross for our *sins, we were forgiven completely—even for the sin of abortion. God loved Beverly in spite of everything she had done, and He forgave her completely, burying her sin in the depths of the sea. In fact, I reminded her that, according to His Word, God could not even remember she had ever had an abortion:*

> I, even I, am he who blots out your transgressions, for my own sake, and remembers your sins no more.
>
> —*Isaiah 43:25*

> You will again have compassion on us; you will tread our sins underfoot and hurl all our iniquities into the depths of the sea.
>
> —*Micah 7:19*

After receiving God's complete forgiveness, Beverly still had to forgive herself. She could not fully enjoy the benefits of what Jesus did for her at Calvary if she did not forgive herself. It wasn't enough to make excuses for her past behavior, saying she was young or pressured or rejected—all of which were true. She had to admit that she had sinned and then forgive herself.

Part of her journey to wholeness would involve her participation in a post-abortion recovery group. I told Beverly of such a group that met at the church, leading many women to freedom. There she would find women going through the same journey and would be led by others who had made it to the other side.

It was crucial that her fiancé be told the truth. While it was highly unlikely that the kind of man Beverly described him to be would reject her because of her past, he had a right to know. Should any physical damage have occurred that would impair fertility, it would affect his life, as her partner, in the process of conceiving a child. She would only live in fear of her secret if she did not tell him. My suspicion was that her honesty would open the door for him to share his own past with her, and the result would be a greater marital bond than could ever come from two people "pretending" to be perfect.

Marriage offers the deepest level of intimacy possible on this earth, and that intimacy needed to start with the discussion of this sensitive issue. Otherwise, their future sexual relationship would be forever clouded. Beverly would not feel "worthy" to enjoy herself, and her fear would suppress any sexual desire she might feel for her husband. This burden would be unfair to her and her unsuspecting husband.

The last thing I asked Beverly to do was to forgive her parents. Whether she did that face to face or said a private prayer alone, she had to release them from their sin against her when they pressured her to have the abortion. Beverly knew that if they had supported her initial desire to keep the baby, they would be enjoying a beautiful seven-year-old grandchild today, who would perhaps be walking down the aisle as a flower girl or a ringbearer. She needed to forgive her parents for their mistakes and do it completely. Only then would she be made whole. Only then could the previous generation be free to embrace the coming generation, as grandparents reach out to new grandchildren. A fresh start could be made, but it depended on her.

Beverly left the office that day, not with a prescription for pills, but with the truth. She never experienced another panic attack. And she took responsibility for her past. She enrolled in a ten-week post-abortion recovery group at the church. The support of the women and the beauty of their testimonies gave her the strength to forgive herself and to accept fully all that Christ had done for her.

She also received the courage she needed to talk with her fiancé. As I had suspected, he had a past as well. When he was nineteen, he had gotten a girl pregnant that he met in a bar, and she had had an abortion. Because he didn't even know her, it seemed like a good idea at the time and he was "off the hook." But now that he saw the other side of it, he realized he needed forgiveness as well. Beverly saw an even deeper level of trust and commitment grow between them out of this experience. They could now share everything together because they had passed this difficult test.

On one trip home to view possible reception locations, she talked with her mother about all that she was learning in the post-abortion recovery classes and how she had let the abortion drive her away from her family. She asked for her mother's forgiveness for the ways she had cut them out of her life and been emotionally cold toward them the past seven years.

Beverly's mother in turn asked for forgiveness for pushing her to have an abortion, and the two shared a long cry together as the walls that had separated them for so long came down. They were now free to enjoy each other again and celebrate the joyous wedding that was upon them. Beverly knew that her mother would share with her father all that had happened, and she was content to let that be enough. She had forgiven him in her heart.

Little by little they became more comfortable together, and the ultimate reconciliation came the day he walked her down the aisle, presenting his daughter, the bride, to her groom. Beverly pictured God the Father presenting her to Jesus, her heavenly Bridegroom, and she knew that she stood there spotless and clean before him.

Chapter Sixteen

SEX AND THE AGING MAN

> May your fountain be blessed, and may you
> rejoice in the wife of your youth. A loving doe, a
> graceful deer—may her breasts satisfy you
> always, may you ever be captivated by her love.
> *—Proverbs 5:18–19*

As a couple reaches their forties and fifties, they will notice certain changes happening to their bodies that will cause them to reevaluate their sex life. Many couples will wrongly conclude that they have reached an age when sexual activity is no longer possible or, at least, no longer desirable.

With the average life expectancy now reaching deep into the eighties and nineties, to abandon sexual activity as one ages is to forfeit some of the best years of marital intimacy. And with the average age of marrying reaching to the late twenties, there would appear to be only two good decades of marital sex available to us if we embrace the common "myths" about sex and aging.

Most of the baby-boomer generation (people now in their forties and fifties) have grown up with the idea that anything can happen if one merely works hard at it. It is a generation ever seeking youth and beauty, aware of the benefits of health and exercise as no previous generation on earth. In the realm of sexual activity and aging, this generation is at a crossroads.

Unfortunately, most baby-boomer couples have parents who grew up in the 1930s and 1940s when sexual activity was rarely talked about or demonstrated at home. They are lacking in role models for marital sex at their age. The mother of the baby boomer may have let herself age prematurely, by today's standards, not making physical fitness a priority. The father may have paid little attention to his wife as she got older, and the two may have grown apart and lived very separate lives.

As a consequence, the romantic involvement of the baby-boomer's parents may have diminished considerably over time. Even if their parents stayed sexually active, their love life was never discussed, and affection was not often publicly shown. Thus, the current generation of middle-aged couples has little in the way of a role model after which to pattern their maturing sexual lives.

For these and other reasons, certain myths about sex continue to this day and influence the lives of otherwise committed Christians.[1] I see these women in my office on a regular basis.

MYTHS ABOUT AGING AND SEX

One myth goes something like this:

> Sex isn't important when one gets older. Other things in life like companionship or recreational activity can keep the marriage together. Even grandchildren can be a source of common interest for an older couple. Sex is really something one does when he or she is younger or wanting a family. After awhile, it isn't that big of a deal anymore.

The second myth says:

> Sexual activity is supposed to fade away due to the process of aging. The body naturally tends to stop being able to be sexually active, and the desire for sex is supposed to go away along with the ability to have it. Since God created our bodies, when our bodies no longer can do the things they used to do, that must be a signal that it is time to stop being sexually active. Otherwise, God would have made us capable of staying at the same level sexually as when we were young.

The third myth is:

> Sex after a certain age is dangerous. Hollywood loves to show movies of older men dying in bed while making love to some younger woman. The marriage of former *Playboy* playmate Anna Nicole Smith to a ninety-year-old man who died within a year seems to add to the credibility of this myth. Many men are afraid they will have a heart attack while having sex and be found by paramedics in an embarrassing position that all the neighbors will hear about.

The fourth myth is more prevalent for women. It says:

> Since I am getting older and am not as attractive physically as I once was, I must not be sexually attractive to my husband. If he still wants sex, it is just to satisfy his own needs and not because he still finds me attractive.

The fifth myth is:

> With the challenges of menopause and erectile dysfunction, it is just too much of a bother to stay sexually active. It is easier for everyone involved if the issue never comes up and we move on in the marriage without it. The amount of work involved is not worth the rewards.

All of these myths are just that—untrue statements. Put bluntly, they are flat out lies. The "baby boomers" are in their forties and fifties now. This has been a generation of tremendous education and achievement, of prosperity and health. They have sought to be physically fit and vibrant, as medicine and technology have offered more to them than any previous generation. As a member of that generation, it is my hope that our children will grow up in a loving home, where the husband and wife continue to model romance and passion, letting the next generation know that sex does not end at an arbitrary age.

Some readers may conclude that, by advocating sex beyond middle age, I have been seduced by this present age of overt sexuality and depravity that is plaguing our culture. In an attempt to retreat from this world filled with blatant sexual sin, many well-meaning Christians also retreat from marital sex whenever difficulties arise in this area of their lives.

Many feel they have no one to talk to about these issues. They would never dream of seeing a sex therapist, whose job, they fear, must be devoted to "helping" perverts be more perverted! Choosing a "safer" route, they conclude, *Why not take the cues my body is giving me as a sign that the time of sexual activity is over?*

One has only to look at the Bible to see that God did not intend for us to stop being sexually active as we age. In the world He created for us to enjoy before sin entered, living the life He designed for us, the physical signs of aging that have slowed us down would not have existed: violent menopause, erectile dysfunction, diabetes, hypertension and medications that have sexual side effects.

BIBLICAL SUPPORT FOR "SEX AFTER SIXTY"

According to Scriptures, there doesn't seem to be an age limit or any instruction for couples to forego intentionally the sexual expression of love in marriage at some particular age. If that were necessary to please a holy God, surely He would give clear guidance for sincere Christians to follow. On the contrary, we read passages like the following:

May your fountain be blessed, may you rejoice in the wife of your *youth*. A loving doe, a graceful deer—may her breasts satisfy you *always*, may you *ever* be captivated by her love.

—*Proverbs 5:18–19, emphasis added*

This passage instructs couples to confine their sexual relationship to the wife of their youth, not seeking other partners, but satisfying their desire with the one with whom they first made covenant. Referring to the "wife of your youth" implies that the man being counseled is now older. And clearly the words "always" and "ever" relate to the perpetual source of satisfaction that the wife's breasts, her sexuality, are to be for her husband, with no suggestion that it should fade away with age.

The Bible simply does not place an age limit on marital sex, either overtly by command or through example of family life recorded in the Scriptures. On the contrary, the Scriptures reveal the lives of couples in the Old Testament who maintained their sexual relationship as they aged. For example, when Cain and Abel, sons of Adam and Eve, were grown men, Cain killed his brother, Abel (Gen. 4:8). After that, it is recorded that Cain was building a city and having his own children, when his mother, Eve, gave birth to a son and named him Seth, saying, "God has granted me another child in place of Abel, since Cain killed him" (Gen. 4:17, 25). As a grandmother, Eve was still bearing children herself.

While we understand that people lived longer in that culture, the Bible doesn't ever imply that people reached a certain age and then quit being sexual in their marriage relationships. In the case of Abraham and Sarah bearing their promised son, Isaac, Abraham was one hundred years old when Isaac was born. Although his conception was a result of God intervening supernaturally, it was the sexual union of this old married couple that brought forth God's promised blessing—in their old age.

Abraham conceived his first son with his wife's maid, Hagar, at eighty-six years of age. This relationship was not God's will for Abraham, so it is unlikely that he received a divine miracle to achieve his erection or ejaculation or that his sperm were made more potent. With no angelic intervention whatsoever, Ishmael was conceived of Abraham.

And when the Lord sought to establish a covenant with Abraham at the age of ninety-nine, He instituted the ceremony of circumcision. God did not tell Abraham that because he had a ninety-nine-year-old penis it didn't need circumcision. We can assume that God expected Abraham to still be using it, and He wanted him to be marked as a covenant man in that way.

PRACTICAL CONSIDERATIONS

Hopefully I have at least opened the door to the idea that God wants you to enjoy sexual activity in marriage into old age. Now I'd like to look at some practical considerations. As we reach middle age (for purposes of this discussion we'll agree on the late forties or early fifties), we may find that our lives offer us far more freedom that when we were younger.

The children have either left the home, or they are teens who do not need (or want) your constant attention. There is more time alone to be sexual as a couple than when your children were small. The threat of being "caught" having sex by your preschooler who wanders into the bedroom at night has long passed. With greater age has also come a diminished need for birth control. Menopause signals the end of fertility and a freedom to enjoy sexual intercourse without the fears of unplanned pregnancy or the hassles of condoms and diaphragms.

Along with age, hopefully, has come career stability and financial success as well. You are no longer climbing your way to the top of the corporate ladder or swimming in a mountain of debt. Wherever you are financially at this stage, you have probably made peace with it and can relax and enjoy life more than when you were younger and just starting out. You have more time to cultivate activities you both share and once again enjoy each other's company without the focus always being on work or children. It is a time to reconnect with your spouse on every level.

By the time you have been married fifteen or twenty years, you should have built a level of trust between you and your spouse that allows you to share almost anything. You will have gone through at least one marital, financial or career crisis by this point and weathered the storm together, forging a strong bond of loyalty.

With such solid foundations in every other aspect of your relationship together, it is a shame that most couples abandon satisfying sexual activity just when it could become the best it has ever been. While the challenges of staying sexually active as one ages must be addressed, the rewards are well worth the effort.

Avoiding growing apart

It is easy to grow apart as one ages. When you were focusing on the kids or the business, there was a common goal. But maybe you, like many couples, did not keep your marriage relationship healthy in the process. Various outside interests, hobbies, clubs and so forth pulled you in two different directions. Now that the children are grown, you have discovered that you have little in common anymore. The level of intimacy has diminished, and sex has become either an obligation or a nuisance, no longer serving to unite you into "one flesh."

Intimacy is key to keeping the sexual fires burning as you age. Little things done during the day can remind the other person that you are thinking about them and desiring them. Notes left in a briefcase or a call at work reminds your spouse that he or she still has value for you. Unexpected flowers or a surprise dinner at a romantic restaurant can be the start of a passionate evening. Even a bath together can be a prelude to greater things.

Diana Hagee, wife of popular evangelist John Hagee, candidly shares her attempts to cultivate intimacy in her marriage amidst a very hectic schedule. In her book *The King's Daughter,* she shares her solution, a program she calls "One Way Every Day."[2] This phrase reminds her and her husband to do one thing each day for each other that is loving, kind and romantic. And it has worked beautifully for years—they are forever courting, forever on the path of romance.

The simple things really make the most impact. When your spouse sees that you think about him or her, he or she will naturally be drawn to you and feel safe with you. The level of intimacy will grow to the point where you are each free to share what is really going on in your personal life as you age.

ADDRESSING PHYSICAL CHANGES

Of course, physical changes will occur as you age—that is inevitable. It must be accepted, and you must accept yourself. Don't compare yourself, or your spouse, to what you used to be. You can never go back there. And don't compare yourself, as we have warned, to what Hollywood says you should look like. Most of what you see there is fake anyway.

Jamie Lee Curtis, at age forty-three, recently had the courage to do a photo shoot for *More* magazine that showed before and after pictures. She wanted women to see what she looked like before she put on the girdle, before the makeup team and hairdressers arrived and before the photos were retouched in the studio. It was important to her to remove the mask and let women know that what they see on television or in magazines is not the mark they should be shooting for—in truth, it doesn't exist.[3]

You need to try to be the best you can be for the age that you are and accept the difference between that and your youth. You must also accept who you are becoming based on the opportunities you can personally afford to implement. There are some who can afford plastic surgery and some who cannot. There are some who will dedicate themselves to a feverish exercise schedule and those who will not or cannot. There are those who are willing to be strict in their diet and never eat certain foods, and there are those who don't want to live under those tight restrictions.

Of course, the results you will get will be different based on what you are willing to invest in the process. There needs to be healthy and honest communication where you can agree, as husband and wife, what you are and are not willing to do to remain as healthy and vibrant as possible.

My wife and I, both in our forties, have made peace with some of the changes that are occurring, but we are both in a state of mild warfare against other signs of the advancing aging process. Neither of us is a fanatic, and we are both realistic about the time commitments we are willing to commit to in order to stay young-looking.

We have also talked about anti-aging techniques that we are unwilling to do, even though we are able to take advantage of them. We are in agreement, and neither has pushed the other to do things that were objectionable. Each couple must make an honest assessment of where they are headed and what they can do to stay healthy and vibrant sexually within their own comfort zone.

Maintaining good health

Staying in good health is obviously a worthwhile goal even if you never have sex. The converse is equally true: If you want to stay sexually active, you have to maintain good health. Almost every disease will have an impact on our sex lives. Diabetes leads to hardening of the arteries and loss of nerve function, major contributors to the high impotence rates among diabetic men. If those same men would lose fifty pounds and eat correctly, not only would the diabetes improve, but diabetes and its effects might never have developed in the first place.

Hypertension also impedes blood flow to the penis, and the medications that are often necessary to treat it have their own side effects on sexual arousal for both men and women. Weight loss, dietary changes and exercise could eliminate hypertension for a large percentage of people.

In an earlier chapter, we referred to the words of the apostle Paul:

> The wife's body does not belong to her alone but also to her husband. In the same way, the husband's body does not belong to him alone but also to his wife.
>
> —*1 Corinthians 7:4*

I believe the biblical instruction here gives your spouse the right to expect you to do whatever you can to stay as healthy as possible. You live in a wonderful age where there are medical aspects of aging over which you do have some control. Because you are "one flesh" with your spouse, you should never stop trying to please him or her but do what it takes to make that possible.

Concerns of men

Men and women enter middle age from somewhat different perspectives. One of the first changes men experience in their sexual activity is a difference in erectile function. The penis will take longer to achieve an erection, and it will likely not be as strong as it used to be. The sight of his naked wife will no longer be enough to ensure an erection, and the erection may fade in mid-coitus.

For men, this change can be negative, because the ability to have and maintain a strong erection has been tied to their self-image as a sexual being. It seemed that in their teens and twenties, erections happened even when they were not desired. Visual stimulation was often all that was needed to become aroused, and a simple kiss could bring the penis to life. Now, those things are no longer enough, which can be a frightening experience for most men. The good news is that this "crisis" of masculinity is really no crisis at all. It will happen to every man just as surely as menopause will come to every woman.

Men falsely believe that once they begin to struggle with erections, it is the end of their sex lives. Instead of reaching out for support and help, they retreat, often abandoning their wives emotionally as well. They reason that if they do not engage in physical touch from kissing, hugging and cuddling, then there is no danger that things will progress to the place where she will want to make love. And he will not have to face his fear of failure and his weakening self-image as a man. This period of vulnerability can be a serious crossroads for any marriage.

The male's philosophy regarding his sexual activity is that if he can't be like he was when he was twenty, he doesn't want to participate. He doesn't stop to think logically about any other arena of life where he acts this way. Most men will still play sports with other men their age and still go to work with men of various ages. They know that each man has his strengths and weaknesses. In the corporate world, the young man may have energy and enthusiasm, but he lacks the wisdom to know how to use his gifts and talents. The older man has risen to a place of leadership, and others look to him for wisdom and knowledge. He is at his peak at middle age.

Even in the church, the term *elder* implies someone who has walked with the Lord for a period of time and is recognized by church leaders as a responsible leader. His wisdom did not come overnight; it was a result of years of experience.

There are many areas where men who are aging can still "contribute to the game." The Senior PGA tour is a prime example. There are men who are in their fifties and sixties making more money on this senior golf tour than they ever did when they were younger, even though they can't hit the ball as far as they used to. The wisdom of experience helps them in the very real game that takes place inside one's own mind. In the area of music, gifted singers continue to make beautiful music, even if the key has to be lowered because they can no longer hit the high notes. They use their wisdom and experience to maneuver through the physical changes and produce a vibrant sound.

Why can't the arena of lovemaking for the aging man be tackled with the same wisdom and skills? Why can't the lessons learned over time be used to navigate the uncharted waters of physical change to achieve wonderful sexual experiences? The fact is that great sex is not only possible in middle age, but also that it has the potential for being better.

When men realize that sex is not just about the penis and penetration, a whole new area of sexual exploration unfolds. Women have instinctively known that they are having sex when they are held in a warm embrace, caressed in a soothing bath or kissed passionately for hours. They do not restrict the idea of sex to vaginal penetration and ejaculation. Maybe because orgasm is not the only factor in successful sexual relationships for women, the transitions of aging are not as abrupt as they are for men. But the wise woman will learn to take advantage of the changes in her husband to explore a new realm of delightful experience.

It is a well-known biological fact that men reach orgasm much faster than women. While men can ejaculate in as little as ninety seconds, women often need forty-five minutes.[4] This wide disparity has often left the women without their fair share of orgasmic experiences. Most men are neither patient nor knowledgeable enough to do what is necessary to see that their partner is sexually satisfied. And because most women do not expect to achieve orgasm each time they have intercourse, their lack of satisfaction is often left unspoken.

But along with age comes the great equalizer. It is as if God has remembered the woman and given to her the gift of time. Because it will now take the man longer to achieve and maintain an erection, the process cannot be rushed, as it once might have been when her husband was younger or because she was tired from wrestling with the kids and just wanted to "get it over with."

Now sexual intercourse is an experience that must be lingered over by the very changes that nature brings to the man. It is all about the journey, not just the destination. The sexual experience can now become truly intimate and not simply a race to the finish. And because the house is not filled with little children or demands of work, there is more time available to explore one another and discover what brings your spouse pleasure.

The man must now bring something to the equation besides the mighty penis. He must learn to be creative and give his wife pleasure regardless of the ability he still possesses to have vaginal intercourse. Foreplay is now the most important thing, and this gives the wife the much-needed time she needs to be fully aroused and orgasmic. As the husband concentrates his efforts on caressing her body and stimulating her clitoris by either tongue or hand, she is free to enjoy and receive instead of simply giving as she has done in the past. She can delight in a truly satisfying sexual experience where her needs have been made primary and her only duty is now to receive. Her experience is such a rare gift that the man who is wise enough to give it will be repaid handsomely.

By placing his concentration on pleasing her first, the male mental pressure to have an erection spontaneously is greatly diminished. Since the focus is no longer on the penis, any anxiety that the man was carrying can also be discarded. Just removing this mental stress can do wonders for his ability to have an erection.

This time of erectile difficulty is also the perfect time for the woman to reach out to the vulnerable man and be the helpmate that God created her to be. When the man is no longer able to achieve erection based solely on sight, she must be careful not to interpret this change as a sign that he is not interested in her anymore or that he is having an affair.

The wife must realize that her husband has no control over his erections and cannot "will" them into existence. In fact, pressure to perform to his previous standard can be an erection-killer. She must never make fun of him or tease him in any way. No other area of life is as vulnerable and exposed for men as this one. Only the most gentle and soothing words of encouragement will allow him to let his wife meet his sexual need.

As this change becomes apparent, the successful wife will find ways of opening the door to communication with her spouse in a way that does not embarrass, place blame or accuse, but honestly offers help. Show him other ways to please you sexually that do not involve penetration. Verbally tell him how much he means to you and that you like it when he does certain things to you. Make foreplay the main activity, and guide him as he learns, maybe for the first time, what you need to be satisfied. Encourage him to seek medical help that is available as well, and offer to go with him to see a urologist.

There are many things that can be done to help erectile difficulties. A trained urologist can suggest an assortment of products to help, depending on the man's unique medical condition. There is almost no one that cannot be helped to have an erection. The main barrier to receiving that help is pride.

Most of the products overcome the weakness of blood flow to the penis that comes with aging. Hardening of the arteries slows the flow of blood to the penis, making the time required to full erection longer and lessening the firmness of the erection. Devices like the *vacuum pump* are placed over the penis to pull blood into it. Once an erection is achieved, a rubber ring is placed around the base of the penis to prevent the flow of blood back out of the penis until intercourse is complete. This device may intimidate both the man and his wife, but it can be successfully woven into foreplay. Men who are on any type of blood thinners cannot use it.[5]

Penile self-injection is a technique where a small needle is used to inject medication directly into the penis to achieve erection. It takes effect within ten minutes and lasts for four hours. The hindrances to this method are the reluctance to inject one's penis and the fact that the erection will not go away for four hours. On the positive side, millions of people self-inject insulin every day and have grown accustomed to it. The fact that the erection lasts so long and is so reliable is also a plus for the wife, who is assured of all the time she needs to achieve her own orgasm. The man can be confident that his erection cannot fade prematurely, and this frees him to linger in lovemaking as well.[6]

As we have discussed in a previous chapter, the development of the drug Viagra has been revolutionary in the field of medicine. Except for a very few specific medical conditions, almost every man can use Viagra, and most will achieve measurable improvement in the strength of their erection as well as its longevity. Because it can decrease blood pressure, it must be used under medical supervision for those men who are taking blood pressure medication or have heart disease. Viagra can be taken one hour before intercourse and, as such, is a discreet sexual aid that can boost a man's confidence.[7]

New drugs are being introduced this year that may prove superior to Viagra in many ways. Your physician can help you decide which one may be right for you.

For those few who are unable to use or achieve results with the previous methods, there is the *penile implant*. This is a device that is surgically implanted into the shaft of the penis along with a pump that is placed inside the scrotum. When an erection is desired, the pump is squeezed to release a liquid that fills the device in the shaft of the penis for as long as needed. The liquid is then drained back into the pump when erection is no longer needed. This is a more complicated task but one that many who suffer from prostate cancer have found will bring them back to sexual function again.[8]

Besides these medical tools, the wife can aid her husband in achieving an erection. The older penis needs more tactile stimulation to become erect.

This means that the sense of touch now becomes more dominant than the sense of sight. Again, God balances it so that just as women begin to feel less physically beautiful, the realm of visual images loses some of its power and is replaced by touch. Both manual stimulation, following the techniques of masturbation, and oral sex are important tools for achieving erection.

Certainly, the man must feel comfortable touching himself and helping himself get a stronger erection without feeling that he is committing sin. There may be times during foreplay, when he is concentrating on his wife's pleasure, that he can also be caressing his penis to achieve an erection so he is ready to enter his wife when the time is right. But there is no substitute for the wife who will reach out a helping hand and let her part of foreplay be directed at helping his erection. As I have mentioned before, oral sex ranks very high on the erotic meter for most men. Using the tongue or whole mouth to bring an erection into existence will be very much appreciated.

In the next chapter, we will look at the middle-aged women and the issues that she faces as she strives to stay sexually alive. It is not uncommon for the man and woman to be facing the challenges of aging at the same time. Insight by the man into the changes occurring in his spouse will help him better understand his role in the ever-changing sexual union.

Chapter **Seventeen**

SEX AND
THE AGING WOMAN

Teach the older women to be reverent in the
way they live . . .

—Titus 2:3

There is probably not a man on this planet who is not familiar with the phase of life called *menopause*. He may not understand it, but he has heard horror stories from others and has dreaded his own wife's passage through this phase. Menopause can be a challenging part of growing older for a woman, both physically and emotionally. Anything that affects the body and the emotions must surely impact sexuality as well.

THE REALITY OF MENOPAUSE

Menopause is defined as the period of time when the available eggs in the ovary have dwindled and estrogen levels have dropped dramatically. It is not a set moment in time, but rather a process that can last several years. We refer to the time when symptoms begin as perimenopause; there may still be a few eggs left, but the estrogen levels are fluctuating so wildly that the woman is miserable. Just as erectile dysfunction is not under the control of the man, so are the symptoms of menopause not under the control of a woman.

In the midst of early menopause, the decreasing estrogen levels cause irritability, depression, hot flashes, sleep deprivation and fatigue. The lack of estrogen to the vagina leads to thinning of the vaginal lining and dryness. This in turn causes painful intercourse. The ligaments that hold the female organs in place can weaken, letting the bladder, uterus or rectum prolapse into the vagina, also bringing discomfort with intercourse. Bladder control can be partially lost, leading to a decreased sexual drive as well.

The loss of estrogen can also independently decrease libido, but there is an overlap of emotions as well that interfere with sexual desire. The cessation of menstrual periods, a blessing for most, also signals the end of fertility. While it is rare to find a woman who still wants to have a child in her fifties, the very

172

fact that she can never have one again can trigger a state of mourning. Even women who have had a tubal ligation find that they become sad when they understand that the last egg is gone. Their hormonal and physiological processes have been geared toward fertility and childbearing. They must face the realization that new life will no longer come from their wombs. For some, this calls for a radical reshaping of their self-image. For others, this means that they are getting "old."

On the positive side, the lack of menstruation frees the woman to be sexually active whenever she wants. She will not be a victim of some ill-timed blood flow or painful menstrual cramps. Birth control is not an issue or a burden. In this new era of freedom from those womanly issues, sex can be for fun instead of carrying the fear of unwanted pregnancy.

Even the sexual drive will be restored as the body becomes accustomed to its new hormonal reality. The ovaries continue to produce a small amount of weak estrogen, and the production of testosterone still continues. With the balance of hormone shifted to the male side, some women even have an increase in libido after menopause. Of course, the relatively dominant testosterone can come with the troubling side effect of increased facial hair!

As women enter menopause, there will be about 15 percent who experience no symptoms at all apart from the universal end to menstruation. They will not complain of hot flashes, mood swings or anything their fellow sisters in menopause are going through. In fact, they may have a difficult time understanding what the other 85 percent are experiencing. But the majority of women will have varying degrees of difficulty as they transition through this phase of life. How much it bothers you will determine what remedies you seek.

Hormone supplements

The main question that comes with menopause is whether or not to take hormone supplements. There is such an ever-changing and evolving body of science surrounding this issue that I almost hesitate to address it. As soon as I put something down on paper, some new scientific study will emerge to refute my advice. It happened to me the summer of 2002 when the Women's Health Initiative (WHI) stopped its study of hormone replacement therapy (HRT) early because it was finding that the women who were taking hormones were doing worse than the women who were taking placebo (or fake) pills.[1] The HERS (Heart and Estrogen/progestin Replacement Study) trial has also shown some problems recently with HRT, as I will discuss.

For many years, there was a body of evidence that showed HRT, specifically estrogen, was beneficial in raising "good" cholesterol and lowering "bad" cholesterol. Because it was assumed that this would be an improvement for the heart, HRT was recommended as a way to prevent heart attacks and strokes. I spent the first decade of my private practice vigorously advocating HRT for everyone.

The problem with the early studies was that the number of patients studied was small and the data were based on questionnaires that asked about past use and present disease. There had not been a large trial of HRT vs. placebo to see what would actually happen in the future. This type of study is much more powerful in reaching conclusions, but it takes a lot longer to complete and requires thousands of participants.

Over the past couple of years, a few of these large studies began releasing their findings. The first study to question the value of HRT was the Heart and Estrogen/progestin Replacement Study (HERS). Women with previous heart disease were recruited in the hope that adding hormones to their system would reverse the effects of hardened arteries and improve their lives. In the first year of the study, those who took the hormones began dying of heart attacks and strokes at a faster rate than those taking the placebo or "sugar" pills.[2] We immediately stopped advocating hormones as a treatment for heart disease but still clung to the hope that healthy women might find prevention for future heart attacks if they could keep their cholesterol levels balanced with the hormones.

The WHI study released early findings in July of 2002 showing no benefit for healthy women who took hormones to prevent heart attacks. In fact, a small number of women actually did worse than expected. This was only seven out of nearly ten thousand women, but it still pointed to a flaw in our thinking about hormones.[3] Just because it seemed to do one thing in the laboratory did not mean it translated to better health in real people. To figure this out required that thousands of women be studied. The four main studies published to date represent over twenty thousand women participating in them. There are further studies we expect to be completed in 2005 and 2007 that may solidify these results.

The other findings from the recent research on HRT are in the area of cancer risk. There seems to be a small but definite rise in the risk of breast and ovarian cancer with continued use of estrogen. Those who took the hormone more than four or five years began to see an increase, and it continued for those taking estrogen ten or more years.[4] These findings will hopefully be further clarified in the next few years.

New advice

My advice to women now is different from what I advocated a couple of years ago. Some of the promise of estrogen is in its prevention of osteoporosis and fractures. Millions of women suffer from osteoporosis and have sustained vertebral fractures, causing their spines to hunch over, or a hip fracture that has left them bound to a walker or wheelchair. A visit to any nursing home in America will reveal hallways lined with old women who are immobile and dependent on others to even take them to the bathroom. Much of this suffering could have been prevented by maintaining better bone health as they aged.

Estrogen is a powerful preventative of spine and hip fractures. For the longest time, it was the only preventative we had that could take calcium and bind it back into the bones. But over the last few years, new drugs have been developed that not only prevent osteoporosis, but also can reverse some of the bone loss that has already taken place. Some of these agents even appear to prevent breast cancer and may decrease the risk of heart disease. These new "designer" drugs called SERMs (selective estrogen receptor modulators) are targeting the areas that need help without the side effects of HRT. With the advent of such therapy, the need for HRT is greatly diminishing.

Natural aids

For those women who are suffering from these unexpected swells of heat and perspiration, awakening them in the night and embarrassing them in the daytime, hot flashes may be the worst part of menopause. There are natural herbal preparations that can help with hot flashes, such as ginseng, black cohosh, red clover and soy. The only herbal preparation that has shown benefit in relieving hot flashes when tested in rigorous medical trials is black cohosh, sold in the United States under the name Remifemin. Herbal preparations do not improve bone density, nor have they shown much effectiveness for osteoporosis prevention. Some serotonin agents, previously used for depression, have been found to improve hot flashes and are often prescribed to women who have had breast cancer and cannot take estrogen.

For those with severe hot flashes or mood swings, there is nothing like estrogen to make them feel "normal" again. If the current data hold true, there is no harm in taking HRT for a few years to aid in the transition of menopause until the hot flashes subside, generally by age fifty-five. This is, of course, provided you have not had breast cancer or heart disease before. Only your doctor can review your individual history and advise you on your options.

From a sexual point of view, many women find it uncomfortable and embarrassing to be in the middle of intercourse when a hot flash takes place. This is an area where an understanding spouse can smooth the rough edges and help his wife deal with her changing body. The temporary decline in sexual desire during this time also requires an accommodating husband.

The physical changes in the vaginal area that can cause discomfort are just another hurdle to overcome.

The good news is that the effects of menopause can be lessened. Just like erectile dysfunction, menopause is a condition that can be improved if the person is willing to seek help and include her spouse in the solution. But like men who retreat from sex because of ED, I see just as many women retreat from sex and decide that their sex life has come to an end during menopause. This reaction to aging is really not a viable option in sustaining a vibrant marriage. It is very unfair to the husband who still desires sexual activity, and it is scripturally wrong for either spouse according to the apostle Paul.

Medical choices

For those of you who have embraced the idea of staying sexually active throughout your marriage, there are more choices to aid your decision than ever before. I have already discussed the pros and cons of HRT, but even for those women who take it, and especially for those who do not, vaginal dryness and painful intercourse can be a challenge. Lubricants such as K-Y Jelly can be a wonderful aid, not only for the woman, but also for the man. With the decrease in erectile strength, a dry vagina can be increasingly difficult to enter, further increasing the man's anxiety about his potency. A well-lubricated vagina can ease his entry and alleviate her pain. Of course, if he has been following the suggestions of increased foreplay, his wife will have had more time to release natural vaginal secretions, and it may not necessary.

Commercially available lubricants only coat the surface of the vagina, and sometimes the loss of estrogen has caused thinning of the lining as well, which renders the vagina more susceptible to trauma. Local estrogen treatment can reverse this problem, using estrogen creams, tablets or even rings that can be inserted into the vagina at prescribed intervals to ease the dryness, irritation and pain that menopause can bring. These agents work locally and do not travel to other parts of the body. They can be used indefinitely with no side effects.

Kegel exercises are a way to tighten the vaginal muscles and improve bladder control. Because the muscles of the vagina are responsible for gripping the penis, a woman with strong vaginal muscles, specifically the pubococcygeal (PC) muscles, will be able to bring her husband to orgasm quite effectively. There are some women who, through childbirth injury or severe loss of vagina muscle tone, find that they are beyond the aid of Kegel exercises and require vaginal surgery to tighten the vagina and/or lift the fallen bladder. A trained gynecologist can be used by God to bring the vagina back to its youthful state.

There are those women who do not find their sexual desire returning as quickly after menopause as they would like. Some of these women are lacking ovaries or have very little natural testosterone production. There are herbal remedies such as those containing DHEA that can build testosterone. There are also oral and transdermal testosterone supplements that can be prescribed. One has to be careful not to take in too much and suffer facial hair growth or deepening of the voice.

For women with concerns about side effects, a testosterone cream can be made that is applied locally to the outer portions of the vagina and clitoris. This not only increases sexual drive, but it can also improve the strength of the outer skin and heal vulvar itching. It must be hand-made by a reputable pharmacist, but nearly every gynecologist is familiar with the formulation required.

A newly approved device has been released by the FDA to help the many thousands of women who experience sexual dysfunction after menopause but for personal or medical reasons are not able to use hormonal therapy. It is called the *Eros Therapy* device and was invented by a urologist.[5] The device is a suction device that is intermittently applied to the clitoris during foreplay to increase the flow of blood to that organ.

The clitoris is then more responsive to stimulation and brings a higher rate of orgasm. In addition, the increased blood flow brings better vaginal lubrication as well. In a recent study of women who used this device at one-minute intervals for five to ten minutes four times a week, there was a dramatic improvement within three months in over 80 percent with no side effects. Improvements included less pain with intercourse, better desire, arousal and lubrication. An unexpected finding was an improvement in bladder control for those who had previously suffered from overactive bladder syndrome.[6] This device is available through UroMetrics by prescription at www.uromctrics.com.

OTHER MEDICAL CONDITIONS

Some men and women will find their health fading as they age. There are certain medical conditions that can present challenges to a couple that desires to remain sexually active. Even the treatment of one disease can impact the ability of other organs to function. Because the woman is not as sensitive to changes in blood flow for her ability to have orgasm, men bear a larger share of these difficulties. But certain medications for high blood pressure, diabetes or depression can affect the ability of both men and women to experience sexual pleasure.

Because there are so many drugs available to us today, I strongly encourage those who have found unwanted sexual side effects with certain mediations to talk to their doctors about alternatives that might be available.

Even the addition of an herb like ginkgo can reverse some of the side effects that medication can have on sexual function. Don't feel resigned to a life without sex simply because some disease has come your way.

Those who have suffered a heart attack are often afraid to resume sex again—it seems like a stupid way to die! But a recent Harvard study found that those who have been able to return to a regular exercise program of three times a week did not have an increased risk of suffering a heart attack because of sexual activity.[7] Again, have the courage to ask your doctor about your individual condition; don't automatically assume that the game is over as far as sex is concerned. You may be thankful to be alive, but don't prematurely bury one part of you out of fear.

Post-mastectomy patients have a difficult time feeling sexually desirable, and it can be a challenge for the husband to show his wife that the loss of a breast has not diminished his attraction to her. Sometimes, counseling with those who specialize in the sexuality of cancer patients can be of tremendous benefit.

Similarly, prostate cancer victims may have physical difficulties in achieving erection that cannot be overcome. But, as we have discussed, there is more to sex than vaginal penetration. Lying naked together in a bathtub surrounded by candles, gently massaging each other and giving one another long, lingering kisses can be as satisfying as any vaginal penetration could ever be. The idea that sex has to be confined to a penis entering a vagina is far too limiting. There are those who would find themselves on the sidelines if that were the case, when the truth is, sex has so many other ways of being expressed.

Many people are troubled by back pain or arthritis and find intercourse to be a challenge. It is not a pleasant experience if it cannot be done without pain. But a bit of creativity and experimentation can reveal position changes that allow for satisfactory sex. The standard missionary position is especially difficult for men who must support their weight (sometimes a lot of weight!) on their arms and knees. The back is also arched in this position, and thrusting maneuvers can be very uncomfortable. Trying to achieve orgasm when several body parts are crying out in pain is no easy task.

Some have found that the man on bottom position with the wife lifting herself onto the erect penis is easier. Alternatively, the man can stand at the side of the bed with his wife at the edge resting her legs against his shoulders. There is even a swing that can be hung from the ceiling, which supports the woman sitting in it while the husband swings her in and out, enabling his penis to experience vaginal motion without his back moving at all. Though swings are sold in specialty stores that most Christian couples would be afraid to venture into, the reward can be great. It is not sin if it is kept between the two of you.

ENJOY ROMANTIC CREATIVITY

While we are on the topic of specialty stores, there is a risk that over time, the bedroom can become a place of boredom. Doing the same things the same way with the same person for thirty or forty years can result in the elements of romance and eroticism being lost to the relationship. God gave to each of us an imagination. The fact that the devil and his crowd have misused it should not keep us from exercising our right to be creative. There are a variety of marital aids such as vibrators, lingerie, massage oils and so forth that can break the monotony of your sexual routines and increase the arousal of both partners. As each of you age, arousal is a bigger challenge. Because you have more privacy and time, since the children are older or gone, there is freedom to experiment in ways you never have before.

As we mentioned, making love outdoors in a hot tub or on a deserted beach can be a great departure from the same old bedroom you have seen for years. A romantic tryst in front of a roaring fire on a cold winter's night costs nothing. If you can afford the occasional hotel room or bed and breakfast, the money spent will be a worthy investment in your relationship.

Don't ever stop being romantic or creative. What your body may lack as it ages can more than be made up for in imagination and romance. Your later years can really be your best years in terms of a satisfying sexual relationship. Don't let the myths of aging prevent you from experiencing the truth that God designed you to enjoy a happy and fulfilling sexual relationship for as long as you both shall live.

Chapter **Eighteen**

INTIMATE AND
UNASHAMED

You...were called to be free. But do not use
your freedom to indulge the sinful nature;
rather, serve one another in love.
                                    —*Galatians 5:13*

With the use of Bible references, medical facts and composite case presentations, I have tried to paint with broad strokes a picture of our sexuality as God sees it. There are many details that could be added, but one book could not contain them all. If I have given you a starting point to explore all that God has for you, I will have succeeded.

It is only recently that a handful of churches and ministries have dared broach the subject of sexuality for Christians. Much of what I have learned has come from medical school, residency and private practice. I have been fortunate to be able to integrate that knowledge with teaching I have received from ministers such as John Hagee and Chip Ingram, authors Willard Harley and Andrew Comiskey, and ministries such as Desert Stream.

But many churches in communities across the United States have no one in their pulpits that will teach their flock that God is interested in their sex lives. Christians have no one to tell them that God designed a level of intimacy in marriage that we will never fully appreciate here on earth but that can continue to grow deeper with each passing year, if we will only learn His ways and follow His instructions.

The secular world has taken a beautiful and holy act and so twisted it in depravity that we fear even to speak about sex. Our own past sin only reinforces the fact that sex can be a weapon with which to wound and be wounded. The scars of sexual sin linger even after the healing of those wounds is complete. God's beautiful gift has become a source of anger, depression, pain, disease and even death. God never intended it to be this way.

It is my prayer that we in the Christian community will begin to reclaim our rights and our heritage. We should be the ones others look to for advice. Our homes and our marriages should reflect all that is good about sex and sexuality. The light of godly sexual relationships should shine brightly in this dark age of abortion, STDs, AIDS, divorce and perversion. There are so many millions stumbling in the fog of sexual "freedom."

It is our duty to make a path for them to follow. That won't happen with a series of self-righteous "dos" and "don'ts." Legalistic barriers will never free those in sexual bondage. Only the truth of God's Word lived out in successful, lifelong relationships will turn this generation and this nation back to God.

In his book *I Kissed Dating Goodbye*, Joshua Harris describes his own struggles with dating and the mistakes made daily by his peers. He calls on his generation to forsake the current destructive and degrading patterns of relationships and to conform to what God designed in the beginning.[1] Joshua has been blessed to be surrounded by godly parents who have modeled God's plan for relationships and, ultimately, for marriage. As I read his book, I couldn't help but remember the immature and painful relationships that litter my own past.

My wife, Sandy, and I were not fortunate in having parents who were Christians when we were growing up. My parents have each been married more than once. Sandy and I made major mistakes in relationships during our teens and early twenties. When we became a couple, we brought significant baggage with us.

Without godly role models, we fall prey to the world system, using relationships to meet our own needs instead of focusing on the needs of others. In our sex-saturated society, we become predators and prey, never tasting the riches of a sexual relationship committed to and orchestrated by God.

But even without a Christian heritage to build upon, because God surrounded us with godly marriages that were five or ten years ahead of our own, Sandy and I have been helped. We have been blessed to watch the pitfalls and struggles that committed couples endure on their journeys together and to see the tremendous fruit of their unions. These Christian couples have learned what Paul taught to the Philippians:

> And this is my prayer: that your love may abound more and more in knowledge and depth of insight, so that you may be able to discern what is best.
>
> —*Philippians 1:9–10*

As Joshua Harris describes it, this biblical definition of love "looks beyond personal desires and the gratification of the moment. It looks at the big picture: serving others and God."[2]

It is my hope that those who have yet to begin their sexual journey will avoid the dangers that lie all around them and that they will stay pure as they await their wedding day. May the ravages of STDs, unplanned pregnancy and abortion be far from them.

It is my prayer that the newly married will avoid the pain of pornography, adultery, abuse and divorce that devour many of the marriages in this country. May the inevitable physical and emotional changes of this body we live in not cause us to abandon romance, intimacy and sexual expression. May we never stop exploring the depths and riches of that person with whom the Lord has joined us in holy matrimony.

This is God's desire, His creation, and He longs to tend to our sexual relationships as He would a cherished vineyard. Anyone who has knowledge of winemaking knows that the oldest, thickest branches of the vine produce the most fruit. The new, young branches are devoted to growing as far away from the vine as they can and filling themselves with beautiful leaves. They produce little fruit. But the mature branch that has been trained and pruned bears much fruit.

So should it be in our marriages. As Bruce Wilkerson portrays so beautifully in his book *Secrets of the Vine*, the master of the vineyard cleans off the dirt of sin, prunes away the endless activities we race after and calls us to stay connected to the vine in order to produce fruit.[3]

So it is with our sex lives. God desires to cleanse us of the pain of STDs or abortion, the shame of rape, incest or sexual abuse. He wants to prune us when our lives become overwhelmed with school, work, children, financial challenges and health concerns. When we veer off in our own direction, seeking fulfillment in pornography, romance novels or soap operas instead of our spouse, He cuts us back until we are forced onto the path He has for our lives. He wants us to stay connected to Him and to each other as we age, producing the richest fruit in our later years.

Sandy and I firmly believe God is for us and that He cares about our relationship in every detail. God can help us bring joy, pleasure and love, in all its forms, to that person with whom He has united us. Only God can make two separate human beings into one flesh. Through extending and receiving forgiveness, we have been vulnerable enough to share our secrets. Through honest communication, we have made our needs known and our desires understood. Through failure we have discovered those empty places in our soul that the other is incapable of filling and that God reserves for Himself.

As we grow older, we are on a journey together, unashamed of the changes we encounter along the way. We are willing to adapt but unwilling to give up. Despite what the generations before us have decided, the thought of not being sexually intimate after a certain age is foreign to us. As one of the "baby boomers," our generation is refusing to concede anything as we age.

My prayer is that this generation of Christian baby boomers will continue to present to the church marriages filled with life and passion as we age. May our children and grandchildren see us as role models, living vibrant lives even into our retirement. The decades of marriage should mold two into one so tightly that younger generations will wish for the day they can achieve that level of intimacy and love. They should understand that the youthful physical stamina of their early sexual relations will pale in comparison to the deep, unfaltering breadth of love they can achieve in their senior years.

May the fire in our eyes tell them that passion still burns after thirty, forty, fifty or sixty years of marriage. May we be able to say at the end of the journey that we achieved what Adam and Eve knew in the Garden—we were *intimate and unashamed.*

Appendix **A**

WORLDWIDE IMPACT
OF HIV/AIDS

The region hardest hit so far by HIV/AIDS is sub-Saharan Africa, that portion south of the Sahara Desert, which is an area comprising the lower half of the continent. The number of people estimated to have HIV/AIDS in this small corner of the world is 28.5 million.[1] This represents nearly one in ten adults living between the ages of fifteen and forty-nine, the prime of life, and the most productive segment of their population.

Of the 14 million children in the world orphaned by the deaths of their parents to AIDS, 11 million live here. Almost 90 percent of the children in the world infected by HIV live in sub-Saharan Africa, and almost 80 percent of the people who have died from AIDS since its origin have been from this region of the world. While the worldwide estimate is that 1 percent of the population ages fifteen to twenty-four are HIV-infected, a frightening statistic by itself, over 5 percent of the boys and a staggering 11 percent of the girls ages fifteen to twenty-four are infected in sub-Saharan Africa.[2]

It is difficult to appreciate the extent of this epidemic when one considers such large numbers. It is only when we look at particular countries that we grasp the tremendous impact HIV/AIDS can have on a nation. In the country of Botswana, 39 percent of the adults ages fifteen to forty-nine are infected.[3] That's more than one in three! Common sense would say that once a country reached such enormous levels of infection, the others would protect themselves and the disease would plateau. But unfortunately, it shows no sign of slowing down and is on the verge of consuming an entire nation. Over half of the women seeking prenatal care in Botswana are HIV-infected, poised to transmit the virus to the next generation.[4]

In the more populous countries of Nigeria and Ethiopia, the number of cases is expected to rise from its current 11 million to nearly 25 million in the next eight years. Nearly one-fourth of all adults will be impacted by this disease.[5]

For those who think the epidemic is confined to the other side of the world, the UNAIDS report brings the sobering reality of AIDS closer to home. The Caribbean is becoming a fertile field for the HIV virus. While globally 1 percent of the population ages fifteen to forty-nine are HIV-infected, the percentage is doubled in the Bahamas, a popular tourist destination for those of us seeking to escape North America.[6]

Among the newly infected, women outnumber men in many countries. Biologically, women are more vulnerable to infection through small vaginal tears during intercourse or cervical inflammation from undiagnosed STDs. Culturally, women in developing countries marry men who are older and have had more sexual partners. Adultery is common, and women have little say about fidelity or even condom use by their straying partners. If the women become pregnant, one-third of their babies will become infected as well.[7]

Cultural traditions play a role in the global spread of HIV/AIDS. One of the most rapid progressions of the disease has occurred in Southeast Asia. The predominant ways the disease is transmitted is by heterosexual intercourse and needle sharing in IV drug use. The majority of sex outside of marriage is with prostitutes, who themselves carry the HIV virus. A study of men in Thailand found that 44 percent had their first sexual experience with a prostitute during their teenage years. In the region called the Golden Triangle, where the world's opium and heroin is produced, the virus is rapidly spreading through the sharing of needles during intravenous drug abuse.[8]

CIA Director George Tenet projects that by the year 2010, India will have more HIV/AIDS cases than any other country with 20 million to 25 million cases. It is primarily being fueled by heterosexual activity, and most of the population has little awareness the disease even exists. As many as half of all prostitutes in Bombay are believed to be currently infected.[9]

Even the culturally conservative country of China is feared to be on the brink of its own epidemic, according to the UN report. Intravenous drug use accounts for nearly 70 percent of the HIV infections, with a practice called "blood-selling" responsible for 10 percent. China's blood-selling industry preys on the poor, rural villagers by pooling many people's blood together, extracting the blood components they want, then injecting the mixed blood back into the donors.[10] While the government has tried to crack down on this practice, it continues to this day. It is feared that the sheer size of the population in this country will make education and treatment of HIV difficult. The government has been slow to acknowledge HIV/AIDS as a reality in their country, and many experts fear that by the end of the decade, 10 million Chinese could be HIV-infected.[11]

CORPORATE GREED

Corporations have seized upon our government's attempts at AIDS prevention with its own brand of greed at the expense of human life. The World Bank has given the African nation of Zambia, where one in ten adults living in urban centers has HIV, a grant of $42 million to fight the spread of AIDS. But it is not being spent on treatment for the sick but on the purchase of condoms. Kenya has gotten a World Bank loan to purchase 300 million condoms over the next five years. Africa is becoming a major importer of condoms as their governments allocate millions of dollars to purchase condoms, having been told by the condom manufacturers and the United Nations that this is the only way to save their nations.[12]

But in Tanzania, where one in nine adults has HIV, the United Nations Population Fund (UNFPA) was forced to withdraw 10 million condoms it had purchased from China when it was discovered that they failed two separate leak tests. Congress increased funding of this UN organization by 36 percent in 2001, but as yet the Bush Administration has not released the funds.

However, Secretary of State Colin Powell testified before the Senate Foreign Operations Subcommittee in June 2002 that he believed the UNFPA condoms should be used.[13] You may remember the controversy over his remarks about condoms on MTV in 2001 in direct contradiction to President Bush.

Appendix **B**

INEFFECTIVENESS
OF CONDOMS

In his book *The Truth About AIDS*, Dr. Patrick Dixon outlines common reasons why couples dislike condoms:[1]

1. To put it on carefully takes precious seconds out of a continuing experience. Some men find that by the time they have the condom on so that it is comfortable (it may need a couple of trics), their erection has disappeared. A woman is left hanging around and rapidly loses her momentum. Trying to find where you put one, opening the package and getting it on correctly may be a joke, but it is disruptive.

2. Many men say that the layer of rubber reduces what they can feel, and some women dislike the thought of a piece of rubber in such a personal area.

3. For many couples a central part of their celebration of oneness is to be lying together, with the man inside, immediately after both are satisfied. Correct condom use requires the man to withdraw immediately, which some see as a rather abrupt and savage end to a marvelous experience.

4. Some find disposing of the used condom rather revolting.

5. The very fact that a condom is being used implies slight anxiety about whether a partner is infected. This can cause tension.

6. Many women feel carrying a condom makes them look promiscuous, when they feel they are not. A further major problem is when to produce it. A romantic evening is turning rapidly into something more. Are you going to show you don't trust the other person by reaching for a condom? Will the other person take offense?

One study of men who were experienced condom users showed that 13 percent of them were exposed to some risk during intercourse because of faulty condom usage. The most common error occurred because the condom was worn inside out, then flipped over and reworn, leading to increased risk of tearing. Another 12 percent of men lost their erections trying to use it. Almost 8 percent began intercourse without a condom, then stopped to put one on. Many others had their condoms break or completely fall off inside the vagina.[2] And these were the "experienced" users!

What about those couples that pledge to use condoms perfectly, aiming for that 3 percent failure rate listed by the government? Why shouldn't condoms be 100 percent effective? The truth lies in the inherent flaws of the material latex. Since 1976, the FDA has regulated condoms to ensure their safety and effectiveness. Each condom is electronically scanned for holes or other defects. The manufacturers test condoms from each batch using a "water leak" test for holes and an "air burst" test for strength. The FDA specifies that no more than one in four hundred can fail these tests, or the entire lot is discarded.[3]

But in real-life trials evaluated by Karen Davis and Susan Weller of the University of Texas, 1 to 6 percent of condoms break. In an analysis of twenty-five studies of condom usage in heterosexual couples with one HIV-infected partner, they found that 1 percent of the previously uninfected partners became HIV-positive each year when using condoms 100 percent of the time. If condoms were not used at all, 7 percent per year became infected. They concluded that condoms reduce the risk of contracting HIV by 85 percent.[4]

Their findings have been widely touted as supportive evidence of condom efficacy and have prompted the FDA to allow condom manufacturers to put such a statement on the label. But is 85 percent a comforting statistic for the possibility of contracting a fatal disease? Has this statistic been shared with the American public? No. The fact is that many physicians do not even know the data exist.

The truth is that the HIV virus is not very infectious compared with other STDs. HIV/AIDS infects only one million of the sixty-five million people in the U.S. living with an STD. Of the fifteen million new cases of STD each year, HIV makes up only forty thousand.[5] So how do condoms fare against these more common STDs?

Oklahoma Congressman Tom Coburn, M.D. commissioned a workshop to address this very question. In June 2000, four government agencies (U.S. Agency for International Development, the Food and Drug Administration, Centers for Disease Control and Prevention, and the National Institutes of Health) came together to evaluate the published data of the effectiveness of latex male condoms on STD prevention.

Twenty-eight experts reviewed 138 papers published before June 2000 to determine the effectiveness of condoms in the prevention of STDs transmitted by penile-vaginal intercourse. They looked at eight STDs: HIV, gonorrhea, chlamydia, syphilis, chancroid, trichomoniasis, genital herpes (HSV 1 and 2) and genital human papillomavirus (HPV). Their report, called

"Scientific Evidence on Condom Effectiveness for STD Prevention," included breakage and slippage rates.[6]

While trying to minimize this area of concern, they did admit that "for many STDs, risk of infection might not be proportional to exposure of a *volume* of semen." As background for their report, it was noted that 55 percent of young men ages fifteen through nineteen do not use condoms consistently. A survey of unmarried women ages seventeen through forty-four showed only 18.5 percent used condoms "every time."[7]

There are differences between STDs in relation to concentration, infectivity (their ability to infect) and mode of transmission (body fluids vs. skin-to-skin contact). There are other factors that determine whether a particular act of intercourse will spread an STD. The health of the infected individual will determine how aggressive his disease may be, as well as the immune system of the uninfected partner. Certain sexual behaviors (vaginal vs. anal intercourse, extended foreplay that tears the skin, intercourse during menses) also affect transmission. A person's gender, age and nutritional status are other determining factors for rate of infection.

The report detailed each STD studied and the effects of condom use on prevention of disease. The most infectious STD is gonorrhea. Each act of intercourse has a 50 percent chance of transmitting the disease on average, with women having a 60 to 80 percent transmission rate with each exposure. The report found no significant risk reduction for women using condoms and no reduction in tubal infertility. There was some protective effect for men who used condoms. Chlamydia, the most common bacterial STD, is also more easily passed to women, and again, condoms failed to protect women compared to those whose partners did not use them. But even men using condoms found no protection against chlamydia.[8]

One of the most common viral STDs is herpes, with forty-five million Americans infected with type 2 virus, and five hundred thousand new cases diagnosed each year. Herpes can be contracted by exposure to bodily fluids or skin-to-skin contact. The ability of the condom to protect against this virus is dependent not only on its intrinsic strength but also on its ability to cover all of the affected skin. Several studies on HSV and condoms found that condom use actually *increased* the spread of HSV.[9]

Syphilis is another STD that can be contracted by skin-to-skin contact, a significant limitation of the condoms. It is easily acquired by contact with only a few organisms. The studies reviewed could show no statistically significant reduction in the transmission of syphilis with condom usage.[10]

More than twenty million Americans are currently infected with one of the more than one hundred types of HPV according to this report. They estimate that more than 50 percent of sexually active adults have at one time been infected with one or more genital HPV types, with the majority being the less aggressive varieties. Because HPV infections can occur on the scrotum, inner thighs and anal region, as well as being isolated on the hands and fingernails of infected persons, it was expected that condoms would only partially protect against transmission. After reviewing the available scientific literature, the panel concluded, "There was no evidence that condom use reduced the risk of HPV infection."[11]

In July of 2001, the panel released its final report to the press, and its conclusions were dramatically different from the evidence found deep within. Citing poor study designs as the reason transmission of most STDs occurred despite condom usage, they called for more research. Their summary states, "The Panel stressed that the absence of definitive conclusions reflected inadequacies of the evidence available and should not be interpreted as proof of the adequacy or inadequacy of the condom to reduce the risk of STDs..."[12]

Their bias had been exposed. This panel was so convinced that condoms were the answer to "safe sex" that when the available scientific evidence failed to support their belief, they blamed the evidence and called for more research! This panel is comprised of the very governmental agencies authorized to protect the American public.

Aside from the statement that condoms did not reduce the risk of HPV, the official press release by the U.S. Department of Health and Human Services touted the condom's 85 percent reduction in HIV transmission and the gonorrhea transmission reduction for men.[13] No other mention was made of the failure of condoms to protect the public from the STDs that comprise more than 98 percent of the infections in this country.[14]

Since Congressman Tom Coburn, himself a physician, originally commissioned the panel, he was able to understand the "politically correct" spin that had been placed on this report. Along with another physician in Congress, Florida Congressman Dave Weldon, Coburn was joined by medical associations representing over ten thousand physicians and medical professionals in a press conference in Washington, DC four days after the report went public. In a joint statement, this group made the following charges:

> We believe the failure of public health efforts to prevent the STD epidemic in America is related to the CDC's "safe-sex" promotion and its attempt to withhold from the American people the truth of condom ineffectiveness...[There is] extensive evidence that the CDC has systematically hidden and misrepresented vital medical information regarding the ineffectiveness of condoms to prevent the transmission of STDs...We believe that the CDC may be in

direct and intentional violation of a federal law (P.L.106-554) passed last year that requires the CDC (and other federal agencies) to communicate medically accurate information to the public and to enforce the use of medically accurate information by contractor, grantees and sub-grantees...

The data in the NIH document, based on real people living real lives, show little or no evidence of condom protectiveness against real STDs...The CDC has promoted condom-use programs that have been used to educate an entire generation. Because they believed condoms would protect them during intercourse, millions of women in our country now suffer from the ravages of diseases, including pelvic infections, infertility, and cervical cancer.

We physicians, who have depended upon the CDC to develop sound public health policy to protect the health and well-being of our patients, are appalled at public health officials who are with-holding the very information we need to educate and care for our patients.[15]

Dr. Coburn stated in a separate interview that the report issued by the government "finally exposes the 'safe' sex myth for the lie that it is. For decades, the federal government has spent millions of dollars to promote an unsubstantiated claim that promiscuity can be safe...Who can ever know the true toll in human lives and healthcare costs that have resulted from the misinformation that has been propagated by the CDC, Planned Parenthood and the rest of the 'safe' sex lobby?"[16] Despite this report, many leading medical groups, including the American Medical Association, the American Academy of Pediatrics and the American College of Obstetricians and Gynecologists, endorse condom use.

Appendix C: Birth Control Methods

Method	% Unintended Pregnancy Within First Year	
	Typical Use	*Perfect Use*
NONE USED	85	85
NATURAL FAMILY PLANNING	25	
Calendar		9
Cervical mucus		2
Temperature		1
WITHDRAWAL	19	4
BARRIER		
Spermicide	26	6
Diaphragm	20	6
Cervical cap	40	26
Condom	14	3
BIRTH CONTROL PILLS*		
Mini-pill	--	0.5
Standard	5	0.1
(*includes injectable, ring and patch)		
DEPO-PROVERA INJECTION	0.3	0.3
IUD	0.8	0.6
Mirena		
ParaGard		
FEMALE STERILIZATION BY TUBAL LIGATION	0.5	0.5
MALE STERILIZATION BY VASECTOMY	0.15	0.1

Appendix C: Birth Control Methods

Advantages	Disadvantages
No cost; creates a baby.	You will likely get pregnant.
No cost; no side effects; no chemicals or hormones.	Requires discipline; high failure rate.
No cost; no side effects; no chemicals or hormones.	Requires discipline; high failure rate.
Inexpensive; almost no side effects.	Requires discipline; high failure rate; some skill required; some women are irritated by the spermicide.
Excellent prevention of pregnancy; can regulate menstrual cycle; may diminish cramps, blood loss, PMS, acne, ovarian cysts; may decrease risk of uterine and ovarian cancer.	$30–$50 per month; must use correctly to be effective; some women have nausea, breast tenderness, weight gain, mood changes, headache; rare serious side effects of heart attack, stroke, liver disease, gallbladder disease.
Excellent prevention of pregnancy; most women cease menstruation; one injection every three months; less responsibility for women to remember to use it; stops uterine cramps, blood loss, PMS, and ovarian cysts; may decrease uterine and ovarian cancer.	$75–$100 every three months; some women gain significant weight; takes six to nine months before conception is possible after use; may bleed irregularly for several months.
Highly effective prevention of pregnancy; inserted in the office; nothing to remember; Mirena lasts five years and stops menstruation; ParaGard lasts ten years; both can be easily removed in the office with immediate resumption of fertility.	May cause PID if patient contracts an STD; may cause an ectopic (tubal) pregnancy; both block implantation if conception is able to occur; cost of $500–$700 up-front.
Highly effective pregnancy prevention; permanent protection; no chemicals or hormones; no side effects.	Relatively irreversible; rare ectopic pregnancy; involves general anesthesia in an operating room setting; cost $1,000–$2,000.
Same as female sterilization; can be done in an office setting under local anesthesia.	Relatively irreversible; cost $300–$500; men find this psychologically difficult to do because of fear of pain, sexual changes or complications (most of which are not likely).[1]

Notes

CHAPTER ONE
A BIBLICAL PERSPECTIVE ON OUR SEXUALITY

1. Joe McIlhaney, M.D., *Sexual Health Today* (Austin, TX: The Medical Institute for Sexual Health), 1999.
2. Diana Hagee, *The King's Daughter* (Nashville: Thomas Nelson), 2001.

CHAPTER TWO
HOW GOD MADE A WOMAN

1. Don Colbert, M.D., *The Bible Cure for PMS and Mood Swings* (Lake Mary, FL: Siloam, 2001).
2. "Relief for PMS," WebMD, retrieved from the Internet at http://my.webmd.com/content/article/11/1668_50285.htm.
3. Andrew Comiskey, *Pursuing Sexual Wholeness* (Lake Mary, FL: Charisma House, 1989), 109–125.

CHAPTER THREE
HOW GOD MADE A MAN

1. "Prostatic Enlargement: Benign Prostatic Hypertrophy," *The National Kidney and Urologic Diseases Information Clearinghouse*, NIH Publication No. 02-3012 (June 2002).
2. Ibid.
3. "What Are the Key Statistics About Prostate Cancer?", American Cancer Society, retrieved from the Internet at www.cancer.org/docroot/cri/content/cri_2_4_1x_what_are_the_key_statistics_for_prostate_cancer_36.asp?sitearea=cri.
4. "Questions and Answers about the Prostate-Specific Antigen Test," National Cancer Institute (January 2001): source retrieved from the Internet at http://cis.nci.nih.gov/fact/5_29.htm.

CHAPTER FOUR
UNDERSTANDING OUR SEX DRIVE

1. Barbara Levy, M.D., "Breaking the Silence: Discussing Sexual Dysfunction," *OBG Management* 14, Issue 3 (March 2002).
2. Ibid.
3. Ibid.

CHAPTER FIVE
HOW BODY IMAGE AFFECTS A WOMAN

1. "Sexual Dysfunction," *ACOG Technical Bulletin*, Number 211, September

1995.

2. Willard Harley, Jr., *His Needs, Her Needs* (Grand Rapids, MI: Revell, 1986), 100.

3. "Christians Are More Likely to Experience Divorce Than Non-Christians," *The Barna Report* (October–December 1999).

4. Don Colbert, M.D., *The Bible Cure for Weight Loss and Muscle Gain* (Lake Mary, FL: Siloam Press), 2000. Don Colbert, M.D., *What Would Jesus Eat?* (Nashville: Thomas Nelson), 2002.

5. 2001 National Plastic Surgery Statistics, Cosmetic and Reconstructive Patients, The American Society of Plastic Surgeons. Source retrieved from the Internet at www.plasticsurgery.org/mediactr/2001_expanded_stats/national.pdf.

6. "Botox 'Parties' Not Just Fun and Games, Advises the American Society for Aesthetic Plastic Surgery," News Release, American Society of Aesthetic Plastic Surgery, May 23, 2002.

CHAPTER SIX
MALE SEXUAL ISSUES

1. "About Erectile Dysfunction," source retrieved from the Internet at www.viagra.com.

2. Ibid.

3. Culley Carson, M.D. and Diana Wiley, *The Couples' Guide to Great Sex Over 40* (New York: Masquerade, 1997), 50.

4. Levy, "Breaking the Silence: Discussing Sexual Dysfunction."

CHAPTER SEVEN
SEXUALITY AND SINGLES

1. "Catholics for a Free Choice," retrieved from the Internet at www.cath4choice.org/youthfacts.htm.

2. The Salt Covenant sermon series by Pastor John Hagee, Cornerstone Church, San Antonio, TX.

3. For more information on abstinence-based resources, visit Worth the Wait's website at www.worththewait.org. Also read Joe McIlhaney, M.D., *Sexual Health Today* (Austin, TX: The Medical Institute for Sexual Health, 1999).

4. Leon Speroff, M.D. et al., *Clinical Gynecological Endocrinology and Infertility*, sixth ed., (Baltimore: Lippincott, Williams & Wilkins, 1999), 390.

5. Abercrombie & Fitch's Pornographic Catalog Brings Embarrassment, Shame to College Student Body President, Says American Decency Association, source retrieved from the Internet at www.americandecency.org/abercrombie.htm.

6. Personal communication by author with Pastor John Hagee, Cornerstone Church, San Antonio, TX.

7. Joshua Harris, *I Kissed Dating Goodbye*, (Sisters, OR: Multnomah, 1997), 93.

8. Lewis B. Smedes, *Sex for Christians* (Grand Rapids, MI: William B Eerdmans, 1976), 128.

9. Harris, *I Kissed Dating Goodbye.*

10. Amy Stephens, "What Really Is 'Mature Teen Sex'?," Focus on the Family website Family.org, retrieved from the Internet at www.family.org/pplace/youandteens/a0008154.cfm.

11. Ibid.

12. Ibid.

13. Fact Sheets: Dads Make a Difference, January 2002, retrieved from Internet at www.teenpregnancy.org/resources/reading/fact_sheets/fatherfs.asp. Also, "Research on Kids," Worth the Wait website at www.worththewait.org/parents/research.html.

14. Laura Meckler, "Teens Having First Sex at Home," Associated Press (September 26, 2002).

15. Grace Kettermann, Ph.D., "How to Teach Your Child About Sex," Focus on the Family website, Family.org, retrieved from the Internet at www.family.org/pplace/schoolkid/A0016711.cfm.

16. Physician Resource Council, "Talking About Sex and Sexuality to Your Adolescent," *The Complete Book of Baby and Childcare* (Wheaton, IL: Tyndale House, 1997).

17. Chip Ingram, Love, Sex and Lasting Relationships, series of six audiotape messages available from Living on the Edge in Santa Cruz, CA.

18. Sexually Experienced Teens, Child Trends Databank, retrieved from the Internet at www.childtrendsdatabank.org/socemo/childbearing/24Sexually ExperiencedTeens.htm.

19. Ibid.

20. Ibid.

21. Youth Risk Behavior Surveillance, *Morbidity and Mortality Weekly Report (MMWR), Recommendations and Reports* 51, no. 38 (September 27, 2002): 856-859.

22. *Newsweek* (December 9, 2002).

23. Press release, CDC/NCHS (June 6, 2002).

Chapter Eight

SEXUALLY TRANSMITTED DISEASES

1. Hunter Handsfield, M.D., *A Practical Guide to Sexually Transmitted Diseases* (Minneapolis: McGraw-Hill, 1996), 5.

2. Workshop Summary: Scientific Evidence on Condom Effectiveness for Sexually Transmitted Disease Prevention (July 20, 2001): Retrieved from the Internet at www.niaid.nih.gov/dmid/stds/condomreport.pdf.

3. STD Statistics, NIAID Fact Sheet, Office of Communications and Public Liaison, National Institute of Allergy and Infectious Diseases, National Institutes of Health (December 1998): Retrieved from the Internet at www.niaid.nih.gov/factsheets/stdstats.htm.

4. An Introduction to Sexually Transmitted Diseases, NIAID Fact Sheet, Office of Communications and Public Liaison, National Institute of Allergy and Infectious Diseases, National Institutes of Health (July 1999): Retrieved from the Internet at www.niaid.nih.gov/factsheets/stdinfo.htm.

5. Ibid.

6. Chlamydial Infection, NIAID Fact Sheet, Office of Communications and Public Liaison, National Institute of Allergy and Infectious Diseases, National Institutes of Health (May 2002): Retrieved from the Internet at www.niaid.nih.gov/factsheets/stdclam.htm.

7. Pelvic Inflammatory Disease, NIAID Fact Sheet, Office of Communications and Public Liaison, National Institute of Allergy and Infectious Diseases, National Institutes of Health (July 1998): Retrieved from the Internet at www.niaid.nih.gov/factsheets/stdpid.htm.

8. STD Statistics, NIAID Fact Sheet.

9. Charlotte Gaydos, M.D. et al., "Chlamydia Trachomatis Infections in Female Military Recruits," *New England Journal of Medicine* 339, No. 11 (1998): 739–744.

10. Kimberly A. Workowski, M.D. and William C. Levine, M.D., M.Sc., "Sexually Transmitted Diseases Treatment Guidelines—2002," *Morbidity and Mortality Weekly Report (MMWR), Recommendations and Reports* 51, RR-06 (May 10, 2002):1–77.

11. STD Statistics, NIAID Fact Sheet.

12. Handsfield, *A Practical Guide to Sexually Transmitted Diseases*, 22.

13. Pelvic Inflammatory Disease, NIAID Fact Sheet.

14. STD Statistics, NIAID Fact Sheet.

15. Pelvic Inflammatory Disease, NIAID Fact Sheet.

16. Workshop Summary: Scientific Evidence on Condom Effectiveness for Sexually Transmitted Disease Prevention.

17. Information in this section is from Syphilis, NIAID Fact Sheet, Office of Communications and Public Liaison, National Institute of Allergy and Infectious Diseases, National Institutes of Health (November 2002): Retrieved from the Internet at www.niaid.nih.gov/factsheets/stdsyph.htm.

18. STD Statistics, NIAID Fact Sheet.

19. Lawrence Stanberry, M.D. et al., "Glycoprotein-D-Adjuvant Vaccine to Prevent Genital Herpes," *New England Journal of Medicine* 347, No. 21 (2002): 1652–1661.

20. Handsfield, *A Practical Guide to Sexually Transmitted Diseases*, 29

21. Dexter Frederick, M.D. et al., "Fatal Disseminated Herpes Simplex Virus Infection in a Previously Healthy Pregnant Woman," *J of Repro Med* 47, No. 7 (2002): 591–596.

22. Richard Sweet and Ronald Gibbs, *Infections of the Female Genital Tract* (Baltimore: Williams & Wilkins, 1985), 183–184.

23. National Herpes Resource Center, retrieved from the Internet at www.ashastd/hrc/helpgrp1.html.

24. STD Statistics, NIAID Fact Sheet.

25. An Introduction to Sexually Transmitted Diseases, NIAID Fact Sheet.

26. Human Papillomavirus and Genital Warts, NIAID Fact Sheet, Office of Communications and Public Liaison, National Institute of Allergy and Infectious Diseases, National Institutes of Health (March 2001).

27. STD Statistics, NIAID Fact Sheet.

28. Laura Koutsky, Ph.D., et al., "A Controlled Trial of a Human Papillomavirus Type-16 Vaccine," *New England Journal of Medicine* 347, No. 21 (2002): 1645–1651.

29. Human Papillomavirus and Genital Warts, NIAID Fact Sheet.

30. Human Papillomavirus and Genital Warts, NIAID Fact Sheet.

31. "HUMAN PAPILLOMAVIRUS: Family Research Council Tells Senators to 'Listen to the Facts,' Pass HHS Bill," *Daily Reproductive Health Report* (October 25, 2000): Retrieved from the Internet at www.kaisernetwork.org/daily_reports/rep_index.cfm?hint=2&DR_ID=618.

32. "Hepatitis in Pregnancy," *ACOG Technical Bulletin* 174 (November 1992).

33. "1998 Guidelines for Treatment of Sexually Transmitted Diseases," *Morbidity and Mortality Weekly Report (MMWR), Recommendations and Reports* 47, No. RR-1 (January 23, 1998): 101.

34. Katherine Chen, M.D., "Hepatitis C: The Silent Epidemic," *OBG Management* 14, No. 2 (2002): 27–45.

35. STD Statistics, NIAID Fact Sheet.

36. STD Statistics, NIAID Fact Sheet.

37. XI International Conference on AIDS, 7–12 July 1996, Vancouver, Canada.

38. Audra Ang, "U.N. Predicts AIDS Epidemic in China," The Associated Press (June 27, 2002).

39. "Trends in Sexual Risk Behaviors Among High School Students, United States 1991–2001," *Morbidity and Mortality Weekly Report (MMWR)* 51, No. 38 (September 27, 2002): 856–859.

40. "Condoms: History, Effectiveness and Testing," retrieved from the Internet at www.avert.org/condoms.htm.

41. Ibid.

42. Ibid.

43. Ibid.

44. Hatcher, *Contraceptive Technology*, 216.

45. Tamar Nordenberg, "Condoms: Barriers to Bad News," *FDA Consumer*, U.S. Food and Drug Administration (March–April 1998).

46. Ibid.

47. Karen Davis and Susan Weller, "The Effectiveness of Condoms in Reducing Heterosexual Transmission of HIV," *Family Planning Perspectives* (Nov/Dec 1999): 272–279.

48. C. M. Roland and M. J. Schroeder, "Intrinsic Defect Effects on NR Permeability," *Rubber & Plastics News* (January 12, 1998): 15.

CHAPTER NINE
UNDERSTANDING AIDS

1. "Human Immunodeficiency Virus Infections in Pregnancy," *ACOG Educational Bulletin* 232 (1997).
2. *Report on the Global HIV/AIDS Epidemic,* Joint United Nations Programme on HIV/AIDS, available on the Internet at www.unaids.org/epidemic_update/report_July02/english/embargo.htm.
3. Ibid.
4. Ibid.
5. Bruce Wetterau, *The New York Public Library Book of Chronologies* (New York: Prentice Hall Press, 1990), 528.
6. Helene D. Gayle, M.D., CDC, "Dear Colleague" letter dated August 4, 2000; retrieved from Internet at www.cdc.gov/hiv/pubs/mmwr/mmwr11aug00.htm.
7. Ibid.
8. Charles Ornstein, "Online Access to Risky Sex," *The Los Angeles Times* (July 26, 2002).
9. Robert M. Grant, M.D. et al., "Time Trends in Primary HIV-1 Drug Resistance Among Recently Infected Persons," *Journal of the American Medical Association* 288 (July 10, 2002): 181–188.
10. Ronald Kotulak, "AIDS Virus Fights Attempts to Create Vaccine," *Chicago Tribune* (May 10, 1987).
11. "Human Immunodeficiency Virus Type 2," last updated October 1998, Centers for Disease Control and Prevention, National Center for HIV, STD, and TB Prevention, Divisions of HIV/AIDS Prevention, retrieved from Internet at www.cdc.gov/hiv/pubs/facts/hiv2.htm.
12. Steven Sternberg, "Government Report on Condoms Stress Abstinence," *USA Today* (July 19, 2001).
13. "Condom Warnings—Beware! Doctors speak out about condom failures," retrieved from the Internet at Pro-Life America, www.prolife.com/condoms.html.
14. Ibid.
15. Ibid.
16. Statement made by the World Health Organization, World AIDS Day 1991, as reported in Patrick Dixon, *The Truth About AIDS* (Eastbourne: Kingsway Publishing, 1994).

CHAPTER TEN
THE WEDDING NIGHT: BASICS YOU SHOULD KNOW

1. Levy, "Breaking the Silence: Discussing Sexual Dysfunction."
2. Carson and Wiley, *The Couples' Guide to Great Sex Over 40,* 50.

CHAPTER ELEVEN
BIRTH CONTROL:
WHAT ARE YOUR OPTIONS?

1. Leon Speroff, M.D. et al., *Clinical Gynecological Endocrinology and Infertility*, sixth ed. (Baltimore: Lippincott Williams & Wilkins, 1999), 1015.
2. "Family Planning by Periodic Abstinence," *ACOG Patient Education* (March 1997).
3. Robert Hatcher, M.D. et al., *Contraceptive Technology*, 17th edition, (New York: Ardent Media, 1998), 215–218.
4. Ibid.
5. Ibid.
6. Ibid.
7. David Grimes, M.D. et al., *Modern Contraception* (Totowa, NJ: Emron, 1997), 158.
8. Hatcher, *Contraceptive Technology*, 215–218.
9. Speroff, *Clinical Gynecological Endocrinology and Infertility*, 1044.
10. "Birth Control Pills," *ACOG Patient Education* (1999).
11. Hatcher, *Contraceptive Technology*, 215–218.
12. Ibid., 516.
13. Ibid., 215–218.
14. Grimes, *Modern Contraception*, 78.

CHAPTER TWELVE
LOVE HAS THREE NAMES

1. I am indebted to Pastors John Hagee and Chip Ingram for their teaching series on love that have inspired millions, including this author, to pursue what God has for them in the area of love.
2. Harley, *His Needs, Her Needs*.
3. Gary Chapman, *The Five Love Languages* (Chicago: Northfield Publishing, 1995), 87–100.
4. Interlinear Transliterated Bible, copyright © 1994 by Biblesoft.
5. Harley, *His Needs, Her Needs*.
6. Chapman, *The Five Love Languages*, 87–100.
7. Harley, *His Needs, Her Needs*.
8. Ingram, Love, Sex and Lasting Relationships.
9. "Born-again Adults Less Likely to Co-Habit, Just as Likely to Divorce," *Barna Research*, August 6, 2001. Available on the Internet at www.barna.org.
10. Ingram, Love, Sex and Lasting Relationships.

CHAPTER THIRTEEN
MARITAL SEX

1. "The Burqa, Chador, Veil and Hijab! Historical Perspectives on Islamic

Dress," Women in World History Curriculum, Lyn Reese, director. Retrieved from the Internet at www.womeninworldhistory.com/essay-01.html.

2. Harley, *His Needs, Her Needs.*
3. Ibid.

CHAPTER FOURTEEN

MARITAL SIN

1. "Born-again Adults Less Likely to Co-Habit, Just as Likely to Divorce," *Barna Research*, August 6, 2001. Available on the Internet at www.barna.org.
2. Andrew Comiskey, "The Wonder and Weakness of Heterosexual Relating," *Power in Weakness 2002*, a seminar given at Dallas-Fort Worth.
3. For more information, visit Andrew Comiskey's website at www.desert-stream.org.

CHAPTER FIFTEEN

THE ABORTION ISSUE

1. Ronald Burkman, M.D. and Anne Moore, "Unintended Pregnancy," *Clinical Courier* 20, No. 20 (October 2002).
2. Laurie Elam-Evans, Ph.D. et al., "Abortion Surveillance," *Morbidity and Mortality Weekly Report (MMWR)* (November 29, 2002).
3. Burkman and Moore, "Unintended Pregnancy."
4. Ibid.

CHAPTER SIXTEEN

SEX AND THE AGING MAN

1. Carson and Wiley, *The Couples' Guide to Great Sex Over 40*, 13.
2. Hagee, *The King's Daughter*, 108.
3. Interview with Jamie Lee Curtis in *More* (September 2002).
4. Carson and Wiley, *The Couples' Guide to Great Sex Over 40*, 50.
5. Ibid., 54–55.
6. Ibid.
7. Source retrieved from the Internet: www.viagra.com.
8. Carson and Wiley, *The Couples' Guide to Great Sex Over 40*, 54–55.

CHAPTER SEVENTEEN

SEX AND THE AGING WOMAN

1. For more information, visit the home page of the Women's Health Initiative website at www.nhlbi.nih.gov/whi/.
2. Stephen Hulley, M.D. et al., "Randomized Trial of Estrogen and Progestin for Secondary Prevention of Coronary Heart Disease in Postmenopausal Women," *Journal of the American Medical Association* 280, No. 7 (August 19, 1998).

3. Jacques Rossouw, M.D. et al., "Risks and Benefits of Estrogen and Progestin in Healthy Postmenopausal Women," *Journal of the American Medical Association* 288, No. 3 (July 17, 2002).
4. A. Z. LaCroix, M.D. and W. Burke, M.D., "Breast Cancer and Hormone Replacement Therapy," *Lancet* 350 (October 11, 1997): 1047–1059. Also, James Lacey Jr., Ph.D. et al., "Menopausal Hormone Replacement Therapy and Risk of Ovarian Cancer," *Journal of the American Medical Association* 288, No. 3 (July 17, 2002).
5. Bruce Jancin, "Vacuum Device Advocated for Treatment of Sex Disorders," *ObGyn News* (September 15, 2002).
6. Ibid.
7. Carson and Wiley, *The Couples' Guide to Great Sex Over 40*, 175.

CHAPTER EIGHTEEN

INTIMATE AND UNASHAMED

1. Harris, *I Kissed Dating Goodbye.*
2. Ibid., 24.
3. Bruce Wilkinson, *Secrets of the Vine* (Sisters, OR: Multnomah, 2001).

APPENDIX **A**

WORLDWIDE IMPACT OF HIV/AIDS

1. *Report on the Global HIV/AIDS Epidemic*, Joint United Nations Programme on HIV/AIDS, available on the Internet at www.unaids.org/epidemic_ update/report_July02/english/embargo.htm.
2. Ibid.
3. Ibid.
4. Ibid.
5. John J. Lumpkin, "U.S. intelligence: Russia, China, India facing skyrockcting HIV cases," The Associated Press (October 1, 2002). Retrieved from the Internet at www.aegis.com/news/ap/2002/AP021002.html.
6. *Report on the Global HIV/AIDS Epidemic*, Joint United Nations Programme on HIV/AIDS, available on the Internet at www.unaids.org/epidemic_ update/report_July02/english/embargo.htm.
7. Ibid.
8. XI International Conference on AIDS, 7–12 July 1996, Vancouver, Canada.
9. Lumpkin, "U.S. intelligence: Russia, China, India facing skyrocketing HIV cases."
10. Ang, "UN Predicts AIDS Epidemic in China."
11. Lumpkin, "U.S. intelligence: Russia, China, India facing skyrocketing HIV cases."
12. Finnigan Sinbeye, "Corporate Activists Promoting Condoms as Panacea to HIV/AIDS," *The Perspective* (May 29, 2002).
13. Matt Pyeatt, "UN Shipment of Condoms Seized by Tanzanian Government,"

CNSNews.com (April 30, 2002): retrieved from Internet at www.cnsnews.com.

Appendix B
INEFFECTIVENESS OF CONDOMS

1. Patrick Dixon, M.D., *The Truth About AIDS* (Eastbourne: Kingsway Publishing, 1994).
2. L. Warner et al., "Assessing Condom Use Practices. Implications for Evaluating Method and User Effectiveness," *Sex Trans Dis* 25, No. 6 (Jul 1998): 273–277.
3. Nordenberg, "Condoms: Barriers to Bad News."
4. Davis and Weller, "The Effectiveness of Condoms in Reducing Heterosexual Transmission of HIV."
5. Workshop Summary: Scientific Evidence on Condom Effectiveness for Sexually Transmitted Disease Prevention (July 20, 2001): Retrieved from the Internet at www.niaid.nih.gov/dmid/stds/condomreport.pdf.
6. Ibid.
7. Ibid.
8. Ibid.
9. Ibid.
10. Ibid.
11. Ibid.
12. "Scientific Review Panel Confirms Condom Effectiveness Against HIV/AIDS," News release from the U.S. Department of Health and Human Services, July 20, 2001. Retrieved from the Internet at www.hhs.gov/news/press/2001pres/20010720.html.
13. Ibid.
14. Workshop Summary: Scientific Evidence on Condom Effectiveness for Sexually Transmitted Disease Prevention (July 20, 2001): Retrieved from the Internet at www.niaid.nih.gov/dmid/stds/condomreport.pdf.
15. Congressman (Ret.) Tom Coburn, Congressman Dave Weldon, M.D., Physicians Consortium, Christian Medical Association and Catholic Medical Association, "It Is Time for the Centers for Disease Control and Prevention (CDC) to Start Telling the Whole Truth About Condoms," *Orthodoxy Today*, retrieved from the Internet at www.orthodoxytoday.org/articles/CoburnCDCSafeSex.htm.
16. "Safe sex myth exposed," *Family E-Flash* 2, issue 29 (July 25, 2001): retrieved from the Internet at www.familiesnorthwest.org/dynpage.cfm?DPID=87.

Appendix C
BIRTH CONTROL METHODS

1. Chart compiled from Hatcher, *Contraceptive Technologies*.

Index

205